Broken Glass, Broken World
Glass in French Culture in the Aftermath of 1870

LEGENDA

LEGENDA is the Modern Humanities Research Association's book imprint for new research in the Humanities. Founded in 1995 by Malcolm Bowie and others within the University of Oxford, Legenda has always been a collaborative publishing enterprise, directly governed by scholars. The Modern Humanities Research Association (MHRA) joined this collaboration in 1998, became half-owner in 2004, in partnership with Maney Publishing and then Routledge, and has since 2016 been sole owner. Titles range from medieval texts to contemporary cinema and form a widely comparative view of the modern humanities, including works on Arabic, Catalan, English, French, German, Greek, Italian, Portuguese, Russian, Spanish, and Yiddish literature. Editorial boards and committees of more than 60 leading academic specialists work in collaboration with bodies such as the Society for French Studies, the British Comparative Literature Association and the Association of Hispanists of Great Britain & Ireland.

The MHRA encourages and promotes advanced study and research in the field of the modern humanities, especially modern European languages and literature, including English, and also cinema. It aims to break down the barriers between scholars working in different disciplines and to maintain the unity of humanistic scholarship. The Association fulfils this purpose through the publication of journals, bibliographies, monographs, critical editions, and the MHRA Style Guide, and by making grants in support of research. Membership is open to all who work in the Humanities, whether independent or in a University post, and the participation of younger colleagues entering the field is especially welcomed.

ALSO PUBLISHED BY THE ASSOCIATION

Critical Texts
Tudor and Stuart Translations • *New Translations* • *European Translations*
MHRA Library of Medieval Welsh Literature

MHRA Bibliographies
Publications of the Modern Humanities Research Association

The Annual Bibliography of English Language & Literature
Austrian Studies
Modern Language Review
Portuguese Studies
The Slavonic and East European Review
Working Papers in the Humanities
The Yearbook of English Studies

www.mhra.org.uk
www.legendabooks.com

RESEARCH MONOGRAPHS IN FRENCH STUDIES

The *Research Monographs in French Studies* (RMFS) form a separate series within the Legenda programme and are published in association with the Society for French Studies. Individual members of the Society are entitled to purchase all RMFS titles at a discount.

The series seeks to publish the best new work in all areas of the literature, thought, theory, culture, film and language of the French-speaking world. Its distinctiveness lies in the relative brevity of its publications (50,000–60,000 words). As innovation is a priority of the series, volumes should predominantly consist of new material, although, subject to appropriate modification, previously published research may form up to one third of the whole. Proposals may include critical editions as well as critical studies. They should be sent with one or two sample chapters for consideration to Professor Diana Knight, Department of French and Francophone Studies, University of Nottingham, University Park, Nottingham NG7 2RD.

Editorial Committee
Diana Knight, University of Nottingham (General Editor)
Bill Burgwinkle, King's College, Cambridge
Janice Carruthers, Queen's University Belfast
Shirley Jordan, Queen Mary, University of London
Neil Kenny, All Souls College, Oxford
Jennifer Yee, Christ Church, Oxford

Advisory Committee
Wendy Ayres-Bennett, Murray Edwards College, Cambridge
Celia Britton, University College London
Ann Jefferson, New College, Oxford
Sarah Kay, New York University
Michael Moriarty, University of Cambridge
Keith Reader, University of Glasgow

PUBLISHED IN THIS SERIES

20. *Selfless Cinema? Ethics and French Documentary* by Sarah Cooper
21. *Poisoned Words: Slander and Satire in Early Modern France* by Emily Butterworth
22. *France/China: Intercultural Imaginings* by Alex Hughes
23. *Biography in Early Modern France 1540–1630* by Katherine MacDonald
24. *Balzac and the Model of Painting* by Diana Knight
25. *Exotic Subversions in Nineteenth-Century French Literature* by Jennifer Yee
26. *The Syllables of Time: Proust and the History of Reading* by Teresa Whitington
27. *Personal Effects: Reading the 'Journal' of Marie Bashkirtseff* by Sonia Wilson
28. *The Choreography of Modernism in France* by Julie Townsend
29. *Voices and Veils* by Anna Kemp
30. *Syntactic Borrowing in Contemporary French: A Linguistic Analysis of News Translation* by Mairi McLaughlin
31. *Dreams of Lovers and Lies of Poets: Poetry, Knowledge, and Desire in the 'Roman de la Rose'* by Sylvia Huot
32. *Maryse Condé and the Space of Literature* by Eva Sansavior
33. *The Livres-Souvenirs of Colette: Genre and the Telling of Time* by Anne Freadman
34. *Furetière's* Roman bourgeois *and the Problem of Exchange* by Craig Moyes
35. *The Subversive Poetics of Alfred Jarry: Ubusing Culture in the Almanachs du Père Ubu* by Marieke Dubbelboer
36. *Echo's Voice: The Theatres of Sarraute, Duras, Cixous and Renaude*, by Mary Noonan
37. *Stendhal's Less-Loved Heroines: Fiction, Freedom, and the Female*, by Maria C. Scott
38. *Marie NDiaye: Inhospitable Fictions*, by Shirley Jordan
39. *Dada as Text, Thought and Theory*, by Stephen Forcer
40. *Variation and Change in French Morphosyntax*, by Anna Tristram
41. *Postcolonial Criticism and Representations of African Dictatorship*, by Cécile Bishop
42. *Regarding Manneken Pis: Culture, Celebration and Conflict in Brussels*, by Catherine Emerson
43. *The French Art Novel 1900–1930*, by Katherine Shingler
44. *Accent, Rhythm and Meaning in French Verse*, by Roger Pensom
45. *Baudelaire and Photography: Finding the Painter of Modern Life*, by Timothy Raser
46. *Broken Glass, Broken World: Glass in French Culture in the Aftermath of 1870*, by Hannah Scott
47. *Southern Regional French: A Linguistic Analysis of Language and Dialect Contact*, by Damien Mooney
48. *Pascal Quignard: Towards the Vanishing Point*, by Léa Vuong
49. *France, Algeria and the Moving Image: Screening Histories of Violence 1963–2010*, by Maria Flood
50. *Genet's Genres of Politics*, by Mairéad Hanrahan
51. *Jean-François Vilar: Theatres Of Crime*, by Margaret Atack
52. *Balzac's Love Letters: Correspondence and the Literary Imagination*, by Ewa Szypula

www.legendabooks.com

Broken Glass, Broken World

*Glass in French Culture
in the Aftermath of 1870*

Hannah Scott

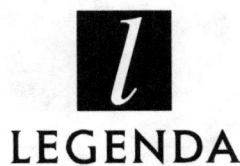

Research Monographs in French Studies 46
Modern Humanities Research Association
2016

Published by Legenda
an imprint of the Modern Humanities Research Association
Salisbury House, Station Road, Cambridge CB1 2LA

ISBN 978-1-909662-87-2 (HB)
ISBN 978-1-781883-18-1 (PB)

First published 2016

All rights reserved. No part of this publication may be reproduced or disseminated or transmitted in any form or by any means, electronic, mechanical, photocopying, recording or otherwise, or stored in any retrieval system, or otherwise used in any manner whatsoever without written permission of the copyright owner, except in accordance with the provisions of the Copyright, Designs and Patents Act 1988, or under the terms of a licence permitting restricted copying issued in the UK by the Copyright Licensing Agency Ltd, Saffron House, 6–10 Kirby Street, London EC1N 8TS, England, or in the USA by the Copyright Clearance Center, 222 Rosewood Drive, Danvers MA 01923. Application for the written permission of the copyright owner to reproduce any part of this publication must be made by email to legenda@mhra.org.uk.

Disclaimer: Statements of fact and opinion contained in this book are those of the author and not of the editors or the Modern Humanities Research Association. The publisher makes no representation, express or implied, in respect of the accuracy of the material in this book and cannot accept any legal responsibility or liability for any errors or omissions that may be made.

Trademark notice: Product or corporate names may be trademarks or registered trademarks, and are used only for identification and explanation without intent to infringe.

© Modern Humanities Research Association 2016

Copy-Editor: Dr Anna J. Davies

CONTENTS

	Acknowledgements	ix
	Abbreviations and Translations	x
	Introduction: Why Glass?	1
1	Glass and Culture in the Aftermath of the Année Terrible	13
2	Shopping for Harmony: Glass, Sound, and the Exhibition Effect in Zola's *Au Bonheur des Dames*	47
3	Breakdowns and Breaking Glass: Glass and Identity Crises in Maupassant's Short Stories	79
4	The Ideal Naturalist? Glass, Popular Culture, and Naturalism in Huysmans's *À rebours*	107
	Afterword	135
	Bibliography	141
	Index	149

In loving memory of my wonderful grandmother
Audrey Churchward
10 April 1923 – 24 May 2015

ACKNOWLEDGEMENTS

A number of people have offered me their support during this project, and I am grateful for this opportunity to thank them. Above all, I am indebted to Susan Harrow, who has been a constant source of guidance, encouragement, and inspiration over the last five years. My thanks also go to Diana Knight, Fiona Cox, Robert Villain, and Nicholas White, who have all generously offered their time, advice, and criticism at various stages in the development of this book.

In Chapters 2 and 3, I draw in part on material from articles which first appeared as 'Symphonic Shopping: From Masculine Visuality to Feminine Aurality in Zola's *Au Bonheur des Dames*', *Dix-Neuf*, 18:3 (November 2014), pp. 259–71, and 'Le Blanc et le Noir: The Spectre Behind the Spectrum in Maupassant's Short Stories', *Nottingham French Studies*, 52:3 (November 2013), pp. 268–80, by kind permission of the editors.

Writing this book would not have been possible without the generous financial support of the University of Bristol Postgraduate Studentship. I would also like to thank the Ecole Normale Supérieure in Paris, who welcomed me to the Rue d'Ulm during my archival research.

H.S., Cambridge, February 2016

ABBREVIATIONS AND TRANSLATIONS

References to texts by the three authors central to this study will be given in abbreviated form. The abbreviated form of the title of each novel, indicated in the key below, is followed by the page number from the original French text, and lastly the page number from the translation where translations are used.

Emile Zola

All works referenced to Henri Mitterand's five-volume edition of *Les Rougon-Macquart* (Paris: Gallimard, Editions de la Pléiade, 1960–67), using the following abbreviations:

LC	*La Curée* (1872), vol. 1
VP	*Le Ventre de Paris* (1873), vol. 1
A	*L'Assommoir* (1877), vol. 2
ABD	*Au Bonheur des Dames* (1883), vol. 3
LD	*La Débâcle* (1892), vol. 5

Translations of Emile Zola's works are from the following editions unless otherwise stated:

The Kill, trans. by Brian Nelson (Oxford: Oxford University Press, 2004)
The Belly of Paris, trans. by Brian Nelson (Oxford: Oxford University Press, 2007)
The Assommoir, trans. by Margaret Mauldon (Oxford: Oxford University Press, 1995)
The Ladies' Paradise, trans. by Brian Nelson (Oxford: Oxford University Press, 2013)
The Debacle, trans. by Elinor Dorday (Oxford: Oxford University Press, 2000)

Guy de Maupassant

All short stories are referenced to Louis Forestier's two-volume edition of *Contes et Nouvelles* (Paris: Gallimard, Editions de la Pléiade, 1974), and abbreviated as *CN*. Translations are from the three-volume *Complete Short Stories* (London: Cassell, 1970) (translator uncredited) unless otherwise stated.

Joris-Karl Huysmans

All works are referenced to Lucien Descaves's eighteen-volume edition of the *Œuvres complètes* (Geneva: Slatkine, 1972), using the following abbreviations:

DE	*Le Drageoir aux épices* (1874), vol. 1
CP	*Croquis parisiens* (1880), vol. 8
EM	*En ménage* (1881), vol. 4
AV	*À vau-l'eau* (1882), vol. 5

AR   *À rebours* (1884), vol. 7
ER   *En rade* (1887), vol. 9

Translations are my own with the exception of quotations from *À rebours*, for which I have used the translation by Margaret Mauldon, published by Oxford World Classics.

All other translations are my own, unless otherwise indicated.

INTRODUCTION

Why Glass?

Crystal palaces and railway stations, greenhouses and arcades, church windows and shop frontages, window panes and mirrors, wine glasses and lamp shades, the most expensive bottles of champagne and the cheapest bottles of *casse-poitrine*: from the monumental to the minuscule, glass became ubiquitous in nineteenth-century France. Once, glass had been the sole province of the rich, making the Hall of Mirrors internationally renowned, and making broken glass windows a poignant symbol of the demise of the traditional elites in 1789. The thirty-nine lower stained-glass windows of the Panthéon were walled up to signal its appropriation by Revolutionaries,[1] and one aristocratic English visitor to France asked: 'Who could, without emotion, behold the windows broken and barred up, [...] where all was gaiety and splendor.'[2] Yet by the latter half of the nineteenth century, burgeoning mass production by France's glassworks had led to some level of vitreous presence throughout society, particularly in Paris. In 1878, nearly 108 million francs worth of glass products were produced in France, despite the loss of several major factories and coke suppliers after the annexation of Alsace-Lorraine.[3] Demand continued at such a rate that glass production doubled between 1878 and 1890, with total output from the major factories (Saint-Gobain, Chauny, Ciry, Montluçon, Mannheim, and Stolberg) rocketing from 10 to 20 million kilos of glass per annum.[4]

This book considers how glass culture influenced French society in the aftermath of the *année terrible* of 1870–71, and ways in which the symbolic associations attached to glass were drawn into literature to expand and enrich its signifying potential. Glass had entered firmly into the cultural — and commercial — imaginary of Paris from the building of the arcades onwards, as Walter Benjamin's *Arcades Project* has so richly illustrated.[5] The World Fairs and Haussmannization brought glass from sheltered arcades to a prominent position in every city vista during the Second Empire. The rationale, then, for turning away in this study from these glory years to scrutinize the two decades following 1870 is the uniqueness of the early Third Republic. Whilst industrialization, urban beautification, commodity culture, exhibition fever, and later the Symbolist movement also touched Great Britain, Germany, Belgium, Austria, and America, to name just a few, the crises of 1870 and 1871 — chasing on the heels of nearly a century of revolution — provide a context which is peculiarly French, and in many cases peculiarly Parisian.

Glass is such a fragile material that it was often the first or even the only material to be destroyed in the combat and bombardments of this terrible year — after all, an explosion did not need to be strong enough to knock a wall down, but a broken window could still give a building the aspect of a ruin with the sight of its jagged remnants. Flying glass could still wound the inhabitants of a comfortable living room; glass could still shock and terrify with the sound of its shattering; and the subsequent void where glass once was could still leave the private interior open and vulnerable. As such a fragile material and one whose destruction had visual, aural, and tactile impact, glass has a particularly poignant and pervasive tie to memories of the fighting. Consequently, glass became a material to be reckoned with in representations and redefinitions of Paris, France, and French identity in the aftermath of 1870–71, including in many canonical literary works of the period.

This is not to claim that there was a sudden and unprecedented awareness of a symbolically-charged material world for nineteenth-century writers and readers in 1870. Gautier had registered his horror at being advertised alongside 'les pessaires élastiques, les cols en crinoline, les biberons en tétine incorruptible, la pâte de Regnault' ['elastic diaphragms, crinoline collars, imperishable rubber feeding bottles, Regnault paste'] in the Préface to *Mademoiselle de Maupin* in 1835,[6] and Balzac had already placed the material world in the trinity of 'les hommes, les femmes et les choses' ['men, women and things'] in the 'Avant-propos' to his *Comédie humaine* in 1842.[7] Flaubert wrote both a history of France in shoes and a 'Théorie du gant' ['Theory of the Glove'].[8]

Yet relatively few scholars of nineteenth-century French studies have turned their attention to the interaction between material culture and literature in nineteenth-century France, unlike their English studies counterparts.[9] This may seem surprising, since French philosophical and sociological thinkers so often turned a critical eye upon object society in the 1960s; characteristic is Jean Baudrillard's influential *Le Système des objets* [*The System of Objects*] (1968), which brought together an anthropological and Marxist approach to reading material artefacts as signifiers of culture.[10] A small number of insightful works in French studies have embraced these ideas, alongside a more substantial engagement from scholars of Anglophone literature. Notably, Brian Rigby's edited collection, *French Literature, Thought and Culture in the Nineteenth Century — A Material World*, draws together essays on topics as diverse as still-life painting, the materiality of signifiers, and the natural world.[11] These essays, in 1993, highlighted important fields of enquiry within material-culture studies and, recently, researchers have begun to explore these pathways in more detail.

Three notable book-length studies — by Janell Watson, Emma Bielecki, and Anne Green — characterize this gradual increase in attention to nineteenth-century French material culture.[12] Watson's research addresses issues surrounding collecting, consuming, and classifying collectors' items in the late nineteenth century; she explores the role of the ostensibly real-world object in an era where representations of reality were gradually evolving from Realist description towards Decadence and Symbolism. For Watson, the sudden and ever-growing prominence of material culture in nineteenth-century texts signals a significant development in attitudes towards commodities and the world of consumption. This has much in common with Bielecki's research into the collector from the July Monarchy to the *fin de siècle*;

Bielecki, too, examines representations of the collector, and she develops and extends Watson's discussion of how writers endeavour — and often struggle — to translate the experience of collecting into language. Green's *Changing France* incorporates a substantial range of archival documents to underwrite this connection between material and literary spheres. Everyday texts such as guidebooks and manuals, Green suggests, helped readers to negotiate emerging cultural phenomena and contemporary concerns — and literature capitalized upon the rich opportunities offered by this proliferation of writing about quotidian life, from exhibitions and transport to food, dress, and photography. All three studies open fertile avenues for future scholarship on French material culture in the nineteenth century and its impact upon the literary writers and readers who lived among these objects.

However, unlike the bibelots, clothing, and exhibited products at the heart of these three studies, glass and glass objects are strikingly resistant to being scrutinized as material phenomena. This is particularly so because glass, prisms, crystals, windows, and mirrors have long had engrained metaphorical associations, which have provided scholars, philosophers, and authors with a means of debating the relationship between writing and the world. M. H. Abrams, in his classic discussion of Romantic poetry *The Mirror and the Lamp*, remarks upon the number of thinkers, from Plato to Caxton, Barclay, Locke, and Rousseau, who take up mirrors as a metaphor for the relationship between artistic or literary representation and its real object.[13] This, Abrams demonstrates, has a cumulative impact, becoming a self-perpetuating way of analysing that relationship.[14] Although Romanticism sought a shift away from that mirror paradigm in favour of a richer variety of comparisons — including the wind-harp, fountains, and organic and geological metaphors — the glass analogy proved tenacious throughout the nineteenth century. Stendhal chose his oft-cited mirror in the roadway, and Baudelaire saw the artist of modern life as a 'miroir aussi immense que cette foule' ['a mirror as immense as this crowd']. For Baudelaire and Gautier, windows were also an effective metaphor; both poets compared literature to a room with windows and shutters closed against the tempest of social unrest, whilst Huysmans described Naturalism as a suffocating room with hermetically sealed windows and doors (*AR*, xxiii).[15]

For Zola, different genres can be represented by different kinds of glass screen or lens. In his correspondence with Antony Valabrègue (18 August 1864), rather than a mirror, he proposes that 'toute œuvre d'art est comme une fenêtre ouverte sur la création. Seulement, entre l'œil du spectateur et la création, il y a, enchâssé dans l'embrasure de la fenêtre, une sorte d'Ecran transparent, à travers lequel on aperçoit les objets plus ou moins déformés' ['every work of art is like an open window upon creation. Except that, between the eye of the spectator and creation, there sits, fitted in the window frame, a kind of transparent Screen, through which objects appear more or less distorted']. As Zola's argument progresses, the window becomes lenticular and the Classical Screen, Zola suggests, is 'un verre grandissant, qui développe les lignes et arrête les couleurs au passage' ['a magnifying glass, which develops the lines and stops the passage of colours'], whereas the Romantic Screen is 'une glace sans tain, claire, bien qu'un peu trouble en certains endroits, et colorée des sept nuances de l'arc-en-ciel' ['a one-way mirror, bright, although a little blurred in some places, and tinted in the seven colours of the rainbow']. By contrast, the Realist Screen — and, we might extrapolate, the nascent Naturalist Screen — is 'un simple verre à vitre, très mince, très clair, et qui a la prétention d'être si parfaitement transparent que les images le traversent et se reproduisent ensuite dans toute leur réalité' ['a simple window pane, very thin, very clear, which claims to be so perfectly transparent that the images merely pass through it to be reproduced in all their reality']. For all its apparent clarity, Zola still recognizes in a way that will not always be as openly admitted in his future writing on Naturalism that, 'si clair, si mince, si verre à vitre qu'il soit, il n'en a pas moins une couleur propre, une épaisseur quelconque; il teint les objets, il les réfracte tout comme un autre' ['as clear, thin, window-pane-like as it may be, it no less has its own colour, some degree of thickness; it tints objects, it refracts them just like any other'].[16] These vitreous metaphors were not replicated explicitly in *Le Roman expérimental* [*The Experimental Novel*] (1880), but the ideas are clearly an embryonic version of those which Zola would later develop at length as an established author, and they reveal the centrality of glass in the thought processes of nineteenth-century authors.

This metaphorical use of glass has translated from literature to scholarship, and numerous studies about the literary and visual culture of this period treat glass only in this rhetorical sense. For example, Morris Dickstein has played on Stendhal's famous definition of the novel in the title of his study on literature's interactions with reality; Trevor Harris has examined repetition and textual 'mirroring' in Maupassant's corpus; and Susanna Barrows has labelled texts which describe social upheavals in the Third Republic as 'a set of mirrors, refracting the world of popular protest in late nineteenth-century France'.[17] These glassy analogies are seductive, but by employing them in a purely metaphorical sense we overlook the very real, ever-increasing material presence of glass for the nineteenth-century reader and writer. Glass objects tend to become transparent in text just as they do in real life.

This is not, however, the case in Elizabeth Emery and Laura Morowitz's fascinating research into the gothic revival; *Consuming the Past* recognizes windows and glass objects as central elements of *fin de siècle* French culture, which were involved in the profound contemplation of French identity that was conducted through material objects during this period.[18] From a cultural-historical perspective, Roger Magraw's article 'Producing, Retailing, Consuming, Spending' touches on the increase in production and consumption of glass within a wider discussion of consumerism in society and literature.[19] Indeed, as is the case in Magraw's article, the question of glass culture is most often raised in scholarship in terms of its contribution to consumer society, often in response to Walter Benjamin's *The Arcades Project*; the role of glass in *creating* the capitalist culture of commodity exchange is juxtaposed with its role in *subverting* that same culture because its transparency makes it 'the enemy of possession'.[20] Like Magraw, Emery, and Morowitz, the present book aims not to look through but to look at glass — as a material, and as a material whose literal involvement in contemporary events endows it with new metaphorical, symbolic associations unique to the *année terrible* generation.

Initially, this research set out to study glass culture more broadly in the years preceding Symbolism and to champion the importance of glass in everyday Parisian culture and literature. It was only on reading accounts in newspapers, diaries, and autobiographies about the Franco-Prussian War and Commune that it became clear just how much writers with first-hand experience of these events returned again and again to harrowing images and accounts of shattering glass. In writing about the events of 1870–71, broken glass became an inevitable symbol for a broken world. Such texts reveal a freight of distressing symbolism being repeatedly latched onto glass. By 1870 glass was physically present on such a scale that it was intertwined with the traumatic events in Paris more than it had ever been in the past. How could the fragility or ethereality of glass be evoked for the *année terrible* generation, even metaphorically, without it calling to mind those times when the shattering of glass had become a frighteningly everyday occurrence? This material had evolved into what Jonathan Lamb has termed a 'thing' rather than an 'object':

> the properties of objects of most interest to us are their mobility in the world of exchange, expressed as commercial and symbolic value, and their interpretability as specimens and curiosities, expressed as knowledge. We are interested in their contribution to the circulation of information, goods, and money because of the importance it imparts to us, the owners of them. Things, on the other hand, are obstinately solitary, superficial, and self-evident, sometimes in flight but not in our direction.[21]

Glass during the *année terrible* defied ownership and control, and writers representing the physical world and property owners alike had to grapple with this stubborn untenability. The shaking and shattering of glass during the Prussian bombardment had a recognized psychological impact on those trapped in Paris. Louis Veuillot wrote in *L'Univers*, 'si l'obus n'entre pas encore dans ma maison, il entre beaucoup dans ma pensée, surtout la nuit. [...] Entre le moment où son départ est notifié par un certain frémissement des vitres et le moment où il éclat, il y a quelques secondes où l'attention se réveille en sursaut, parfois très puissamment. Il vient à l'esprit quantités d'idées' ['if no shells have yet entered my house, they often enter into my thoughts, especially at night. [...] Between the moment their launch is hailed by a certain trembling of the windows, to the moment they explode, there are a few seconds when the mind is awoken with a start, sometimes very powerfully. All kinds of ideas come into your head'].[22] It is easy to overlook this from today's perspective, removed as we are from the contemporary milieu of sights and sounds; but in the late nineteenth century, this distressing symbolism was capable of weaving its way into a wide spectrum of texts for a generation of readers and writers.

Naturally, not *every* contemporaneous individual would associate *every* sight and *every* mention of glass after 1870 with these terrible events. An object is, as Roland Barthes has phrased it, 'polysémique, c'est-à-dire qu'il s'offre facilement à plusieurs lectures de sens' ['polysemantic, that is to say that it lends itself easily to several different readings'].[23] I do not suggest that glass shed all of its pre-existing metaphorical connections to signify solely anxiety and trauma; on the contrary, glass retained many of its former associations. In 1873, the Hall of Mirrors was used for a state banquet to impress the Shah of Persia, and indeed the glazing of the Hall was actively choreographed to signify French culture in all its glory, as had been its intention under Louis XIV, Louis XV, and Louis XVI. During the first course, the windows were draped by blinds so that the mirrors and crystal chandeliers could glitter to their best effect in the candlelight; with the arrival of the main course, the blinds were raised and the vast grounds of Versailles, lit by torches, appeared beyond the towering windows.[24] Clearly, there is no sense of disquiet here, and the organizers were evidently aware that, despite the demise of the monarchy, the visual splendour of mirrors, crystals, and windows was enough to sustain the old aura of grandeur and national magnificence. Popular expressions involving glass did not fade into taboo following these national crises, and phrases such as 'boire dans le verre de quelqu'un: vivre avec lui sur le pied de la plus grande familiarité' ['drinking out of someone's glass: to live with someone on terms of the greatest familiarity'] and 'courir comme un verrier déchargé: courir légèrement et très-vite' ['to run like an unburdened glazier: to run lightly and very fast'] were still recorded in current usage by Larousse's 1874 edition of the *Grand dictionnaire universel du XIXe siècle*. In literature, Jean Moréas was able to use glass as a metaphor for passing time in 'Les Cantilènes' ['Cantilenas'] (1883–86) as '[le] mirage fruste et kaléidoscope frivole' ['rough mirage and frivolous kaleidoscope'], without this kaleidoscope necessarily evoking a specifically revolution-related sense of temporal anxiety.[25] Maupassant's travel narrative *Sur l'eau* [*On the Water*] (1888) described the sea at sunset as '[un] miroir calme et démesuré [où] tombent les nuées, les nuées d'or, les nuées de sang, les nuées de feu; elles y tombent, s'y mouillent, s'y noient, s'y traînent' ['a calm, expansive mirror where the clouds fall, clouds of gold, clouds of blood, clouds of fire; there they fall, there they are soaked, there they drown, there they linger'];[26] but the reader could well be enchanted by the image of natural beauty rather than necessarily recalling the implicit vision of mirrors among blood and fire akin to the *semaine sanglante*. However, for the reader who had not entirely shunned the discomforting events of recent history from their minds, glass seems to have retained a capacity to evoke these distressing underlying associations.

The symbolic associations of glass that I explore in this book were by definition relatively restricted geographically and were short-lived. By 1890, a new generation came of age — politically and socially — who had never known anything but the Third Republic, and who had little or no recollection of the *année terrible*, its broken glass, its sensory affect, or its direct psychological impact. Whilst the transmission of their parents' memories, nationalistic fervour, bitterness against Germany, and suspicion of the lower classes would have had a significant impact on the political beliefs of the new generation, this could not transmit the painful symbolism which only first-hand experience of 1870 and 1871 could attach to glass. In this respect, glass fails to adhere to Lamb's definition of the 'thing' quoted above; Lamb suggests that 'the transformation from object into thing tends to be final and irreversible, not dialectical'.[27] Glass, on the contrary, could potentially exist both as thing and object in the physical and literary worlds of nineteenth-century France.

The present book shares the anthropological conviction of Baudrillard and of more recent scholars such as Daniel Miller and Janet Hoskins that all people, from Polynesia to London, have relationships with objects that are as complex and intimate as their relationship with language — and these object relationships are perhaps harder to understand as no object dictionary could ever be codified with any degree of universality.[28] Jonathan Lamb notes, in his study of the popular English eighteenth-century autobiographies of inanimate things, that the very fact that people who have lost an object of sentimental value are often prepared to pay a reward — which usually far exceeds its commercial value — demonstrates that our feelings towards the objects in our lives go beyond simple consumerist desires.[29] However, rather than taking on the impossible task of writing a 'language' of objects for a distant century as Baudrillard does for the 1960s, it is perhaps more plausible to examine the ways in which material objects are couched *in language* by French writers.

In this respect, my methodology bears a considerable resemblance to Isobel Armstrong's approach in her wide-ranging study of glass in Victorian England. This book strikes, to my knowledge, a unique balance between cultural history and literary analysis in either English or French studies; she places literary texts, newspapers, and ephemera on a par in order to examine the language(s) of glass in the factory visit, the glass-breaking street protest, the Crystal Palace, and the optical toy, grounding her conclusions in extensive archival research. Although Armstrong rarely mentions France, much of her study forms a useful corollary to the legacy of anxiety, change, and modernization left over from the Second Empire for Third Republic France. She observes, for example, that 'glass culture is at the centre of the debates of what I have called Victorian modernism — labour, political radicalism, the "free" human subject, spectacle in an industrial society, the politics of evolution in astronomy and under the microscope. Glass culture constitutes these debates through an anxiety of mediation'.[30] All of this is also true of glass culture in the French context. Where I differ from Armstrong is in the relative weight of attention I give to cultural-historical and to literary study. Whereas Armstrong uses literary sources to illuminate her exploration of a wider language of glass in culture, I engage in closer reading of literary texts, and place a stronger emphasis on readerly experience at the intersection between literary and material worlds. Such close reading dovetails more closely with Anne Green's work, although rather than seeking to extend Green's panoptical approach beyond the Second Empire into the Third Republic, instead I focus on one material exclusively: glass.

For Emile Zola, Guy de Maupassant, and Joris-Karl Huysmans, the three authors who are explored in detail in the present study, there is a keen sense that glass plays a fundamental and deliberate role in their writing in the years following the *année terrible*. Though they differ considerably in their individual approaches, they all reveal that glass has gained and can gain new signification in spite of its barely-there transparency. These authors recognize the burden of symbolism which glass carried through the 1870s and 1880s, evoking conflict, destruction, identity crises, and social fragility. They exploit this symbolism to enrich and expand the signifying power of their literature. This is not to imply that glass was absent or void of symbolic potential in more esoteric works; indeed, glass, crystals, and prisms are often endowed with emblematic, mystical qualities by Symbolist authors. Patrick McGuinness has noted, for example, how the Belgian writer Maeterlinck uses glass as a recurrent symbol for language's ability to reveal visual forms but divorce the subject from feelings and sensation.[31] However, the relatively small audience for such authors implies a different role for glass in their works. In contrast, Zola, Maupassant, and Huysmans were three of the most popular and iconic authors in the early Third Republic, and their writing reached — and was expected to reach — a sizeable audience. They could thus deliberately play upon mass experiences and concerns; the witnesses of 1870 and 1871 were so numerous that authors could use glass as a recognizable symbol of trauma, distress, and crisis in an unprecedented fashion. In these novels and short stories, associated strongly with the detailed universes of Realism and Naturalism, their readers are led to a greater awareness of meaning inscribed in material culture.

Chapter One of this book sets out the nature of glass culture for the *année terrible* generation, glancing both back towards the Second Empire and forwards into the first two decades of the Third Republic through a variety of newspapers, magazines, medical reports, guidebooks, catalogues, advertisements, paintings, and literary works. This broad view then turns inwards to examine the set of affects and meanings attributed to glass which were specific to the Prussian siege, bombardment, and the Paris Commune. This cultural-historical contextualization makes it possible to gain some sense of how readers in the aftermath of 1870–71 — and particularly Parisian readers — might have seen what is invisible to us today within representations of the material world. Three very different works — Zola's *Au Bonheur des Dames* [*The Ladies' Paradise*], Maupassant's short stories, and Huysmans's *À rebours* [*Against Nature*] — engage with glass and its conflicting significations within this cultural milieu.

Chapter Two explores *Au Bonheur des Dames* (1883), Zola's retrospective glance at a Second Empire department store, filled with vast windows, roof panels, mirrors, wine glasses, bottles, lamps, lifts, and galleries. This novel associates the visual seductiveness of glass with women's weakness for shopping from the very first lines, and the masterly entrepreneur, Octave Mouret, carefully positions glass surfaces to optimum visual effect. Yet if we read between the lines and focus on the women's experience of shopping, the power of the visual is called into question. The sight of mirrors and glass frequently distresses the shoppers — for these women, glass offers images associated with vulnerability, destruction, and oppression. This chapter shifts the focus away from the visual, and seeks a reading of the oral and aural in the text. First, in terms of the female clientele's pleasure in sound; in making and hearing noise, for which the reverberating glass surfaces of the store are essential. Secondly, in terms of sound as a rebellion against oppression on a larger scale; as an escape from the dominant culture of the eye. This chapter questions how this divided sensory experience of glass reflects upon divided society more generally, and what lesson it offers for the future of Third Republic society.

Maupassant's use of glass in his *Contes et nouvelles* (those published 1870–1889) stands in striking contrast to Zola's conciliatory approach. In Chapter Three, I discuss how these short stories — especially the *Contes cruels et fantastiques* — repeatedly locate glass on the borders between everyday normality and trauma, between sanity and psychological collapse. Unlike Zola's largely positive bent, suffering is in the foreground of Maupassant's writing, and it is associated emphatically with glass. This chapter examines different ways in which Maupassant manipulates the freight of symbolism attached to glass in the aftermath of the *année terrible*, both within the narratives and at the diegetic level. It questions how contemporaneous readers might have approached such distressing imagery and texts, and what might have impelled them to keep reading in spite of the unpleasant memories being evoked.

Chapter Four turns to Huysmans's *À rebours* (1884), a novel generally celebrated as the crowning glory of French Decadence. However, this chapter challenges this assumption, reading Des Esseintes's engagement with material culture — particularly glass — alongside archival documents from catalogues, World Fair brochures, guidebooks, and advertising to question whether he really does go beyond the mainstream. I go on to consider the strategic placement of glass objects, and how they are used to glaze over the events of 1870–71 for Des Esseintes, casting light upon the relative aesthetic positions of Des Esseintes and of the text itself. Unlike Maupassant and Zola, Huysmans's innovative text carries few lessons for wider society; it is concerned about recent history only in so much as it influences the evolution of literary aesthetics in the approaching *fin de siècle*. Although these three authors differ considerably in their treatments of glass, each one addresses the problem of representing glass and the physical world for the contemporaneous reader; they explore influences and interactions between literary aesthetics and material culture, and seek to address the impasse of writing fiction in the wake of the *année terrible*.

Notes to the Introduction

1. Marie-Hélène Huet, 'Unsettled Memories: the Revolution Buries its Dead', in *Unfinished Revolutions: Legacies of Upheaval in Modern French Culture*, ed. by Robert T. Denommé and Roland H. Simon (University Park, PA: Pennsylvania State University Press, 1998), pp. 121–37 (p. 128).
2. Quoted in William Scott, *Terror and Repression in Revolutionary Marseilles* (London: Macmillan, 1973), p. 10.
3. Jules Henrivaux, *Le Verre et le cristal* (Paris: Dunod, 1883), p. 1.
4. Maurice Steckel, *Notice sur l'emploi des glaces et des verres* (Paris: Melet, 1890), p. 28.
5. Walter Benjamin, 'Paris, Capital of the Nineteenth Century', in *The Arcades Project*, trans. by Howard Eiland and Kevin McLaughlin (Cambridge, MA: Belknap Press, 1999), pp. 14–26.
6. Théophile Gautier, *Mademoiselle de Maupin*, in *Œuvres complètes: Romans, contes et nouvelles*, ed. by Anne Geisler-Szmulewicz, 5 vols (Paris: Honoré Champion, 2004), I, p. 122.
7. Honoré de Balzac, 'Avant-propos', in *La Comédie humaine*, ed. by Pierre-Georges Castex, 12 vols (Paris: Gallimard, 1976), I, p. 9.
8. Letter to Louise Colet, *Correspondance*, ed. by J. Bruneau and Y. Leclerc, 5 vols (Paris: Gallimard, 1973–2007), II, pp. 419–20, 26 August 1853; *Carnets de Travail*, ed. by P. M. de Biasi (Paris: Baillard, 1988), p. 234.
9. The study of material culture has proved fertile in the discipline of English literature since the late twentieth century. Edited collections by Janis Stout, Luisa Callè, and Patrizia Di Bello explore a wide variety of objects and their symbolic value within the literature of the nineteenth and early twentieth centuries in the Anglophone world, from needlecraft in Willa Cather, to the book as a luxury object in the *Yellow Book*, to design and material aesthetics in John Gray's decadent poetry (Janis Stout, *Willa Carther and Material Culture: Real World Writing, Writing the Real World* (Tuscaloosa: University of Alabama Press, 2005); Luisa Callè and Patrizia Di Bello, *Illustrations, Optics and Objects in Nineteenth-Century Literature and Visual Cultures* (Basingstoke: Palgrave Macmillan, 2010)). Christoph Lindner extends this period in his analysis of narratives of commodity culture from the Victorian to the Postmodern, grounding his ideas in the theories

of Marx, Baudrillard, Lukács, and Adam Smith to draw connections between the authors Gaskell, Trollope, Thackeray, and Conrad, and a number of post-modern cultural phenomena (*Fictions of Commodity Culture: From the Victorian to the Postmodern* (Aldershot: Ashgate, 2003)). His consumption-focused approach is complemented in many ways by Elizabeth Outka's *Consuming Traditions*, which considers the relationship between mass culture and high literature in what she calls the 'commodified authentic'; she argues that early-modernist writers did not simply reject or embrace commodity culture, but that they explored both commercial and non-commercial aesthetic forms to create a peculiarly Edwardian style (*Consuming Traditions: Modernity, Modernism, and the Commodified Authentic* (Oxford: Oxford University Press, 2009)).

10. Jean Baudrillard, *Le Système des objets* (Paris: Gallimard, 1968)
11. Brian Rigby (ed.), *French Literature, Thought and Culture in the nineteenth century — A Material World: Essays in Honour of D. G. Charlton* (Basingstoke: Macmillan, 1993).
12. Janell Watson, *Literature and Material Culture from Balzac to Proust* (Cambridge: Cambridge University Press, 1999); Emma Bielecki, *The Collector in Nineteenth-century French Literature: Representation, Identity, Knowledge* (New York and Bern: Peter Lang, 2012); Anne Green, *Changing France: Literature and Material Culture in the Second Empire* (Cambridge: Cambridge University Press, 2012).
13. M. H. Abrams, *The Mirror and the Lamp: Romantic Theory and the Critical Tradition* (New York: W. W. Norton, 1953), Chapter 2.
14. Ibid., p. 31.
15. Stendhal, *Le Rouge et le Noir*, ed. by Béatrice Didier (Paris: Gallimard, 1972), p. 414; Charles Baudelaire, 'Paysage' in *Les Fleurs du Mal*, in *Œuvres complètes*, ed. by Claude Pichois, 2 vols (Paris: Gallimard, 1975), I, pp. 1–178 (p. 82); 'Préface to *Emaux et Camées*', in *Poésies complètes de Théophile Gautier*, ed. by René Jasinski, 3 vols (Paris: A. G. Nizet, 1970), III, p. 3; Baudelaire, 'Le Peintre de la vie moderne', in *Œuvres complètes*, II, pp. 683–724 (p. 692).
16. Zola, *Correspondance*, ed. by Alain Pagès (Paris: Flammarion, 2012), pp. 110, 115, 116.
17. *A Mirror in the Roadway: Literature and the Real World* (Princeton, NJ: Princeton University Press, 2005); *Maupassant in the Hall of Mirrors: Ironies of Repetition in the Work of Guy de Maupassant* (Basingstoke: Macmillan, 1990); *Distorting Mirrors: Visions of the Crowd in Late Nineteenth-Century France* (New Haven and London: Yale University Press, 1981).
18. Elizabeth Emery and Laura Morowitz, *Consuming the Past: The Medieval Revival in fin-de-siècle France* (Aldershot: Ashgate, 2003), especially Chapter 5.
19. Roger Magraw, 'Producing, Retailing, Consuming, Spending', in *French Literature, Thought and Culture in the Nineteenth Century: A Material World, Essays in Honour of D. G. Charlton*, ed. by Brian Rigby (Basingstoke: Macmillan, 1993), pp. 59–85.
20. As summarized by Isobel Armstrong, *Victorian Glassworlds: Glass Culture and the Imagination 1830–80* (Oxford: Oxford University Press, 2008), p. 89.
21. Jonathan Lamb, *The Things Things Say* (Princeton, NJ: Princeton University Press, 2011), p. xi.
22. Louis Veuillot, 'Pensées de nuit d'un bombardé', *L'Univers*, 18 January 1871.
23. Roland Barthes, 'Sémantique de l'objet', in *Œuvres complètes*, ed. by Eric Marty, 3 vols (Paris: Seuil, 1993–95), II, p. 71.
24. 'Chronique du mois', *La Mode nouvelle et miroir parisien*, July 1873, p. 162.
25. Jean Moréas, *Œuvres* (Geneva: Slatkine, 1977), pp. 130–31:

> 'Le TEMPS dit: Je suis le Temps, un et simultané,
> Et je stagne en ayant l'air de celui qui s'envole,
> Mirage fruste et kaléidoscope frivole,
> Je vous leurre avec l'heure qui n'a jamais sonné.'

26. Guy de Maupassant, *Sur l'eau, Blanc et bleu, Livre de Bord* (Paris: Louis Conard, 1921), p. 114.
27. Lamb, p. xi.
28. Daniel Miller, *The Comfort of Things* (Cambridge: Polity Press, 2008); Janet Hoskins, *Biographical Objects: How Things Tell the Stories of People's Lives* (London and New York: Routledge, 1998).
29. Lamb, p. 38.
30. Armstrong, p. 362.
31. Patrick McGuinness, 'Belgian Literature and the Symbolism of the Double', in *From Art Nouveau*

to *Surrealism: Belgian Modernity in the Making*, ed. by Nathalie Aubert, Pierre-Philippe Fraiture, and Patrick McGuinness (London: Legenda, 2007), pp. 8–22 (p. 16).

CHAPTER 1

Glass and Culture in the Aftermath of the *Année Terrible*

> Indispensable aux usages de la vie domestique, le verre a fourni aux sciences physiques et chimiques leurs plus précieux instruments. C'est le verre qui a permis à la photographie de reproduire l'image de la nature. C'est le verre qui a fourni ces admirables lentilles de télescopes, qui permettent de sonder l'espace céleste, et qui nous révèlent les lois présidant aux mouvements des astres. C'est au verre qu'on doit le microscope, qui nous fait découvrir l'infiniment petit et nous initie aux phénomènes de la vie chez des êtres dont, sans le verre, nous n'aurions même pas soupçonné l'existence. C'est au verre enfin que l'on doit les phares, ressource des navigateurs en détresse, et ces précieux instruments de guerre dont les regards curieux plongent jusqu'à dans les rangs ennemis pour leur dérober leurs secrets.
>
> [Indispensable for domestic life, glass has also supplied the physical and chemical sciences with their most precious instruments. It is glass that has allowed photography to reproduce nature's image. It is glass that has supplied those admirable telescope lenses, which make it possible to penetrate the celestial realm, and which reveal the laws governing the movement of the stars. It is to glass that we owe the microscope, which allows us to discover the infinitely small and initiates us to the phenomena of life which, without glass, we would not even have thought existed. It is to glass, finally, that we owe lighthouses, the salvation of sailors in distress, and those precious instruments of war through which the curious eye may delve into the enemy ranks and unveil their secrets]
>
> MAURICE STECKEL, *Notice sur l'emploi des glaces et des verres.*[1]

The evolution of monumental and commercial Paris over the nineteenth century would have been inconceivable without glass. Technological advances in glass-making launched a trajectory for architectural innovation that traversed the 1840s, Haussmannization and the World Fairs, Art Nouveau, the Pompidou Centre (1977) and Louvre Pyramid (1989), to the present day Tour Triangle (currently due for completion in 2020 at the Porte de Versailles). Although this influx of glass architecture was by no means unique to Paris, it was nonetheless seen to be so by Parisians, and indeed the French glass industry was rivalled only by the English in the whole of Europe. The official catalogue of the 1878 World Fair lauded the making of 'glaces' (for mirrors or high-quality window panes) as 'une industrie essentiellement parisienne' ['an essentially Parisian industry'],[2] and Paris was praised as a world-leader in 'la vente du verre, des cristaux, des glaces, et de la gobleterie' ['the sale of glass, of crystal, of high-quality glass panels, and of drinking glasses'].[3] Another booklet boasted that the French cut-glass producers Baccarat, Buquet, and Maes far outshone Bohemian crystal,[4] and a guidebook to Paris declared that tourists would be unable to resist slowing their pace to admire the extensive shop windows on the Rue de la Paix.[5]

This 'essentially Parisian industry' attracted significant investment from producers and purchasers alike. In 1878, France was producing 15 million francs worth of window glass, 25 million francs of mirror glass, 14 to 15 million francs of glass tableware, 11 to 12 million francs of crystal glass, and 40 million francs worth of glass bottles (bearing in mind that each bottle cost only between 12 and 30 centimes) — in all, a total of 105 to 110 million francs worth of glass, of which only a third was exported.[6] With mass production came considerable reductions in price; a 1 m^2 domestic mirror which would have cost 205 francs in 1802 cost just 30 francs 23 centimes in 1889, and a large 4 m^2 mirror cost 3 644 francs and 136 francs respectively.[7] Consequently, mirrors proliferated throughout the Parisian public sphere. Immense mirrors were commissioned from the Saint-Gobain glassworks for the Hôtel Continental de Paris, the Eden-Théâtre de Paris, and for the foyer of the Opéra Garnier — the latter measuring a prodigious 17.6 m^2 and 19.5 m^2. Mirrors became fundamental to the urban improvements conducted by Haussmann, and they affirmed the aesthetic and economic glory of the Second Empire.

Developments in glass-making technologies were never far removed from developments in nearly every other field since glass components were essential to a vast array of sciences and technologies, as the epigraph to this chapter demonstrates. Both the 1867 and 1878 World Fairs included displays of the latest innovations in lenticular technology for lighthouses, and the 1889 World Fair featured a revolving lighthouse lamp on top of the Eiffel Tower.[8] Scientific developments were quickly embraced by popular culture, as a passion for Progress inspired an avid enthusiasm for each new advancement. The microscope lens not only made it possible for scientists to penetrate the hitherto invisible world, but even ladies of leisure were encouraged to experiment around the home. The magazine *La Mode nouvelle* suggests: 'la cassonade nourrit deux insectes microscopiques. [...] Prenez une forte loupe, ou mieux, un microscope, et vous assisterez à ce drame perpétuel qui constitue la cassonade. Mais si vous aimez la cassonade, ne la regardez pas de trop près!' ['brown sugar feeds two microscopic insects. [...] Take a strong magnifying glass, or better still, a microscope, and you can watch the perpetual drama taking place in the sugar bowl. But if you like sugar, don't look too closely!'].[9]

Photography was perhaps the most popularized technology which flourished thanks to innovations in glass making — two thousand photographic businesses had registered premises in France in 1878, and in that year the industry made more than 30 million francs. Not only was glass vital to photography for providing camera lenses, but there was also a trend in the 1870s for printing photographically-reproduced images onto small panes of glass. During the 1872 *étrennes* season, for example, the *État* newspaper advertised *diaphanographies* — '[une] riche collection de *Photographies sur verre* publiée par la maison Goupil et Cie.' ['a rich collection of *Photographs on glass* published by Goupil and Co.'] — including reproductions of fine art works to be hung in the bourgeois home as a modern form of stained glass which, the reader is assured, 'doivent faire le plus de plaisir aux gens de goût' ['will surely give the utmost pleasure to people of good taste'].[10]

Glass objects were integral to many diverse aspects of the 1878 World Fair. There was a whole Class dedicated to 'Cristaux, Verrerie, et Vitraux', subdivided into *cristaux, gobeleterie, glaces, verre à vitres (blancs et colorés), bouteilles, émaux, miroirs*, and *vitraux peints* ['Crystal, Glassware, and Stained-glass': *crystal, drinking glasses, high-quality glass panels, window glass (clear and coloured), bottles, enamels, mirrors*, and *stained glass*]. Yet even classes not overtly associated with glass still relied upon glass as an integral material — from the 'Meubles à bon marché et meubles de luxe' ['Budget furniture and luxury furniture'], where six different companies exhibited their particular brands of mirrored wardrobe;[11] to 'Objets de voyage et de campement' ['Travel and Camping equipment'], where the manufacturer Bouju displayed cases of miniature travel-size glass bottles and pocket-size ink-wells;[12] to the 'Bimbeloterie' ['Fancy goods'] group, which included objects as diverse as the company Lapierre Fils Ainé's 'lanternes magiques en fer-blanc et dessins sur verres' ['tinplate magic lanterns with images on glass'] and Poudra Fils's 'kaléïdoscope, kaléïdogènes, [et] lorgnettes divers' ['kaleidoscopes, kaleidogenes, and various lorgnettes'].[13]

Not only did glass become more affordable during this period, but its durability also improved, allowing 'des dallages, des pavages, des revêtements, des caniveaux, des urinoirs, etc.' ['flagstones, paving, protective coating, gutters, urinals, etc.'] to be made from glass, and thus making it possible for glass to spread throughout the urban landscape.[14] Large sheets of glass of ever-increasing proportions could be rolled; Maurice Steckel recorded that the largest window panes to be displayed by French companies measured 6.53 m by 3.23 m at the 1855 World Fair, 6.66 m by 4.40 m in 1878, and finally the 'volume vraiment extraordinaire' of 8.13 m by 4.08 m in 1889.[15] This increased size and durability allowed glass to become an ever-more prevalent and prominent architectural feature of the exterior as well as the interior of public buildings, particularly in Paris. Old crown-glass panes had been uneven, bubbled, and vulnerable to the vibrations of passing vehicles with a breakage rate of 25–30%; consequently, urban buildings had rarely used glass on a large scale except in the sheltered arcades. However, new pouring, rolling, and eventually dipping methods permitted shops, hotels, and luxurious apartments to employ larger, clearer windows with only a 5–6% breakage rate.[16] For example, Paris's premier hotel, the Grand-Hôtel, had its entire courtyard glazed over in 1878, with more than 600 m² of glass panelling. This was deemed so impressive that the image chosen for the core of the Hotel's advertising strategy in 1878 depicted the courtyard instead of the monumental front of the Hotel.[17] Furthermore, proprietors could benefit from numerous new insurance policies to protect their vitreous investments, including special deals for exhibitors at the 1878 World Fair.[18] The influence of such insurance policies was felt throughout the streets of the capital city; indeed, Steckel considered that 'l'assurance contre le bris des glaces a été l'auxiliaire le plus efficace de la transformation des magasins et de l'embellissement des rues et des boulevards' ['insurance against glass breakage has been the most efficient auxiliary for the transformation of shops and for urban beautification'].[19] So effective were these new, large shop windows in attracting admiration and custom that by 1890 the insurance provider *La Parisienne* alone had sold some 40 000 policies.[20]

As mirrors and large windows became more affordable but retained their high-life associations, cafés and restaurants lined their walls with glass to attract a wealthy bourgeois clientele — indeed, by 1878 this was such a ubiquitous trait of the fashionable café that Huart and Draner offered a warning in their comic guide to Paris that 'les prix varient avec les dorures, les glaces, et les peintures qui ornent les murs' ['prices vary with the gilding, the mirrors, and the paintings which line to walls'].[21] So engrained was this analogy between modernized Paris and glass that, throughout the literature and art of the latter half of the century, glass décor appears as a metonym for bourgeois Parisian society. It becomes a symbol which could rapidly invoke an entire social scene. Baudelaire's famous depiction of Haussmannized Paris in 'Les Yeux des Pauvres' ['The Eyes of the Poor'] (1869) depicts 'les nappes éblouissantes des miroirs' ['the dazzling sheets of the mirrors'] and the wide café window as typical features of the new bourgeois social scene.[22] Likewise Huysmans, to highlight the segregation of the classes, places his impoverished chestnut-seller in the cold street outside a brightly lit bar, '[où] s'alignent, vives, engageantes, scintillant sur une planchette posée devant une glace, des régiments de bouteilles' ['where, lined up, lively, engaging, sparkling on a shelf in front of a mirror, stand regiments of bottles'] (*CP*, 77). Edmond de Goncourt depicts an ostentatious café in *La Fille Elisa* (1877) whose proprietrix reigns 'au milieu des fioles colorées, reflétées dans la grande glace' ['amongst coloured flasks, reflected in the large mirror'].[23] All of these mirrors and windows call upon the reader's awareness of glass décor and architecture in their real lived experience of nineteenth-century society.

Similarly, the visual arts depict mirror-lined and glass-filled establishments, from Degas's *L'Absinthe* [*Absinthe*] (1873), Forain's *Bar aux Folies-Bergères* [*Bar at the Folies Bergères*] (1880), Caillebotte's *Dans un café* [*In a Café*] (1880), to many of Manet's paintings, including *Au café* [*At the Café*] (1878), *La Serveuse de Bocks* [*The Waitress*] (1879), and the famous *Le Bar aux Folies-Bergères* [*Bar at the Folies Bergères*] (1882) in which glass is central to its modernity. Huysmans later identified the mirror as one of the key features of this Caillebotte work in his *Écrits sur l'art* [*Writings on Art*], specifically singling out the 'grande glace au cadre d'or piqueté par des points de mouches, [qui] réverbère les épaules du monsieur debout et répercute tout l'intérieur du café' ['large mirror with a gilded frame flecked with fly-spots, reflecting the shoulders of the man standing before it, and redoubling the whole interior of the café'] as no mere backdrop, but as essential to the interpretation of the painting.[24]

These large, strong glass panels were rapidly installed from the mid-century onwards and they created a monumental Parisian landscape at the forefront of Western architectural innovation. In 1889 the Saint-Gobain glassworks could boast that their glass had been used in a lengthy catalogue of prominent architectural projects, listing in their brochure:

> l'Hippodrome, l'Administration, des Pompes funèbres, la Société du Val d'Osne, les ateliers Marinani, Mignon et Rouart, le Comptoir d'Escompte, le Muséum d'Histoire naturelle, le Musée du Luxembourg, les gares d'Orléans,

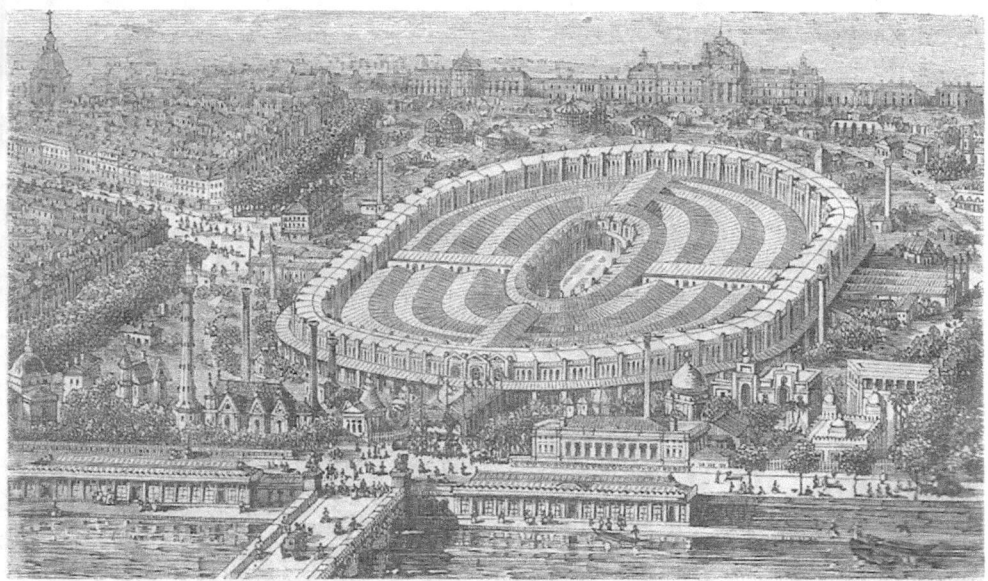

Fig. 1.1. The glass-roofed rotunda of the Paris World Fair of 1867, on the Champs de Mars; engraving from Alfred Joanne, Collection des guides Joanne (Paris: Hachette, 1867). (With thanks to Wikimedia Commons user Bourrichon.)

du Nord, de l'Est, de Saint-Lazare, le Trocadéro, l'Hôtel de Ville, les ateliers de la Compagnie de l'Ouest à Levallois-Perret, tout le Palais des Machines à l'Exposition de 1889, et la plupart des toitures vitrées de cette Exposition.[25]

[The Hippodrome, the central Administrative offices, the general Undertakers, the Val d'Osne Company, the Marinani, Mignon and Rouart workshops, the Central Bank, the National History Museum, the Luxembourg Museum, the Nord, Est, and Saint-Lazare railway stations, the Trocadero, the City Hall, the workshops of the Compagnie de l'Ouest at Lavallois-Perret, the whole of the Machinery Hall at the 1889 World Fair, and most of the other glazing for the current Fair.]

Glass had become so integral to the modern, bourgeois Parisian cityscape in the 1870s and 1880s that Flaubert's notes for the conclusion of *Bouvard et Pécuchet* predict satirically that 'Paris deviendra un jardin d'hiver' ['Paris will become a winter garden'].[26] This Fourieresque dreamworld was less fantastic than Flaubert may have realized, given that projects were proposed in 1875 to glaze over the Palais-Royal after it had been repaired following fire damage,[27] and that among the designs for the 1889 World Fair was a plan to cover the entire Champs Elysées, trees and all, with a glass roof (although neither of these plans ultimately came to fruition).[28]

Hoping to go one better than London's 1851 Crystal Palace, all of Paris's nineteenth-century exhibition halls were constructed predominantly from glass and iron, with the belief that these materials would instantly convey France's enviable position at the forefront of modernity (see Figures 1.1, 1.2, and 1.3). Glass formed the walls and floors of aquaria at the World Fairs, including 'tunnel' style aquaria in

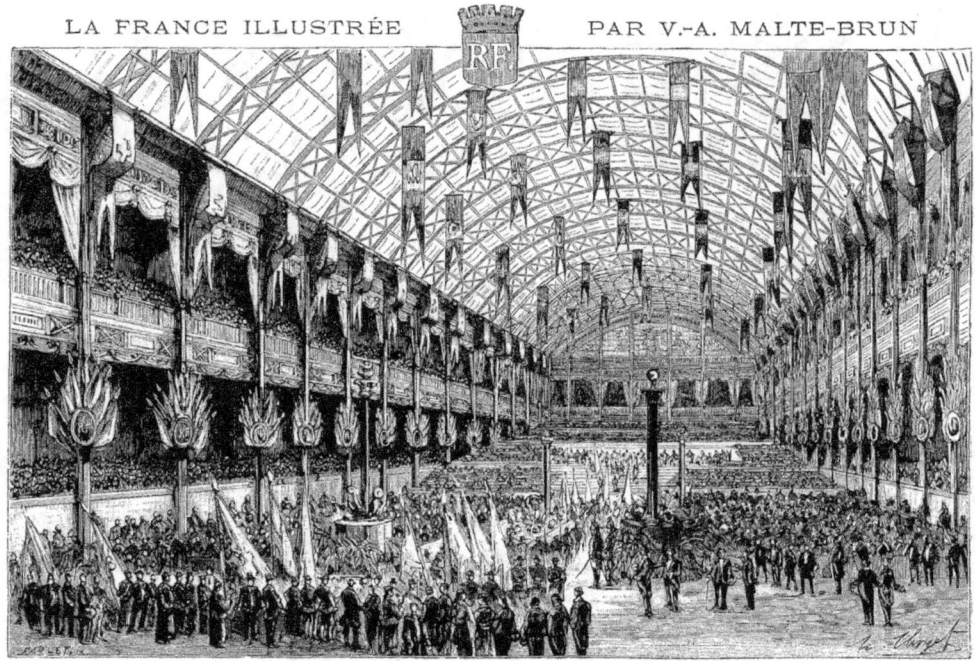

Fig. 1.2 (above). Awarding of prizes at the Paris World Fair of 1878, in the main exposition hall of the Palais de l'Industrie. Engraving from Victor Adolphe Malte-Brun, *La France illustrée* (Paris: Rouff, 1881).

Fig. 1.3 (opposite, above). Dutert's great 'Galerie des machines' at the Champs de Mars, as photographed in the *Album de l'Exposition 1889* (Paris: Gaulon, 1889).

Fig. 1.4 (opposite, below). The fresh water aquarium of the 1867 Paris World Fair.

1867 and 1878 where glass panels allowed visitors to glimpse the sea creatures from all angles (see Figure 1.4).[29] In 1878, miles of glass-fronted *vitrines* offered the sight — but not the touch — of everything from the French Crown Jewels to a chocolate model of the Colonne de Juillet.[30] A towering pyramid was constructed from 40 000 liqueur bottles,[31] and in the Spanish colonial section a replica of the Alhambra gate was built from multi-coloured bottles.[32] Visitors impressed by this vitreous fairyland could even take away a metonymic souvenir by buying a drinking glass with their name engraved into the surface.[33] By the 1889 World Fair, glass became the vehicle for electric light and its immensely popular spectacles, such as the colour-changing fountains which used glass slabs with variable stained-glass filters slotted underneath the spouts to shine polychrome light into the towering flumes of water.[34]

Anne Green has revealed through her extensive archival research that, 'glossing over the dubious legitimacy of the new regime, texts surrounding the [1855 and 1867] exhibitions were suffused with images [...] that implied the exhibitions had evolved as a natural and inevitable manifestation of the essential nature of Frenchness'.[35] The same could be said of the Third Republic's World Fairs in the wake of 1870; the blood that the Republic had on its hands was glossed over in images of purity and transparency, manifested in vast, glittering, and unbroken oceans of glass

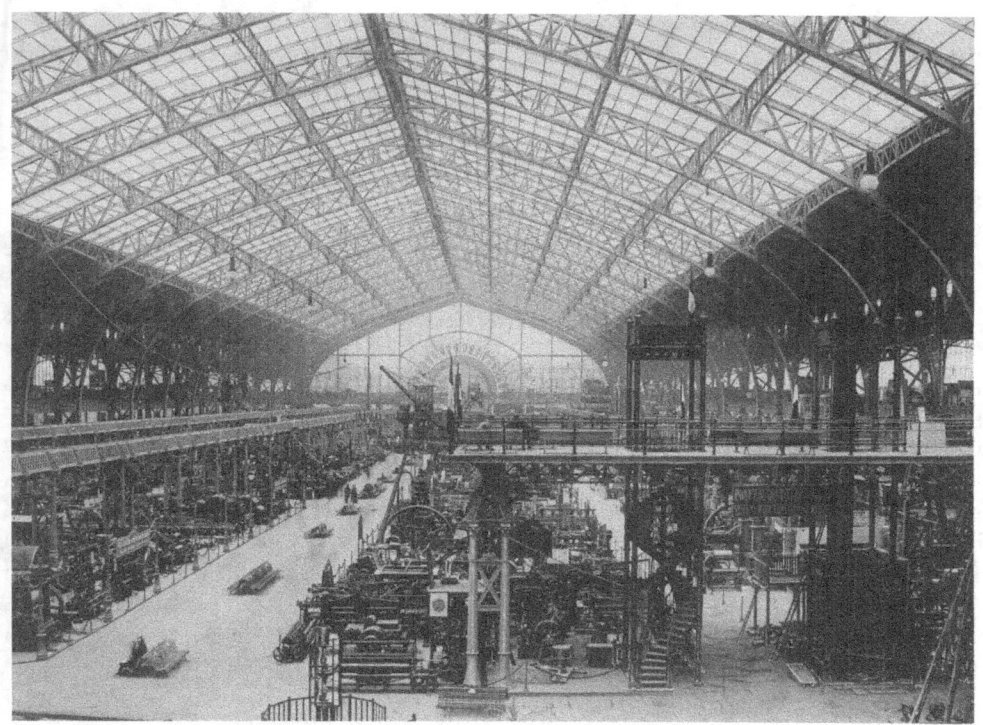

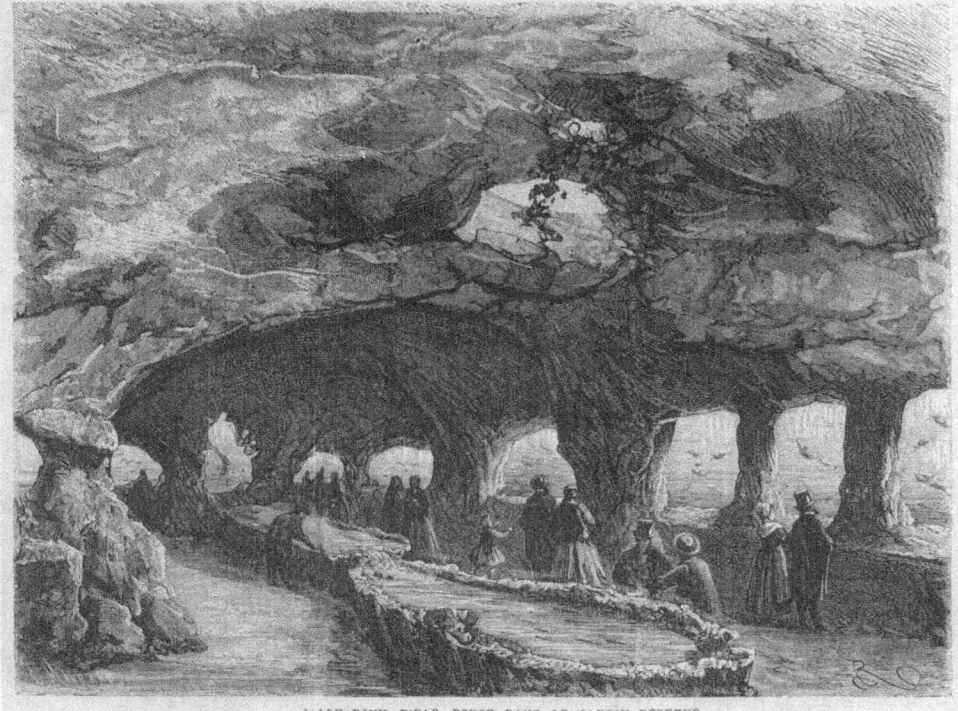

L'AQUARIUM D'EAU DOUCE DANS LE JARDIN RÉSERVÉ

architecture, each bigger and more splendid than the last. Indeed, a proposal to turn the Tuileries ruins into a winter garden — complete with the Arc du Triomphe du Carroussel as the main entrance — in time for the 1878 Fair manifests this desire, quite literally, to glaze over the past.[36]

Glass and the Private Sphere

Glass came to fill not only the public spaces of Paris but also its homes as the nineteenth century progressed — starting with increasingly large windows which stood between the private bourgeois interior and the public world outside. This transparent cloister held the bourgeois wife and children at a safe distance from the promiscuity of the public sphere. In Berthe Morisot's paintings of domestic life, glass windows, conservatories, and glazed panels characterize the crystal fortress of the bourgeois home. In *Dans la salle à manger* [*In the Dining Room*] (1875), the dining room window to the woman's right forms a corollary with the carefully-sealed, glass-fronted cabinet to her left; just as the glass cupboard door keeps the family's best crockery safe from wandering hands, so the window does with the wife. In *Dans la veranda* [*On the Veranda*] (1884) and *Poupée dans la veranda* [*Doll on the Veranda*] (1884), the women and girls are so very nearly in the outside world of the gardens, yet the thinnest of black lines indicates that glass still stands between them and even a domesticated exterior.

However, whilst windows hold the noise, dirt, and pungency of the public sphere at bay, they simultaneously display the vulnerability of the private sphere. They pose a certain physical impediment, but they remain a visual and to some extent aural point of access; they are at once a solid boundary and a point of potential permeability. Any window overlooking a significant thoroughfare would reverberate with every passing omnibus, and urban windows would collect layers of dust and soot which could only be cleared from the bourgeois line of sight by the intervention of a working-class window cleaner. Richard Terdiman identifies, in his work on modernity, the window as 'an architectural oxymoron' which allows 'the stable separations of the world [to be] problematized and upset' with a 'mingling of inside and outside'.[37] After the destruction of the *année terrible* which left so many broken windows around the city, this mingling of inside and outside was revealed in extremis — one guidebook to the Parisian ruins would actively invite the wandering tourist to step right through a shattered window on the Avenue des Gobelins to get a glimpse of a once-private courtyard: 'En enjambant une des larges fenêtres que le feu a léchées, on trouve, derrière, un jardin dévasté mais verdoyant, et, dans une serre aux vitres brisés, un Apollon du Belvédère en plâtre, calme comme il sied à un immortel' ['on stepping through one of the broad windows that has been licked by flames, one finds a garden beyond, devastated but verdant; and, in a greenhouse with shattered glass, a plaster Apollo Belvedere, with all the calmness befitting an immortal'].[38] This demonstrates that, fundamentally, mere, insubstantial glass is all that ever stops the passer-by from breaching the boundaries of the private home.

The problematic mingling of private and public is implied in many of the window-focused paintings of the period, particularly those by Gustave Caillebotte.

Although on the surface these paintings display the bourgeois eye's domination of the world beyond the window, they also imply the disconcerting permeability of bourgeois space. For example, the male viewer in Caillebotte's *Jeune homme à la fenêtre* [*Young Man at the Window*] (1875–76) overlooks the Boulevard des Malesherbes through the wide-open windows of his balcony. On the one hand, his assertive stance, legs apart, places the world outside at his command; both visually and, by implication, psychologically and socially. We do not see his face, but his line of sight seems to rest upon a woman in the distance, as though enjoying the fantasy that his dominant, elevated position could easily translate into sexual domination too. Yet on the other hand such pleasant, casual fantasies entail an implicit threat to the confident male because they involve the invasion of their private space by outsiders. This is hinted at obliquely by the reflection of the outside world which creeps into his room; the buildings opposite are reflected in his window panes which, in their open position, bring the image of the external world inside his personal kingdom.

Moreover, this painting seems to form a pair with *L'Homme au balcon, Boulevard Haussmann* [*Man on the Balcony, Boulevard Haussmann*] (1880), in which a slightly older and slightly wealthier man leans with considerable swagger against the rail of a fourth-floor balcony. The window, once again, places a reflection of the exterior world within the space of the interior; but now, rather than the room belonging to this man, the fact that he still wears his top-hat indicates that he too has infiltrated from outside. Whose room is this? Is his confident posture a sign that he knows he can seduce (or has already seduced) the woman he is visiting at this address? Or does the striped awning imply the *cabinet particulier* of a restaurant — that parody of the private sphere — in which he awaits a scene of seduction as the evening light starts to slant over the street beyond? In either case, the public may clearly seep into the private sphere, and the glass bastions erected to protect it are easily breached. Indeed, both paintings could be juxtaposed with Henri Gervex's *Rolla* (1878). In this work, the young man stands in a similar position overlooking a Parisian street, but turns back into the apartment slightly to face the consequence of his realized desires. He casts a jaded eye over the prostitute in his bed before (as the Alfred Musset short story goes) committing suicide by poisoning himself.

By contrast with these young men and their open windows, Caillebotte's respectable spouse in *Intérieur* (1880) is safely ensconced behind a closed window, and this bored bourgeoise gazes into the street below whilst her husband reads the newspaper. Under its sheen of protection, the glass pane also contributes to a feeling of constriction and imprisonment here, amplified by the curtains, by the husband's amputated form, and by the subtle mirroring of this woman with another equally constrained woman in the apartment opposite. Furthermore, this painting brings to mind both literary and medical cases of women soliciting men from windows, including the wealthy Baroness in Maupassant's 'Le Signe' ['The Sign'] (*CN*, II.725);[39] the poor woman in Vallès's 'Le Dépôt' ['The Depot'];[40] the man with a persecution complex which leads him to believe his wife is hailing lovers from their window;[41] and the fifteen-year-old girl afflicted with acute nymphomania who calls out of her window to every passing soldier.[42] Glass windows represent the architectural weak spot in the separation of the public, masculine and private, feminine spheres. Caillebotte's nonchalant husband may, then, have reason to fear his wife attracting the desiring gazes of other men from behind the seemingly hermetic window pane. As Isobel Armstrong points out, '[being] intended for the passage of sight, every window comes with a future history of seeing blent into it. It anticipates the gaze of innumerable eyes, from inside to out, outside to in'.[43] It is perhaps for this reason that rather than window glass being described as 'clear' in French, it was generally called *verre* or *cristal blanc* — a whiteness which aspires to a more substantial opacity than the window really has. More dramatic still, as the husband peruses the paper — Huysmans suggests he is idling away his time over the *faits divers*[44] — there is an oblique connection to the distressingly frequent accounts of suicide by self-defenestration, particularly by women, during this period. When the frustrations of the bourgeois private space arrive at their breaking point, the cloistering window is flung open by the bourgeois woman, desperate for escape and unable to bide passively in her crystal prison any longer — be it the fiancée in despair, the unhappy wife, the pure bourgeois adolescent, or the new mother.[45] Indeed, this method of suicide was sufficiently common among women at this time to merit a place in Maupassant's *chronique Sur l'eau* [*On the Water*],[46] in Jules Vallès's series of Parisian vignettes, *Le Tableau de Paris* [*Parisian Scenes*],[47] and to have its own section 'Précipitation par la fenêtre' ['Self-Defenestration'] in Legrand du Saulle's book *Les Hystériques* [*Hysterics*] (1883).

Glass objects also became heavily inscribed within the boundaries of the bourgeois domestic sphere. Ladies' magazines offered tips for how to frost glass, how to avoid breaking glasses and lamps, how to engrave glass, how to avoid fly-spots on mirrors, how to make a special glue for repairing glass, and how to pierce glass.[48] Miniature mirrors and glass pieces were encased — without any practical need — into every object upon which a woman might expect to place her hands in the course of a day, from sewing boxes, to glove boxes, jewellery boxes, watch boxes, and handkerchief boxes. In the forty-one pages of the Bon Marché's *Exposition des articles pour Etrennes* [*Seasonal Gifts Exhibition*] catalogue in 1882, there were thirty-eight gifts incorporating glass, many of which were available in a variety of different woods or fabrics but which could not be bought without their piece of glass.[49] Glass was considered so indispensable to bourgeois comfort that even transatlantic ships were equipped with mirrors (after considerable research into how to avoid deterioration by moisture), and any benevolent mistress of the household was encouraged to furnish her maid's room with a mirror and a drinking glass.[50] The latest children's toys incorporated glass parts, such as the mirrored wardrobes for dolls' houses advertised by the Bon Marché,[51] and games using optical technologies such as *chromatoscopes*, *lamposcopes*, *réflectoscopes*, and *praxinoscopes*.[52]

Large fireplace mirrors became a necessary feature of any self-respecting middle-class household. In *Le Drageoir aux épices* [*A Dish of Spices*] (1874), Huysmans describes a theatre production in a popular *quartier* which, in order to set the scene of a bourgeois salon, simply furnishes the stage with 'une fausse cheminée surmontée d'une glace peinte en étain, la fenêtre coutumière au fond' ['a fake chimney-piece, with a mirror hanging over it painted in tin, the standard window in the background'] (*DE*, 117). Indeed, for all his professed rejection of modern fashions, Edmond de Goncourt's coffee-table photographic book of his house at Auteuil shows that the fireplace in nearly every room had a substantially-sized mirror hanging above it.[53] Flaubert describes just three key features of Frédéric's new apartment after his inheritance as recognizable signs that he has 'made it': window shutters, window curtains, and a Venetian mirror.[54] Such mirrors could even show off social connections as well as material wealth for the *arriviste*, by displaying the calling-cards of illustrious visitors; the lady of the house or her guests could admire their good looks and her social conquests simultaneously. The upper-class female writer in *La Mode nouvelle* mocks these 'esprits enfantins [qui] se plaisent [...] à plaquer (ce qui, entre parenthèses, est de très mauvais goût), sur les glaces des cheminées, des vélins surmontés de couronnes ducales ou des armes d'un marquisat, d'un comté, d'une baronnie quelconque' ['those childish minds which take pleasure [...] in exhibiting on the fire-place mirror (with, incidentally, very bad taste), visiting cards printed with ducal crowns or the crest of a marquis, a count, or some baronet'].[55] Yet for all its *mauvais goût*, this remained common practice, and a social critique from 1888, *Le Miroir du monde* [*The Mirror of the World*], makes use of an engraving of a mirror stuck with calling cards to frame a page of its text.[56]

As one might expect, the ex-aristocracy and upper echelons of the bourgeoisie who had first adorned their homes with extremely expensive mirrors later sought to denigrate the petty bourgeoisie for their parvenu desires to do likewise. Octave Uzanne, in his unsympathetic portrayal of the lower-middle classes, declares that: 'toute petite bourgeoise française nubile est la proie de deux rêves, deux ambitions, deux cauchemars qu'elle parvient toujours à réaliser: l'informe boîte à supplice musicale qu'on nomme piano d'Erard, et l'armoire à glace, [...] dont la fabrication est aussi innombrable que les grains du sable de la mer' ['every nubile French petty bourgeoise is prey to two dreams, two ambitions, two nightmares that she always manages to realize: the shapeless musical torture box known as the Erard piano, and the mirrored wardrobe, [...] which are made in greater quantities than sand in the sea'].[57] This is not so much a critique of mirrors as a recognition of their desirability — the upper bourgeoisie are simply irked that mirrors no longer retain the exclusivity that they once did, since they are unwilling to forfeit glass culture themselves to retain their class distinction. To avoid finding themselves on a level with the petty bourgeoisie, the upper classes instead began purchasing Venetian mirrors — as the monarchy did before Louis XIV stole Venice's secret production methods through industrial espionage. However, whilst this meant that the upper classes knew their mirrors were more expensive and exclusive than those in the average middle-class household, it did very little to change the overall appearance of the salon, or the fundamental role of glass in their experience of *fin de siècle* life.

For all the distinction that the upper bourgeoisie might have sought to establish from the petty bourgeoisie, they could concede that the middle classes were more like them than the working classes, whom they considered not merely people of inferior taste but virtually another species. The whole of the bourgeoisie, then, may be united in finding comfort in glass's ability to, as Armstrong suggests, filter and/ or exclude the poor from middle-class and (ex-)aristocratic horizons.[58] However, this engrained and increasingly ubiquitous association between glass and all sections of the bourgeoisie does not always entail the comforting class exclusivity vis à vis the working classes that one might imagine. When some amount of glass became affordable to even the lower classes, it allowed the bodily and domestic characteristics of the classes to be blurred. Roger Magraw has noted, for example, that the mass production of cheap mirrors reduced the physical distinction between bourgeois and working-class men because the latter were able to adopt the fashion for being clean-shaven in the 1860s.[59] Sufficiently credible glass reproductions of precious gems were available by 1887 that less wealthy women could elevate the public perception of their financial status: the company Fremy and Feil announced at the Académie des Sciences that they could make aluminium-based glass in sufficient quantities to provide a viable industrial replacement for rubies and sapphires.[60] Such glass objects would become a means by which the lower classes mimicked the bourgeoisie and attempted to claim a place on the ladder of social ascent.

This aspirational impulse is frequently translated into literature; for example, Zola gives glass a central symbolic role in Gervaise's ambition for a modest bourgeois lifestyle in the canonical tale of the Parisian working classes, *L'Assommoir* (1877). When Gervaise and Coupeau start their own laundry, the large glass windows of the shop repeatedly form a descriptive focal point — Zola portrays them variously as brand-new and glistening with cleanliness; reverberating with sun in the summer's heat; covered in steam during the winter; first curtained and then open to the street during Gervaise's party; and ringing with the sound of drunken singing (*A*, 497, 503, 543, 564, 585). Later, the purchase of a glass-globed clock will mark the high point of Gervaise's social ascent, before it becomes a recurrent symbol of her declining finances, morals, and self-respect (*A*, 476, Chapter 9). She dusts it meticulously, guards it jealously, stores her savings book under it religiously; then, as her descent hastens, the glass globe houses pawnshop receipts in place of the savings book, it gathers dust, and it must eventually and reluctantly be sold.

Indeed, the presence and character of glass objects found in the working-class home and district subvert the meaning conferred upon glass by all levels of bourgeois society. Mirrors signify little in relation to the poor except in direct mimicry or burlesque of the bourgeois material world — and very often an erotic one. Mirrors may adorn the prostitute's parody of bourgeois luxury, or may become an erotic metaphor in Goncourt's *La Fille Elisa*, in which *passer devant la glace* [to pass before the mirror] becomes 'une expression qui désigne l'entrée de faveur accordée, par la maîtresse d'une maison, à l'amant d'une fille' ['an expression designating special access to the brothel for the lover of one of the prostitutes, granted by the madam'].[61] When Huysmans's eponymous heroine Marthe finds a wealthy lover who rents her an apartment, her first move is to furnish it with 'les glaces à cadres trop dorés' ['mirrors with overly-gilded frames'] in an attempt at becoming the comfortable bourgeoise she has long resented.[62] Indeed, Huysmans highlights that glass may reflect both literally and metaphorically the transgression of class boundaries. In 'L'Ambulante', Huysmans depicts a prostitute's room in which the familiar, vertical domestic mirror is translated onto the horizontal plane over the bed (*CP*, 64), and in 'Damiens' the bourgeois narrator can no longer recognize the harrowed face in the mirrored ceiling of a prostitute's bed as his own (*CP*, 116–18). The secure bourgeois subject is splintered as the mirror is perverted from its habitual context and associations — this mirror is as much a comment upon the bourgeois interior as upon the lower class's engagement with material culture.

Yet in working-class domestic arrangements generally, mirrors rarely feature beyond the small shaving mirror. In his 1883 history of glass, Jules Henrivaux notes that even in the 1880s, mirrors remained sufficiently luxurious to the lower-class eye that 'plus d'un écriteau qui annonce un appartement orné de glaces pend encore au-dessus de la porte des maisons de certains quartiers de Paris' ['more than one sign advertising an apartment decorated with mirrors can still be found hanging above the door of properties in certain areas of Paris'].[63] It is also possible for glass to take forms specific to the impoverished *quartier*. The windows of the poor often appear in texts, but their obscure glass has little in common with the large, clear panes of Haussmannized Paris. Whereas the bourgeois home attempts to use glass to delimit and guard its physical boundaries, the poorer household spills beyond its windows. One striking point of contrast between bourgeois and the lower-class windows is their spatial relation to fabrics. The windows of the wealthy are rarely described or painted without their complement of curtains and drapery, testified to by the ever-increasing number of pages of window dressings offered in the Bon Marché catalogues through the 1870s and 1880s. Curtains and drapes seem to be sought as a reinforcement for the protection to the interior already provided by glass. Zola, in *La Curée* [*The Kill*], divides the space accessible to the ultra-rich from the rest of society by layering the large glazed windows at the Monceau mansion with 'les rideaux de soie rouge drapés aux fenêtres du rez-de-chaussée' ['the crimson silk curtains hanging at the ground-floor windows'] (*LC*, 332/17). Conversely, the windows of the poor are often surrounded by fabric on the *outside*, as tawdry, dirty domestic clutter drifts into the public space. At Zola's Hôtel Boncœur, the windows are framed with drying rags (*A*, 415), and Huysmans's sketch of the Bièvre evokes 'un tas de masures [...] aux fenêtres pavoisées de linge sale' ['a pile of hovels [...], their windows bedecked with dirty laundry'] (*CP*, 90).

The windows of the poor, with their cluttered and tainted glass, are epitomized in Marc Trapadoux's article on the *chiffonnier* business (that occupation so often used to incarnate the poor in nineteenth-century literature), centred on a shop on the Rue Mouffetard during the Second Empire. His commentary begins with a lengthy depiction of specifically lower-class manifestations of glass:

> À une fenêtre, des peaux de lapins prennent l'air en compagnie d'une culotte de velours. [...] La devanture de la boutique se compose d'un haut et long vitrage, — évidemment emprunté aux démolitions. Les carreaux et les châssis sont de toutes dimensions. Les vitres sont de toutes nuances, depuis le cristal jusqu'au vert bouteille, jusqu'à l'opale. [...] Derrière ce vitrage, pas de rideaux, mais si peu de transparence qu'il m'eût été impossible de voir dans l'intérieur.[64]

> [At a window, rabbit skins take the air in company with a pair of velvet knicker-bockers. [...] The shop frontage is made up of a high and long display window, — obviously borrowed from the demolitions. There are panes and frames of every dimension. The glass comes in every colour, from crystal clear to bottle green, to opal. [...] Behind this window, not a single curtain, but it was so scarcely transparent that it was impossible for me to see inside.]

This pell-mell collection of glass fragments overlays the scraps of capitalist modernity. Rabbit skins and velvet knickerbockers spill outside the window, while the dubious quality of the glass veils the interior without the need for any proper curtains. This adds a further dimension to Charles Knight's 1851 remark that second- or third-hand shops exhibit 'luxury arbitrarily becoming waste without transition: the gaze of need not desire is at work'. Such rag-picker shops 'display goods [...] to all appearances useless, yet all for sale', effecting an intensification of the exclusion of the working classes from the fantasmagoria of commodity culture.[65] Indeed, whereas Benjamin considered the faded arcades as the best revelation of the illusions of capitalism, I would contend that such *chiffonnier* shops provide an even stronger symbol. Although the unwanted commodities enshrined by the arcades do offer a certain faded version of capitalist culture, the products in the rag-picker shop also incorporate the rapid death of the commodity which, having been bought, quickly ceases to satisfy and is rapidly thrown away again in the eternal cycle of novelty. The impoverished *quartier* is as easy to ignore as the arcades for the bourgeois who is comfortable in his illusions. However, for the poor the rag-picker shop with its distorted and distorting glass windows and with its lack of comforting illusions is an ever-present reality — a daily, magnified view of the underside of commodity culture.

The exclusion of the poor from the delights of leisured society is further symbolized by glass, as Armstrong observes, through the 'history of labour and transformation embedded in its material prior to its existence as a finished product'.[66] Indeed, of all the possible materials, Marx chose glass to exemplify how objects can represent 'crystallized labour-time'.[67] For the worker, the mirror or glass window in the glittering new urban landscape signified not ownership and control of a visual space, but exhausting labour for the pleasure of others. Glass provided dozens of forms of specialized work outside as well as inside the glass factory, from installing glass into street lamps or glazed roofs, to frosting glass, staining glass, cutting glass, and engraving glass.[68] In 1878, a review of the glass industry noted that glass and crystal production employed 16 478 men, 1 992 women, and 4 951 boys in 162 factories, in addition to 2 795 men, 209 women, and 130 boys in mirror production.[69] Whilst it is not within the scope of the present book to provide a detailed account of the glass industry, this study examines ways in which glass straddles the class divide, and how glass brings visual paradoxes and troubling meanings into the urban landscape which go beyond the concerns of commodity fetishism. Troubling meanings which come to a climax when glass became inextricably intertwined with conflict for the 1870–71 generation.

Glass and the Franco-Prussian War

In many ways, glass culture crossed from the Second Empire to the Third Republic without change; it continued to become more prevalent in society, and it continued to grow in usefulness in science. The bourgeoisie's investment in glass as a signifier of their privileged, protected social position and its values, present before the Franco-Prussian War and the Commune, persisted through the *fin de siècle*.

The vulnerable and changeable characteristics of glass had not gone unnoticed by literary authors prior to 1870, either. As the Vaubyessard ball reaches its climax in *Madame Bovary* (1857), the heat builds and a servant breaks a window, revealing to Emma the poverty-stricken faces of the peasants outside — and, as Kathryn Oliver Mills has noted, Flaubert comments here on bourgeois privilege enforced by a transparent but obstinate social barrier since the Revolution.[70] Glass had been adopted in the press as a symbol of disaster and suffering on a localized scale before, as it would come to be on a wider scale in the aftermath 1870. For example, newspapers often recorded brawls or accidents in which glass mutilated the victims — in Lyon, during a fight over pricing at a café, 'X... s'approcha de l'un [des hommes] et lui asséna sur la tête un coup de bouteille; puis, la bouteille s'étant brisée, il lui porta un second coup avec le tesson resté entre ses mains. La victime s'affaissa aussitôt, baignée dans son sang' ['X... approached one of them and struck him a blow to the head with a bottle; then, the bottle having broken, he gave him another blow with the shard that remained in his hands. The victim collapsed immediately, bathed in his own blood'].[71] At the scene of an explosion on a train between Marseille and Toulon, a *fait divers* recounts that 'presque tous les morts ont eu les yeux arrachés de l'orbite, et la figure criblée d'éclats de vitres' ['almost all the dead had their eyes torn from their sockets, and their faces riddled with shards of glass'].[72]

Although the window at the Vaubyessard ball is typical of Flaubert's genius for creating symbols, it should be noted that most writers who sought to describe urban destruction in the nineteenth century before 1870, including Haussmannization, generally fell back upon a body of familiar clichés; Eric Fournier's study of the ruins of Paris from 1850–71 observes that 'pour vaincre l'indicible, les écrivains ont presque systématiquement recours à une grille de comparaison formée d'images connues [...] issues des registres de la culture classique gréco-latine et chrétienne [et] des catastrophes naturelles' ['to overcome the inexpressible, writers almost systematically fall back upon comparisons formed from familiar imagery [...] coming from the registers of classical Greco-Latin and Christian culture [and] natural disasters'].[73] These analogies were once more recycled to describe the *année terrible*, particularly the Prussian siege and the ruins left by both the war and the Commune; but glass, of course, does not appear in the familiar language of Classical or Biblical metaphors. The advent of glass among these more predictable metaphors can thus be considered an innovation peculiar to the experience of 1870 and 1871.

In England and Germany, social unrest had been associated with glass in the 1830s and 1840s, and particularly around 1848. Isobel Armstrong has discussed the fascination with breaking and with broken glass at the start of the Victorian era. Armstrong observes that the temptation for workers to break windows lies in the fact that to break a window was a means to challenge upper- and middle-class attitudes to property, perspective, and space — yet once the window was broken, the well-to-do were no less fascinated by the sight of this destruction. Importantly, Armstrong recognizes that the historical meaning of glass-breaking may change over time; that window smashing by the suffragettes in the 1910s or by the Nazis on Kristallnacht in 1938 endow glass with various and often contradictory connotations at different points in history.[74] This was indeed the case for glass-breaking in the wake of 1870 in Paris. The bombardment by the Prussians was a watershed at which glass-breaking had ceased to be localized, anecdotal, or metaphorical. By 1870 glass was present on such a scale that every heavy artillery shell inevitably shattered a window or glass roof, and thus glass became a symbol of the harrowing shared experience. The witnesses of 1870 were so numerous that authors could use glass as a recognizable symbol of suffering and distress in an unprecedented fashion, and in the manifold accounts in newspapers, letter, and diaries from 1870–71 writers remarked upon glass being boarded up, being shaken, and being shattered again and again.

Published accounts of the war and siege returned repeatedly, almost obsessively, to the presence of glass during these troubled months. In the course of 1869–71, the diarist Henri Dabot writes of crowds breaking lantern glass in street protests in May and June 1869; of contemplating his own death in front of his mirror; of National Guards filling the Hôtel de Ville windows with red flags in October; of seeing elephant meat in the window display of the Palais-Royal restaurant in December; of being covered with shattering glass from shell fire in the street; of the destruction of the Musée de Cluny's windows; of damage to stained glass at Saint-Etienne-du-Mont; and of a letter from a friend reporting that their windows at some distance from Paris still shook with the reverberations of shelling in January 1871.[75] Newspapers thought it worthy of report when the windows of each major building were boarded up or sand-bagged to guard against the risk of bomb damage. During the Prussian siege, the *Journal officiel* reported the measures being taken to protect windows along the Louvre's upper galleries, in the École des Beaux-Arts, the Sainte-Chapelle, and the Louvre statuary gallery, and recommended that ground-floor apartments and shops protect their windows against shrapnel.[76] In the path of the battle across north-eastern France, Prussians smashed their way through the windows of people's homes, not just from a distance with heavy artillery as in Paris, but with all the heated fury of hand-to-hand fighting. Drawing on his own experiences for his novel *Miss Harriet: Souvenirs d'un blessé*, Hector Malot recounts that as the Prussians entered the village of Etrépagny, 'le bourg fut occupé par eux [...]: les portes, les fenêtres qui étaient fermées furent enfoncées à coups de crosses et de haches. La résistance était impossible' ['they occupied the town: closed doors and windows were broken down with rifle butts and axes. Resistance was impossible'].[77] Indeed, there is an uncomfortable irony in the words selected by *La Cloche* for a premature victory cry in September 1870. One journalist asserted that '[la République] est rentrée magnanime, sans effusion de sang, sans autre violence que des carreaux cassés' ['[the Republic] has returned, magnanimous, without bloodshed, without the slightest violence except a few broken windows']:[78] little was it realized in September 1870 how many more windows would have to be broken before the Republic could in fact be established securely, and how traumatic the breaking of those windows would be.

The grand buildings of monumental Paris, including its crystal palaces, were forced to adopt war-time functions, and were very frequently damaged during the Prussian bombardment — to the point that the sight of their shattered ruins became a commonplace of daily life during the final months of the siege.[79] The large gallery of the 1867 Palais de l'Industrie was used as an arsenal and encampment,[80] and the large *serres* of the Jardin des Plantes were used as an ambulance station before being destroyed by a shell in January 1871.[81] The quantity of glass in the Paris cityscape was particularly vulnerable to each of the 7 000 falling shells. These damaged some 1 600 public buildings and 1 400 private homes,[82] as 'les éclats criblèrent les façades des maisons voisines en brisant les devantures des boutiques, les vitres, les candélabres' ['shards riddled the facades of the neighbouring houses, breaking shop frontages, windows, candelabras'].[83] Reports of a considerable number of shell explosions and munitions store explosions all made specific references to mass shattering of glass from the shockwaves: for example, an explosion which occurred as a shopkeeper tried to defuse a shell in the Passage de l'Opéra was reported as 'l'image du plus effrayant désordre. Tout était brisé, haché, confondu; les glaces, les vitrines avaient été réduites en menus fragments' ['the image of the most terrifying disorder. Everything was broken, chopped up, confused; the mirrors, the windows had been reduced to tiny fragments'].[84] Indeed, broken windows were so ingrained in the experience of the war that a popular song borrowed the melody of 'Encore un carreau de cassé' ['Another Broken Window Pane'] to create the song 'De tous les moblots il n'en restera plus' ['Of all the Soldiers, None Will Remain']. Having first reported the boarding-up of windows, at the end of the siege the *unboarding* of windows was reported as one of the first signs of restored safety. The reduced threat to glass was seen to represent a reduced threat to the interior and to personal safety more generally. As one of the first signs of improving conditions on 4 February 1871, Henri Dabot remarks that 'les Delalain font déboucher leurs fenêtres. Le pain est un peu moins répugnant' ['the Delalains have had their windows unblocked. The bread is a little less disgusting'].[85]

Windows did not only enter into powerful memories of the siege once they had been broken; rather, they formed part of the new daily routines which came to define siege life. They provided fundamental reconnaissance positions for civilians and the military alike, and their elevated position permitted the increasingly desperate Parisians some degree of visual access to ongoing events. Edmond de Goncourt depicts a night spent at his window watching gunfire across the cityscape and its reflections in the glass of the new Haussmannized districts to the west of Paris:

> De ma fenêtre, voici ce que je vois — la couleur d'une canonnade. [...] Par ici, par là, des scintillements des vitres de villas, toutes lointaines, pareil à des scintillements de lustres de cristal. Plus proche, les maisons du Parc des Princes, de Billancourt, toute la bâtisse jusqu'à la Seine, détachée en violet sur des bouquets d'arbres pâles.
>
> [From my window what I see is the color of a cannonade. [...] Here and there the sparkling windows of distant villas like the sparkle of crystal chandeliers. Nearer at hand the houses at Parc aux Princes and Billancourt and all the built-up area near to the Seine standing out in violet against clumps of pale trees.][86]

The desperation of Parisians to gain some control over events also made windows a focus for suspicions. A mania spread for interpreting any lights or anything slightly out of the ordinary at a window as evidence of a Prussian spy sending secret signals.

Rampal, in his mémoire, mentions that Parisians saw a spy in 'celui qui éclaire la fenêtre de sa mansarde à une heure avancée de la nuit' ['the person with a light in the window of their attic room at an advanced hour of the night'],[87] and the magazine *La Mode nouvelle et Miroir parisien* later published an article observing that 'on était persuadé que les espions mettaient la nuit à profit pour correspondre avec l'assiégeant au moyen de verres de couleur' ['people were convinced that spies made the most of the night-time to communicate with the besieging army using coloured glass'].[88] Not just coloured glass, but even everyday objects could be read as highly symbolic *when placed near a window*. The anonymous writer of a rather hysterical letter reported with distaste in 1871 that:

> toute la journée ce ne sont que mouvements, enlèvements ou remplacements de rideaux, suspensions de paquets de légumes ou débris de verdure aux appuie-mains des *fenêtres*, changements de vêtements ou plutôt de camisoles, qui sont blanches les jours où nous subissons des pertes. Un petit cerf-volant, indiquant probablement le départ d'un ballon, était suspendu dernièrement avant 6h du matin à l'une des *fenêtres* du cinquième étage du no 4, rue Philippe de Girard. [...] J'ai aussi vu un gros radis noir sous cloche en dehors d'une *fenêtre* au troisième et du no 191, des torchons et parfois des bandes blanches du largueur de deux ou trois doigts sont aussi fixés à l'angle gauche des *fenêtres*. Les chats que l'on tient constamment auprès des *fenêtres* paraissent avoir aussi, BIEN À LEUR INSU, un rôle quelconque dans ces signaux qui sont généralement faits par des femmes.[89]

> [all day there is nothing but movement; curtains drawn open or shut, packets of vegetables or remnants of salad hung at the handrail of the *windows*, clothes or rather camisoles changed, which are white on the days we suffer losses. A little kite, probably indicating the departure of a balloon, was recently suspended before 6am at one of the *windows* of the fifth floor, No. 4 Rue Philippe de Girard. [...] I also saw a large black radish under a bell cover outside a *window* of the third floor, and at No. 191 there were cleaning cloths and sometimes white bands of fabric two or three inches wide fixed to the left-hand corner of the *windows*. Cats, which are kept constantly at the *window*, also seem to have, QUITE WITHOUT THEIR KNOWLEDGE, some role in these signals that are generally made by women.]

Indeed, accounts of the war by bourgeois women suggest that their experience was particularly mediated by glass and windows — owing to their more domestic lifestyle, to their exclusion from active combat, and to the lack of feminine urban pursuits once the parks had become encampments and the shops were emptied of produce. The vast glass display windows which had been installed and welcomed with such enthusiasm in the Second Empire were now only noteworthy for their eerie lack of products and food, and for the occasional uncanny display of the carcass of a butchered zoo animal from the Jardin des Plantes.[90]

Mme Marie Sébrun's journal is saturated with references to windows and glass, around which her entire experience of the siege is structured. It is at her window that she sees flashes of gun fire ('à la fenêtre, je vois chaque éclair précéder le coup!' ['at the window, I see each flash before the impact!']), that she listens to the sound of drums ('Ran, ran, ran, plan, plan, plan... C'est l'école des tambours qui se tient sous mes fenêtres... Quel concert!' ['Ratta ratta ratta, tat, tat, tat... The drum school is practising under my windows... What a sound!']), and that she hears gunfire in the night ('le canon tonne de tous côtés sans cesser! Je ne puis dormir! Je me suis levée pour écouter à ma fenêtre' ['the canons are firing on all sides without respite! I couldn't sleep! I got up to listen to them at my window']). It is due to bombs raining down outside the windows that her friend leaves Paris ('Mme V★★★ [...] me dit que les obus pleuvaient devant ses fenêtres' ['Madame V★★★ [...] tells me that shells were raining down outside her windows']).[91]

It is also notable that glass came to signify trauma primarily for those who had firsthand experience of the conflict; accounts of the destruction during the Franco-Prussian War and siege of Paris from writers who were spared direct contact rarely mention glass, as is the case in George Sand's journal from the siege months.[92] English battlefield tourists, who had sufficient physical and cultural separation from the Franco-Prussian War to view it with pleasant curiosity, collected shards of mirror glass among their souvenirs; *La Cloche* reported with disgust that, '[L'Anglais] ne dédaignait ni les lambeaux de pantalon rouge, ni les squelettes de vieilles chaussures ratatinées par la pluie. Un éclat de miroir, une grosse botte sans semelle parut surtout faire son bonheur' ['[The Englishman] considered shreds of red infantry trousers and the skeletal remnants of old shoes shrivelled by the rain to be worthy souvenirs. A shard of mirror, a large boot without a sole seemed above all to bring him joy'].[93]

Other new glass technologies were also implicated in the events of the siege. In a variety of ways which would have been impossible without glass, anxious Parisians grasped at any possible way of finding out what was happening. A number of forms of glass lens became essential. Numerous accounts show officers and (generally female) civilians using telescopes and binoculars in the hope of glimpsing the Prussians and divining their plans: in September, 'des hauteurs de Rethel, on apercevait à l'horizon un immense nuage de fumée. À l'aide des lunettes d'approche on distinguait des maisons en flammes' ['from the heights of Rethel, an immense cloud of smoke was visible on the horizon. With the aid of telescopes, houses in flames could be glimpsed'];[94] in October, 'sur le versant du Trocadéro [...] stationnent des multitudes de curieux tâchant à grand renfort de longues-vues et de lorgnettes de découvrir si le soleil ne fait pas briller à l'horizon quelque casque ou quelque fusil de Prussien' ['on the slopes of the Trocadero [...] crowds of curious onlookers gather, trying, with a great variety of telescopes and eye-glasses, to catch a glimpse of the sun glinting on the helmet or the gun of some Prussian on the horizon'].[95]

The photographic lens was also essential for maintaining contact with the outside world. Messages were reduced using photography onto a precursor of microfilm so that homing pigeons and balloons could carry as many messages in and out of the city as possible.[96] Photography was used to catalogue the corpses of unidentified bombardment victims in case their families should come looking for them after the siege.[97] Glass was also employed in some rather more unusual attempts at re-establishing contact with the outside world, such as floating glass globes into the city along the Seine — although when the river froze over during the unusually harsh winter of 1870, the ice trapped the glass globes, crushing them or leading to their discovery by the Prussians.[98]

Even when the siege ended, glass did not shed its associations with the distressing memories of the preceding months — not least because reports of the morale-destroying capitulation to the Prussians at Sédan habitually mention that it was signed in a glass pavilion,[99] followed by the signing of German unification in the Hall of Mirrors at Versailles. As people returned to their homes on the outskirts of Paris, the sight of endless broken windows was recorded in journals and newspaper articles. At Enghien-les-Bains, the only property to avoid having its windows broken was the mairie, where the Prussian colonel had stayed; one journalist was struck with how 'ses croisées intactes, ornées de rideaux blancs forment un triste contraste avec les fenêtres détruites des autres immeubles' ['its intact window panes, trimmed with white curtains, strike a sad contrast with the broken windows of the other buildings'].[100] Similarly, at Montmorency, he remarked that 'les carreaux brisés ont été remplacés par des planches et des torchis de paille pour arrêter le vent, la pluie et la neige' ['the broken window panes have been replaced by planks and clumps of straw to block out the wind, rain, and snow'].[101] The glass industry itself was struck by the loss of territory and the financial downturn precipitated by the Franco-Prussian War. Mirror-glass production fell from 270 000 m^2 to 200 000 m^2 per annum in the aftermath of the capitulation; prices rose from thirty to thirty-eight francs per metre; the Saint-Louis, Meisenthal, Goetzenbruck, and M. Maréchal glassworks were lost to the new German state; coke supply chains were interrupted by the annexation; and thirteen glass factories closed following financial difficulties in the 1870s.[102]

While this by no means constituted an irreparable blow to the glass industry, it did mark a decline in the industry until the 1890s — and, moreover, it reveals that glass was influenced in terms of both production and perception by the *année terrible*. One company produced a liqueur whose bottle was patriotically labelled 'Souviens-Toi!' ['Remember!'].[103] The Clichy glass company (whose factory had been forced to close for the duration of the conflict once the banlieues became a battleground) crafted dinner services named after people and places significant to the Franco-Prussian War, including 'Alsace', 'Lorrain', and 'Strasbourg'.[104] A rather eccentric correspondent for *La Ligue commerciale anti-allemande* [*The Anti-German Commercial League*] even wrote to the *Charentais* newspaper vociferating in favour of a boycott on lamp-shades made with German glass:

> [J]e commence en mettant sur la sellette un vilain personnage, *le verre de lampe allemand*. [...] Dernièrement, donc, j'ai acheté, en passant, des paraverres (une invention française, les Allemands n'inventent pas), et [...] ô déception! mon verre d'étude s'est trouvé cassé le lendemain matin. [...] J'ai questionné, et enfin, j'ai su que le paraverre est excellent, mais aussi, j'ai appris, à ma grande confusion, que le verre était *un produit allemand*; je ne m'en doutais pas. Envoyer chez le lampiste acheter un verre français et le mettre en service à côté de son semblable teuton a été l'affaire de quelques instants. J'ai eu la patience de poursuivre la comparaison; j'en suis aujourd'hui au quatrième germain et mon français se porte parfaitement. [...] Je continuerai l'expérience, messieurs les Allemands, et je saurai combien vous m'aurez volé cet hiver sur le verre de lampe seulement. [...] Lorsque j'irai dans un magasin, je dirai poliment; veuillez me montrer la marque française, ou je vais chez le voisin.[105]

[I begin by highlighting a nasty character, *the German lamp glass*. [...] So, recently, I bought, in passing, some glass lampshades (a French invention, the Germans don't invent), and [...] oh my disappointment! My study lamp was broken the next morning. [...] I asked some questions and found out, finally, that the lampshade was excellent, but I also learned that the glass was *a German product*; I did not doubt it. To send a servant to buy a French glass shade and put it into action alongside its Teutonic counterpart was the work of an instant. I had the patience to pursue the experiment; today I am on my fourth German shade, whilst my French one is still in perfect shape. [...] I will continue the experiment, German sirs, and I will find out how much you have robbed from me this winter in lamp glass alone. [...] When I go into a shop in the future, I will politely ask; please show me the French brand, or I'll take my business to your neighbour.]

The writer seems determined to direct his *révanchisme* into, specifically, revenge for any German involvement in the breaking of glass.

Glass in the Commune

The centrality of glass to the events of and the narration of conflict was perpetuated during the Paris Commune of 1871. Zola directly compares the experience of the Prussian siege and the approaching *semaine sanglante* in *La Débâcle* in terms of trembling windows: 'à Vanves, à Issy surtout, le bombardement faisait rage, toutes les vitres de Paris en tremblaient, comme aux journées les plus rudes du siège' ['at Vanves and especially at Issy, the bombardment raged away, rattling all the windows in Paris, just as in the most terrible days of the siege'] (*LD*, 875/477). Indeed, it is notable that Zola felt shaking and shattering glass had made a sufficiently significant impact upon those who lived through 1870–71 that it would still resonate with his readers in 1892. Far from Benjamin's belief that glass has no aura because it defies attachment and denies its own potential status as ruin, glass is now emphatically associated with memories of ruins.[106] Glass did now have a unique aura — an aura which evoked the harshest memories of the *année terrible*.

There were many similarities between the treatment of glass during the Franco-Prussian War and Commune. Windows were once more protected or boarded up to guard against damage; a guidebook to the ruins after the Commune remarked that, in the Faubourg du Temple, 'les prévoyants locataires avaient collé des bandes de papier sur les vitres de leurs fenêtres pour les empêcher de se briser au bruit du canon, mais ce qu'ils ne purent protéger c'est la maison elle-même et dans son entier' ['the far-sighted tenants had stuck strips of paper on their window panes to stop them from breaking with the noise of the canons, but what they could not protect was the house itself and in its entirety'].[107] As in the Prussian siege, explosions obliterated the glass around the city in dramatic scenes of destruction. For example, there was a vast explosion at the Champs-de-Mars gunpowder store, after which a witness wrote 'on ne voit que vitres cassées, toits effondrés, volets arrachés, arbres ébranchés, déracinés...; des Invalides au Champs-de-Mars, nous marchons sur le verre, la toile, l'ardoise [...]. Sous cet épouvantable ébranlement, au Corps législatif des fenêtres sont brisées, blessant, sous leurs débris, un grand nombre d'ouvrières' ['everywhere there are broken windows, collapsed roofs, torn shutters, trees stripped of their branches, uprooted...; from the Invalides to the Champ de Mars, we walk upon glass, tiles, slates [...]. Under this terrible shock, the windows of the Corps Législatif were shattered, injuring a great number of workers with the debris'].[108] Another explosion at the Quai d'Orsay munitions store hit the nearby houses with 'une horrible secousse qui a pulvérisé leurs carreaux, crevé les moindres cloisons' ['a terrible shock which pulverized the window panes, crumbled the very walls'].[109] At a house neighbouring a munitions explosion near the Palais de Luxembourg, 'les vitrages d'une galerie inférieure sont tombés à l'état de pluie fine et coupante, couvrant le sol d'une poussière diamantée' ['the glass panelling of a lower gallery was reduced to a fine, slicing rain, covering the ground in diamond dust'].[110]

Lenses and windows were again central to the daily rituals of life in Paris during the Commune, as the city's inhabitants tried to find out what was to befall them. Telescopes and binoculars were taken to elevated ground for a vantage point just as they had been during the Prussian siege.[111] However, windows were not just look-out posts this time but also became gun emplacements. Prior to the summary killings on 18 March 1871 on the Rue de Rosiers, a prisoner recalled that 'la foule [...] avait brisé les carreaux de la fenêtre et, à chaque instant, nous voyons un canon de fusil s'abattre vers nous' ['the crowd [...] broke the panes of the windows and, at every moment, we saw the barrel of a gun being pointed down at us'].[112] Shooting from windows was so frequent that the Communards published a decree declaring that: 'Art.1: Les persiennes ou volets de toutes les fenêtres demeureront ouvertes. Art. 2: Toute maison de laquelle partira un seul coup de fusil ou une agression quelconque contre la garde nationale sera immédiatement brûlée' ['Article 1: all window blinds and shutters must remain open. Article 2: any house from which a shot is fired or any aggression is effected against the National Guard will immediately be set on fire'].[113] The Communard officials wanted to see the glint of comfortingly unbroken, unobscured, unopened windows to be sure that no gun barrel could be levelled at them as they passed along the streets.

The closer physical proximity between the two opposing forces also resulted in more dramatic damage to glass than during the Prussian siege. Instead of glass being destroyed by long-range heavy artillery alone, in May 1871 the streets and buildings of Paris were themselves the battlefield, and so they became more heavily scarred both physically and symbolically. This included fighting within the grounds of glass factories: in April 1871, the National Guard tried to attack the Meudon glassworks where several hundred government policemen were billeted, and the resulting violence rendered much of the site unusable.[114] Windows and mirrors were destroyed across Paris, and writers seem again to have felt compelled to record this in minute detail. *La Cloche* recounted, among many examples, that 'une compagnie a tiré sur une autre compagnie qui passait sur le boulevard des Filles-du-Calvaire. [...] Une balle a brisé la glace du marchand de vins qui se trouve au coin du boulevard. On la voit profondément enfoncée dans la glace étoilée' ['one company shot at another company as they passed on the Boulevard des Filles-du-Calvaire. [...] A bullet broke the mirror in a wine merchant's on the boulevard corner. It is now visible, sunk deeply into the radiating fractures of the mirror'].[115] The Avenue de Neuilly suffered considerable damage, to the point that 'les détonations ont fait sauter les vitres à toutes les maisons' ['the explosions blew up the windows of every house'].[116] A guidebook to the ruins mentioned that 'il n'est pas de maisons, tout le long de son immense avenue [de Neuilly] qui n'ait eu au moins ses vitres brisées, sa toiture crevée, ses murs écornés' ['there is not a single house along the immense Avenue [de Neuilly] that has not had at least its windows broken, its roof caved in, its walls damaged'], and that the glass halls of the Palais de l'Industrie suffered so many hits that 'on ne saurait mieux la comparer qu'à une toile d'araignée, aux mailles ténues' ['there is no better comparison than a spider's web with its delicate threads'].[117] The *Cloche* newspaper also evoked this striking image, noting that 'le Palais de l'Industrie a reçu dans sa frêle toiture une grêle de balles, venant de la terrasse des Tuileries. Les vitres, par centaines, sont brisées' ['the Palais de l'Industrie received a hail of bullets on its fragile roof, coming from the Tuileries terrace. Glass panels were broken in their hundreds'].[118] The fire at the Hôtel de Ville was of such intensity that all the windows were blown into shards by the flashover.[119] Indeed, the damage at one shop's windows near the Hôtel de Ville was so notable that it would be remarked upon by Maurice Steckel in his reference work on glass some eighteen years later after the 1889 World Fair:

> [N]ous croyons devoir mentionner aussi, ne serait-ce qu'à titre de curiosité, l'effet produit sur une glace, en 1871, par l'explosion de l'Hôtel de Ville. Cette glace, qui se trouvait à la devanture d'un magasin de coutellerie, a éclaté sous l'action de la chaleur. Les fentes qui la sillonnaient avaient la forme de gerbes ayant leur base dans la partie supérieure de la devanture, et s'épanouissant à droite et à gauche, comme pourraient le faire les gerbes lumineuses d'un feu d'artifice renversé. Ces ramifications avaient une forme si régulière qu'on les aurait crus produites par la main habile d'un artiste.[120]

> [we believe we should also mention, even if just as a point of interest, the effect produced on a shop window in 1871 by the explosion at the Hôtel de Ville. This window, found at the front of a cutlery shop, shattered under the heat. The cracks which ran across its surface took the form of sprays with their roots in the upper part of the window, and spreading out to the right and left like the branches of an upside-down firework. These effects had such a regular appearance that you would have thought they had been created by the skilled hand of an artist.]

The shattering of glass was so common that it even became newsworthy to report that the mirrors at the Grand Café Parisien, worth four hundred thousand francs, were *not* broken in the fires or in combat.[121]

Edmond de Goncourt writes frequently of windows and broken glass in his diary entries about the Commune, just as he did during the Prussian bombardment. He recounts a number of occasions when he used windows to observe the ongoing battles, particularly during the climax in May.[122] Goncourt recorded images of broken glass across the city: en route for the Champs du Mars, he noted that 'les rues par lesquelles je passe n'ont plus un seul carreau. On marche sur de la poussière de vitre, et je vois une marchande de verre cassé, remplir, en un instant, sa voiture, du verre qu'elle ramasse à pleine main de fer' ['the streets along which I pass have

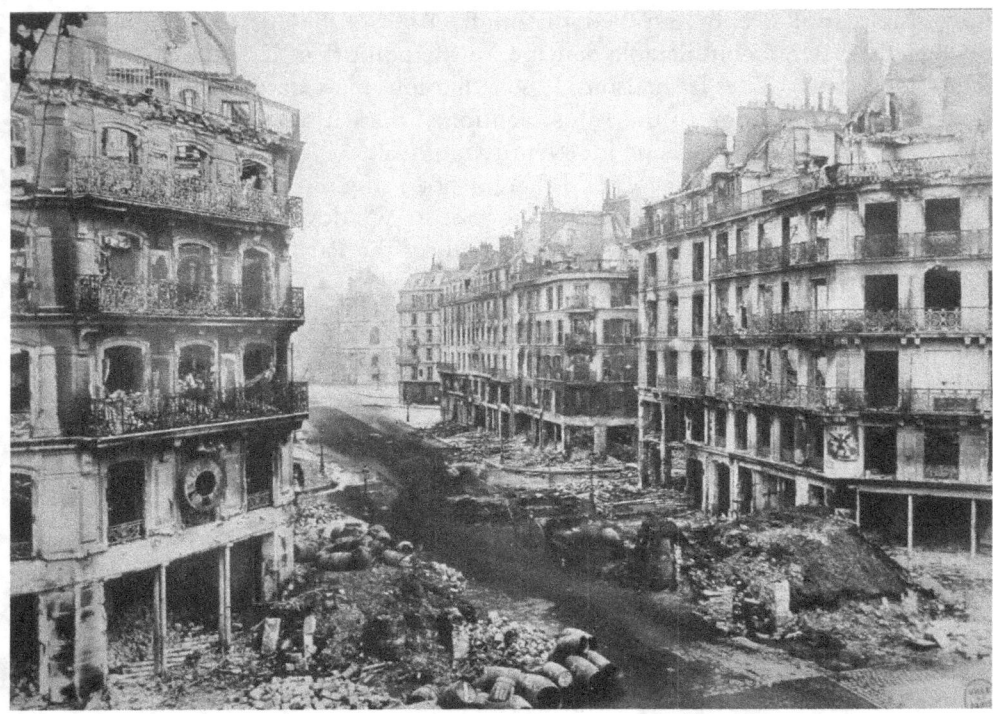

Fig. 1.5. The rue de Rivoli, damaged by fire and street fighting, in May 1871.

no windows panes; I walk on powdered glass, and I see a broken-glass merchant fill her barrow in a moment with glass that she has gathered up by the shovelful']; in his house, he wrote that 'on marche sur les plâtras et les fragments de glaces mêlés aux éclats d'obus et aux balles' ['we walk on plaster and broken glass mixed with shrapnel and bullets']; and upon the explosion of the Fort d'Issy, he noted that the Rue de Bac shopkeepers were 'tout épaourés [sic] de la danse de leurs vitres' ['terrified by the shaking of their shop windows'].[123] The breaking of glass, by crossing the sensory boundaries of sight, hearing, and touch, seems to root itself more deeply and more durably in the memory.

The ghosts of this destruction would endure, living on in daily newspaper updates about the ongoing repairs, in innumerable diaries describing the events, and in a flood of photographic collections — over 735 photographs of these ruins have survived to this day, hinting at the much more considerable number which must have been taken at the time (see figures 1.5 and 1.6).[124] One journalist commented with derision that 'de tous côtés, nous avons remarqué des appareils de photographie braqués sur ces preuves de nos discords civiles' ['on every side, we noticed cameras pointing towards this proof of our civil discord'].[125] One collection, *Album historique, Paris incendié 1871*, refers specifically to the damaged windows time and again in its captions, enumerating the 'fenêtres béantes' ['gaping windows'] of the Tuileries Palace and the Hôtel-de-Ville, the 'fenêtres disparues' ['absent windows'] of the Palais-Royale, and noting that the Théâtre de la Porte-Saint-Martin's

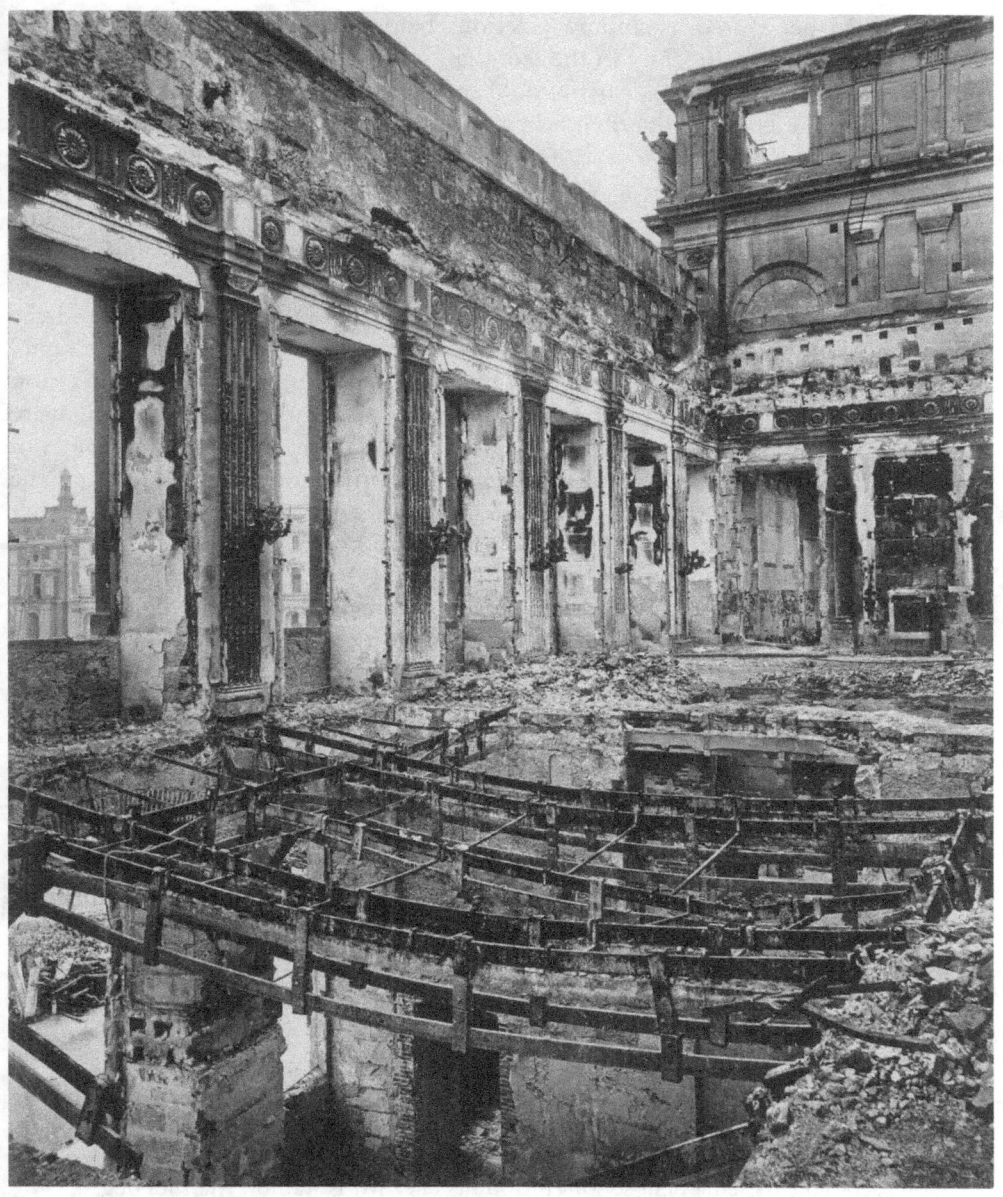

Fig. 1.6. Disaster as art at the Hôtel de Ville: a print on silver from Alfred d'Aunay, *Les Ruines de Paris et de ses Environs 1870-1871: Cent Photographies.*

windows had been used as sniping positions before it too was burned down.[126] Indeed, there is a certain irony in the fact that, while the working-class Commune foundered, the working-class *vitrier* would see considerable financial benefits from the destruction. Henri Dabot remarks in a footnote to his diary: ' — On sonne! c'est le vitrier; il vient remettre les carreaux cassés. Oh! la bonne aubaine. Les carreaux sont très rares et les vitriers ne veulent travailler qu'à des prix exorbitants' [' — There's the doorbell! It's the glazier; he has come to replace the broken window panes. Oh, what a godsend! Glass panes are so scarce and glaziers will only work at exorbitant prices'].[127]

There is a further dark side to the symbolic associations between glass and the Commune. Bourgeois accounts of this crisis never fail to decry excessive alcohol consumption by the Communards.[128] Drinking and drunken violence are not, of course, in themselves automatically features of glass culture — after all, were alcohol to have been available in tin, plastic, or carton in 1871, it would not have had the slightest moderating influence upon the amount consumed by the populace. However, where the line between this unruly drinking and glass culture blurs is in its textualization. Bottles and glasses are not merely vessels containing drink, but become its metonyms in text and image. In Republican descriptions of Commune scenes, it becomes impossible to recreate their world in the mind's eye without visualizing the materiality of glass bottles and drinking glasses. Paul de Saint-Victor asserted in his vitriolic book of 1871 that the Commune not only resulted in drunken behaviour, but was in fact the *result of* alcoholism. He declared that 'la bouteille fut un des instruments du règne de la Commune. Elle abrutissait avec le vin et l'eau-de-vie les bandes imbéciles qu'elle expédiait à la mort' ['the bottle was one of the Commune's instruments of power. It rendered the bands of imbeciles stupid with wine and brandy and sent them off to their death'].[129] Figurative though this expression clearly is, it is noteworthy that the bottle and not the wine or the brandy is the active subject of the verb. In an account of pillaging at the Second Arrondissement *mairie* by Communards, there is a focus throughout on bottles and glass; moreover, this focus juxtaposes the refined glassware familiar from the Baccarat and Murano display cases at the World Fairs with the vulgarity of the drinkers:

> Une bouteille de vin blanc, débouchée depuis trois semaines, leur donna l'idée d'une petite orgie. Donc ils vidèrent cette bouteille, et toutes celles sur lesquelles ils purent mettre la main, soit dans la salle à manger, soit dans les caves où ils descendirent. Sept verres alignés sur une table semblent indiquer que sept voleurs seulement se sont introduits chez M. Rataillot. Mais les dégâts commis prouvaient que le nombre des coupables a dû être plus grand. L'orgie commença. Les pillards brisèrent un magnifique service de Sèvres, une bonne partie de la vaisselle et plusieurs meubles de prix. Ils n'épargnèrent qu'une bouteille d'eau de Seltz.[130]

> [A bottle of white wine, uncorked three weeks beforehand, gave them the idea for a little orgy. So they emptied this bottle, and every other they could get their hands on, both in the dining room and on descending into the cellars. Seven glasses lined up on the table seem to suggest that only seven thieves entered Monsieur Rataillot's house. But the amount of damage proves that the

number of culprits must have been much larger. The orgy began. The robbers broke a magnificent Sevres dinner service, a large quantity of the tableware and several valuable pieces of furniture. They spared nothing but a bottle of soda water].

The only objects which survive this destructive orgy are a bottle of soda water and seven glasses, the seven vitreous substitutes for the intruders who drank from them. They remain behind after their human counterparts have left as if to survey the destruction with satisfaction and to pass on its story. This metonymic association between Communards and glass is made all the more pointed by the frequent images of the *pétroleuses*; the glass bottle used for their fire bombs is as readily associated with their violence as the grey gun-metal of today's artillery is with the explosions of modern warfare. In the petrol bomb, glass, like the Communards, goes on a suicide mission to cause as much damage as possible before finally being crushed to pieces.

In the years following the Commune, this metonymic link between glass and working-class alcoholism did not immediately fade. We can detect it, lingering, in depictions of the poor and their insatiable desires for drink, violence, and sexual depravity. Even Jules Vallès struggles to attach positivity to the working-class glass of alcohol; there is nothing noble in his description of the Chiffonniers in the *Tableau de Paris*, whose shot glasses and filth-covered sticks are their two crucial identifying features: 'ces patriarches [qui] chient et boivent, [qui] ne semblent disposés à lâcher ni leur verre, ni leur crochet' ['these patriarchs [who] shit and drink, [who] seem indisposed to let go of either their glass or their hook'].[131] The disturbing, hyperbolic, and constantly inebriated character of Pierrot in Huysmans's *Pierrot Sceptique* [*Skeptical Pierrot*] oscillates between bottles of alcohol and acts of violence, drinking at length with the Sidonie before severely beating his dead wife's former nursemaid and needlessly shattering a barbershop window with a broom handle.[132] The link between the Parisian poor, alcohol, and revolt is even satirized in a comic-yet-cautionary tale about Paris's compulsive return to revolt. Alfred Franklin's *Les Ruines de Paris en 4875* [*The Ruins of Paris in 4875*] is a pseudo-archaeological/ethnological narrative about the excavation of nineteenth-century Paris three thousand years into the future. The very first artifacts uncovered by the exploratory team are alcohol bottles. As soon as the fictional Nouméan men (who are undertaking the dig) begin to drink with the local Parisi tribe, they become mutinous, shout socialist slogans, and force the officer in charge to sail away without his crew — after which he places his journal in a glass bottle and casts it into the sea in the hope that it, at least, might survive.[133] Indeed, it seems symptomatic of the bourgeois fear of the poor and of their Communard past that while bourgeois mirrors and windows are so often plagued by vulnerability and instability in texts, the wine bottle proves stubbornly resilient to the travails of time.

Glass in the Aftermath of the *Année Terrible*

In the wake of the intensely traumatic experience of the *année terrible*, Parisians needed to find a way to cope with the recent past — not just politically, but also symbolically. Most often, Paris and Parisians sought to cover the scars and repress the recent defeat and civil war. This brings to mind Freud's subsequent remark in *Beyond the Pleasure Principle* that war trauma shares much in common with hysteria — not just for its motor symptoms, but also because its victims mostly suffer from memories.[134]

Dozens of street names were changed to efface their Second Empire or Germanic connotations,[135] buildings were hastily repaired,[136] and Parisians strove to resume their pleasure-seeking pursuits. In a satirical article on the Parisian propensity for selective rewritings of history, a journalist for *La Cloche* quipped with deliberate flippancy: 'Vingt années qu'il faut éliminer! Qu'est cela, bon Dieu? Nous avons étouffé bien d'autres choses. Ne faut-il que des barres sur du papier' ['Twenty years that need to be eliminated! But what's that, good God? We've stifled plenty of other things. What more does it take than a few crossings-out on some paper'].[137] There are clear (albeit possibly unconscious) attempts to deal with the trauma of these years by cataloguing and conceptualizing the ruins. Special-edition guidebooks to the ruins demonstrate an impulse to render the traumatic events familiar and comprehensible — not only by creating new, recognizable landmarks from the ruins, but also by absorbing them into familiar aesthetic traditions. For example, the *Guide à travers les ruines* [*Guide through the Ruins*] romanticizes the remains. Its authors write that the Ministry of Finance 'qui n'avait jamais été qu'un monument médiocre, est devenu une ruine superbe. [...] C'est une forêt de pierres, inextricable, pleine d'ombres, fantastique et puissante. La nuit lui prête d'incroyables aspects' ['which had never been more than a mediocre edifice, has become a superb ruin. [...] It is a forest of stones, inextricable, filled with shadows, fantastic and powerful. The night lends it an incredible appearance']. They go on to affirm that '[la vue de l'Hôtel de Ville] est encore la plus merveilleuse. Le monument se présente alors obliquement avec ses fenêtres ouvertes sur le ciel, donnant un paysage d'arbres roussis, comme aux temps d'automne' ['[the sight of the Hôtel de Ville] is still the most marvellous. The monument lies obliquely with its windows open to the heavens, producing a landscape of charred trees like visions of autumn'].[138] Familiar tropes are imposed upon the incomprehensible to provide a familiar vocabulary with which it may be articulated and conceptualized, and glass — in shards or under repair — is conspicuously absent from all such texts.

However, glass — by now an essential, everyday substance — had become so emphatically associated with these years of crisis that the impulse to cover over the past was not as easily satisfied as it may at first appear. In France after 1871, handling symbolism in the material world was no easy process. Everyday sights were now tainted with memories of the *année terrible* — all the more so because the blanched face of Haussmannized Paris had little other symbolism inscribed upon its new walls and streets. As Bergson asserted at the end of the century, 'il n'y a pas de perception qui ne soit imprégnée de souvenirs. Aux données immédiates et présentes de nos sens nous mêlons mille et mille détails de notre expérience passé' ['there is no perception not imprinted with memories. To the immediate and current data received from our senses we mix thousands and thousands of details from our past experience'].[139]

Even when mirrors had been repaired, window panes had been replaced, and black fire-scars had been scoured from around window frames, there is a sense that the recent traumas had merely been repressed rather than forgotten. Indeed, the problem of how even to attempt to express 1870–71 was a pressing concern for writers of every kind. There had been little time between the Franco-Prussian War and Commune for writers to get their thoughts onto paper, but from June 1871 a vast number of diaries and memoires of both conflicts went to press, with more literal than literary testimonies of personal experiences and prejudices. During the summer and autumn of 1871, these texts dominated every bookshop — and when other titles finally started to reappear, a relieved journalist for *La Vie parisienne* declared: 'des livres vont bientôt paraître qui seront véritablement des livres, et sur la couverture desquels on lira autre chose que: *Paris brûlé*, *Les Ruines de Paris*, *Le Massacre des otages*, *Les Membres de la Commune*, *Le Procès des pétroleuses*, etc. etc.' ['books will soon appear that will really be books, and whose covers will read something other than: *Paris Burned*, *The Ruins of Paris*, *The Massacre of the Hostages*, *The Members of the Commune*, *The Trial of the Pétroleuses*, etc. etc.'].[140]

However, in spite of his desire for fresh reading material, he recognizes the difficulty of writing fiction in the aftermath of such crises: 'Que voulez-vous demander à la poésie ou au roman? La fiction se sent annulée, écrasée par le fait' ['What do you want from poetry or the novel? Fiction feels undone, crushed by fact'].[141] Zola, too, acknowledged this impasse. In his 'Lettres parisiennes' column in May 1872, he wrote at length on the flood of war novels that the preceding year of peace had produced:

> Le flot montant des publications sur la dernière guerre s'arrête et l'heure vient où la critique peut chercher si quelque perle n'a pas été roulée dans tout ce sable et tous ces cailloux. [...] C'est n'est pas au sortir d'une crise affreuse qu'on peut la juger et en mettre toutes les phases en leur place. [...] Les récits personnels [...] gardent toute la fièvre de la lutte, s'ils sont écrits au lendemain même des faits. Faux souvent, ayant mal vu et racontant mal, tirant des conséquences qui ne se vérifie point, ils ont le grand mérite de vivre ce qu'ils racontent et de rester comme des documents pour les historiens qui viendront. [...] Tout cela bon à être trié dans dix ans.[142]

> [The rising flood of publications about the last war is waning and the time has come when critics can sift through them all and see whether a pearl hides among all the sand and pebbles. [...] The first days of respite from a terrible crisis are not the best time to judge events or to put them in order. [...] Personal narratives [...] still carry all the fever of the struggle if they are written the day after those events took place. They are very often inaccurate, when the subject has observed poorly or narrates badly, and they draw conclusions which cannot be proven. But these are certainly valuable as a record of the vivid lived experience of the events, and as documents which allow the stories to live on for future historians. [...] All of that will be ripe for sorting through in ten years].

While Zola himself would wait not ten but twenty-one years to write his historical novel about 1870–71, *La Débâcle* (1892), he would write indirectly of these crises in almost all of the Parisian novels of the *Rougon-Macquart*. Colette Wilson has explored many of these oblique references in detail, including the famous scene at the top of the Vendôme Column in *L'Assommoir*, the presence of the Tuileries Palace before its destruction in every passing reference to the Tuileries gardens, and Florent's entry into Paris in *Le Ventre de Paris*.[143] One aspect not covered by Wilson's thoroughgoing book is material culture at a more minute level; the next chapter seeks to tease out Zola's play on glass, consumerism, and the memories of 1870–71 in his iconic shopping novel, *Au Bonheur des Dames*.

Notes to Chapter 1

1. Steckel, pp. 1–2.
2. Reprinted in R. Gentilini, *La Société anonyme des manufactures de glaces et produits chimiques de Saint-Gobain, Chauny et Cirey à l'exposition universelle de 1889* (Paris: Publications du journal *Le Génie Civil*, 1889), p. 22.
3. Commissariat Général, *Catalogue officiel: Groupe 2–6, Section française, classes 6 à 68* (Paris: Imprimerie Nationale, 1878), p. 151.
4. Pourcin, *Visite à l'exposition universelle: itinéraire* (Paris: Au Petit Financier, 1878), p. 40.
5. They would be 'captivés [...] par les merveilles de luxe [...] qui s'étalent aux vitrines des somptueux magasins' (*Guide des étrangers à l'exposition universelle et Itinéraire dans Paris* (Paris: n. pub., 1878), p. 51).
6. Louis Clémandot, *Visites des ingénieurs anciens élèves de l'Ecole centrale des arts et manufactures à l'exposition universelle de 1878* (Paris: n. pub., 1878), p. 3.
7. Gentilini, p. 22.
8. *L'Exposition universelle de 1867 illustrée*, ed. M. Fr. Ducuing (Paris: n. pub., 1867), I, pp. 19–22; R. Tamisier, *Les Annales de l'exposition universelle de 1878* (Paris: n. pub., 1878), p. 7; Emile Goudeau, 'Ascension à la Tour Eiffel', *Revue de l'Exposition universelle de 1889*, 2 (1889), 280–88 (p. 286).
9. 'Chronique du mois', *La Mode nouvelle et Miroir parisien*, November 1871, p. 260.
10. *L'État*, 28 December 1872.
11. Commissariat Général, pp. 135–39.
12. Ibid., p. 386.
13. Ibid., pp. 391, 393.
14. R. Gentilini, p. 24.
15. Steckel, p. 40.
16. Breakage statistics from Louis Clémandot, *Visites des ingénieurs anciens élèves de l'Ecole centrale des arts et manufacture à l'exposition universelle de 1878* (Paris: n. pub., 1878), p. 16.
17. For example in the advertisement printed by Paul Joanne's best-selling guidebook series, the *Paris-Diamant* (Paris: Hachette, 1878), p. 44.
18. G. Dorville, *Les Renseignements sur l'exposition universelle de 1878: Guide des exposants* (Paris: n. pub., 1877), p. 65.
19. Steckel, p. 49.
20. Ibid., p. 50.
21. Adrien Huart et Draner, *Guide comique dans Paris pendant l'exposition* (Paris: n. pub., 1878), p. 53.
22. Charles Baudelaire, *Le Spleen de Paris*, in *Œuvres complètes*, I, pp. 272–374, (p. 318).
23. Edmond de Goncourt, *La Fille Elisa* (Paris: La Boîte à Documents, 1990), pp. 81–82.
24. J.-K. Huysmans, *Ecrits sur l'art, 1867–1905*, ed. by Patrice Locmant (Paris: Bartillat, 2006), p. 169.
25. R. Gentilini, p. 24.
26. Flaubert, *Bouvard et Pécuchet*, in *Œuvres complètes*, 16 vols (Paris: Club de l'honnête homme, 1971), V, p. 274.

27. *La Mode nouvelle et miroir parisien*, November 1875, p. 290.
28. Listed in Walter Benjamin, *The Arcades Project*, p. 165.
29. See *La Mode nouvelle et miroir parisien*, May 1878, p. 68.
30. R. Tamisier, p. 117; T. de Wyzewa, 'Le Palais de l'alimentation', *Revue de l'exposition universelle de 1889*, 2 (1889), 137–44 (p. 142).
31. Adrien Huart and Draner, *L'Exposition comique* (Paris: n. pub., 1878), p. 49.
32. *La Mode nouvelle et miroir parisien*, November 1878, p. 257.
33. Ibid., July 1878, p. 131.
34. See, among other reports, F. G. Dumas, 'Fontaines lumineuses', *Revue de l'exposition universelle de 1889*, 1 (1889), 341–46.
35. Green, p. 6.
36. Antoine Mattei, *Projet d'un jardin d'hiver public à faire dans la cour des Tuileries* (Paris: De Dubuisson, 1876), p. 2.
37. Richard Terdiman, *Present Past: Modernity and the Memory Crisis* (Ithaca, NY and London: Cornell University Press, 1993), p. 165.
38. Ludovic Hans and J.-J. Blanc, *Guide à travers les ruines. Paris et ses environs, avec un plan détaillé* (Paris: A. Lemerre, 1871), pp. 53–54.
39. In 'Le Signe' (1886), the wealthy Baroness sees a prostitute signaling to customers from the window opposite the Baroness's own apartment. The Baroness is impressed with the simplicity of this system, so tries to mimic the gesture before her mirror, then at her own window. To her astonishment, a man sees her gesture and forces his way into the apartment. The Baron is due home soon, so the Baroness decides the quickest way to get the man to leave is to fulfil his expectations.
40. Vallès recounts the story of a young woman in prison; she tells Vallès that '[mon amant] ne sait pas que je suis en carte, il me croit une étudiante, comme tout le monde... Je suis inscrite à la Préfecture, malheureusement, — ou plutôt heureusement, je ne pourrais pas vivre avec ce qu'il me donne, et il me quitterait. Hier je me suis mise à la fenêtre, parce que c'est demain que tombe mon garni, j'ai appelé un vieux, les agents m'ont vue...' ['[my lover] doesn't know I'm locked up, he thinks I'm a student, like everyone else... I'm signed up at the Préfecture, unfortunately, — or rather fortunately, since I couldn't live on what he gives me and he'd leave me. Yesterday I took up the window, because my rent's due tomorrow, I signalled to an old man, and the policemen saw me...'] (Jules Vallès, *Le Tableau de Paris* (Paris: Messidor, 1989), pp. 167–68).
41. 'R..., 34 ans, bourgeois: [il croit que] sa femme regarde souvent par la fenêtre; il est brun, et l'un de ses enfants est blond' ['R..., 34 years old, bourgeois: [he believes that] his wife often looks out of the window; he is brown-haired, and one of his children is blonde'] (Legrand du Saulle, *Le Délire des persécutions* (Paris: Plon, 1871), p. 208).
42. 'Une enfant de quinze ans [...] honnêtement élevée par ses parents, appelle par la fenêtre tous les soldats qu'elle voit passer' ['A child of fifteen years old [...] honestly brought up by her parents, calls out of the window to every passing soldier'] (Legrand du Saulle, *Les Hystériques: état physique et mental, actes insolites, déliciteux et criminels* (Paris: J.-B. Baillière et fils, 1883), p. 592).
43. Armstrong, p. 115.
44. Huysmans, *Écrits sur l'art*, p. 167.
45. The 'Fait Divers' column of the *Revue parisienne* reported a certain Mlle G..., aged 20, whose fiancé was sent on manoeuvres with the army; in her despair that she would never see him again and that her future was ruined, she threw herself from a third-floor window (6 August 1870, p. 2). The *Cloche* reported that Mme X..., aged 22, was in a critical condition after leaping from a sixth-floor window. During a minor domestic dispute, she threatened to throw herself from the balcony and although the maid tried to prevent Mme X... from jumping, she succeeded only in reducing her mistress's momentum; Mme X... fell onto the second-floor balcony and rebounded inside (2 May 1872). A few weeks later, the *Cloche* announced that the sixteen-year old Marie de B... had thrown open a sixth-floor window, called out to warn pedestrians below, and jumped to her death. Nobody had been able to discover what drove this girl of unimpeachable morals to suicide (23 May 1872). And Legrand du Saulle's medical writings on hysteria recount one case in which a new mother threw herself from a third-floor window after a quarrel with her husband (*Les Hystériques*, p. 375).

46. Maupassant recounts the tragic tale of a wife who, after a lifetime of dedication to her husband, discovers his infidelity and throws herself out of an attic window (*Sur l'eau, Blanc et bleu, Livre de Bord*, p. 159).
47. In the chapter 'Hôpital des fous — Sainte-Anne', Vallès describes the recent death of a mad woman who repeatedly tried — and eventually succeeded — to throw herself out of her window (Vallès, p. 60).
48. *La Mode nouvelle et Miroir parisien* ('Science de la ménagère', January 1872, p. 35; February 1872, p. 38; September 1874, p. 224; October 1872, p. 255; June 1876, p. 159; October 1882, p. 224).
49. *Au Bon Marché, Maison Aristide Boucicaut, Articles pour Etrennes* (Paris: n. pub., 1882), p. 8.
50. 'Chronique du mois', *La Mode nouvelle et Miroir parisien*, July 1876, p. 162; 'Lettre d'une mère à sa fille', *La Mode nouvelle et Miroir parisien*, April 1876, p. 85.
51. *Au Bon Marché, Maison Aristide Boucicaut, Nouveauté, Articles pour Etrennes* (Paris: n. pub., 1885), p. 4.
52. *Chromatoscopes, lamposcopes*, and *réflectoscopes* were variations on the magic lantern, all designed by M. Lapierre, and the *praxinoscope* was a spinning circular box designed by M. Reynaud, with the phases of an action printed inside and reflected by 'un prisme garni de petits miroirs où les images viennent se réfléchir tour à tour de telle sorte que l'action qu'elles représentent semble véritablement s'accomplir' ['a prism with small mirrors attached in which images are reflected one after another so that the action really seems to take place'] (see Marius Chaumelin, *Chefs-d'œuvre et curiosités de l'industrie à l'Exposition universelle de 1878* (Paris: Larousse, 1878), p. 8).
53. Edmond de Goncourt and Fernand Lochard, *Maison d'Edmond de Goncourt à Auteuil: Photographies et gravures représentant l'intérieur des appartements avec légendes manuscrites par Edmond de Goncourt* (n. pub., 1883), pp. 6, 7, 9, 10, 11.
54. 'Ils trouvèrent leur ami dans sa chambre à coucher. Stores et doubles rideaux, glace de Venise, rien n'y manquait' (Gustave Flaubert, *L'Éducation sentimentale*, in *Œuvres complètes*, p. 160) ['They discovered their friend in his bedroom. Blinds, reversible curtains, a Venetian mirror, nothing had been forgotten'].
55. 'Chronique du mois', *La Mode nouvelle*, February 1870, p. 130.
56. Octave Uzanne, *Le Miroir du monde: notes et sensations de la vie* (Paris: Quartin, 1888), p. 14.
57. Ibid., pp. 36–37.
58. Armstrong, p. 89.
59. Magraw, pp. 61–62.
60. Henrivaux, p. 448.
61. Edmond de Goncourt, *La Fille Elisa*, p. 97.
62. J.-K Huysmans, *Marthe, Histoire d'une Fille*, in *Œuvres complètes*, II, p. 109.
63. Henrivaux, pp. 10–11.
64. Marc Trapadoux, 'Le Métier du chiffon', in *Paris qui s'en va, Paris qui vient: publication littéraire et artistique*, ed. by Léopold Flameng (Paris: Alfred Cadart, 1859–60), n. pag.
65. Charles Knight, *Cyclopedia of London* (n. pub., 1851), p. 761.
66. Armstrong, p. 5
67. Karl Marx, *Capital. A Critical Analysis of Capitalist Production*, trans. by S. Moore and Edward Aveling, ed. by Frederick Engels (London: Lawrence and Wishart, 1974), p. 47.
68. Among the services listed in *Société centrale des architectes: Série des prix applicables aux travaux de bâtiments exécutés pour le compte des particuliers dans la ville de Paris 1883* (Paris: Imprimerie et librairie centrales des chemins de fer, 1883).
69. Henrivaux, Supplement — p. 1.
70. Kathryn Oliver Mills, *Formal Revolution in the Work of Baudelaire and Flaubert* (Newark, MD: University of Delaware Press, 2012), pp. 98–99.
71. 'Nouvelles et fait divers', *La Revue Parisienne*, 6 August 1870, p. 2.
72. *Journal officiel de la République français*, 15 February 1871, p. 91.
73. Eric Fournier, *Paris en ruines: Du Paris haussmannien au Paris communard* (Paris: Imago, 2008), p. 123.
74. Armstrong, pp. 10–11, p. 69.
75. Henri Dabot, *Griffonnages quotidiens d'un bourgeois du quartier latin, du mai 1869 au 2 décembre 1871* (Péronne: E. Quentin, 1895), pp. 2, 4, 75–76, 80–81, 124, 136, 138, 152, 159, 171, 239, 245.
76. *Journal officiel de la République*, 25 September 1870, p. 1597; 26 September 1870, p. 1599; 2 October 1870, p. 1612; 5 October 1870, p. 1619; 13 January 1871, p. 26.

77. Hector Malot, *Miss Harriet: Souvenirs d'un blessé* (Paris: Flammarion, 1895), p. 241.
78. *La Cloche*, 6 September 1870.
79. *Souvenirs d'un garde nationale pendant le siège de Paris et sous la Commune par un volontaire suisse. La Capitulation* (Neuchâtel: J. Sandoz, 1871), p. 209.
80. *La Cloche*, 14 September 1870.
81. *Journal officiel de la République française*, 10 January 1871, p. 19; 13 January 1871, p. 26.
82. Fournier, p. 40.
83. Etienne Dejoux, *Souvenirs du siège de Paris* (Paris: Moulin, 1871), pp. 100–01.
84. *Journal officiel de la République française*, 16 February 1871, p. 93.
85. Dabot, p. 153.
86. Edmond de Goncourt, *Journal: Mémoires de la Vie Littéraire, 1866–1886*, 2 vols (Paris: Laffont, 2014), II. p. 72 [*Paris under Siege, 1870–71: From the Goncourt Journal*, trans. by George J. Becker (Ithaca and London: Cornell University Press, 1969), pp. 115–16].
87. Benjamin Rampal, *Souvenirs du siège de Paris* (Marseille: n.pub., 1871), pp. 17–18.
88. *La Mode nouvelle et Miroir parisien*, March 1871, p. 5.
89. Ibid., p. 6 (my emphases).
90. Dabot, p. 124.
91. Mme Marie Sébrun, *Journal d'une mère pendant le siège de Paris* (Paris: Didier, 1872), pp. 80, 48, 125, 105, 252.
92. George Sand, *Journal d'un voyageur pendant la guerre* (Paris: Michel Lévy frères, 1871).
93. *La Cloche*, 19 January 1872.
94. *L'Espoir*, 2 September 1870.
95. *Journal officiel de la République française*, 10 October 1870, pp. 1629–30.
96. Ibid., 15 November 1870, p. 1703.
97. Ibid., 28 January 1871, p. 55.
98. Rampal, p. 14.
99. For example, in *Journal officiel de la République française*, 8 September 1870, p. 1537.
100. 'Exploits prussiens', *La Cloche*, 16 February 1871.
101. *La Cloche*, 16 February 1871.
102. *Observations présentées à l'Assemblée nationale par les Fabriques de Glaces françaises* (Paris: n. pub., 1874), p. 2; *La Cloche*, 13 March 1871.
103. On show at the Exposition de Lyon in 1872 (*La Mode nouvelle et Miroir parisien*, November 1872, p. 259).
104. Roland Dufrenne, Jean Maës and Bernard Maës, *La Cristallerie de Clichy; une prestigieuse manufacture du XIXe siècle* (Clichy-la-Garenne: La Rose de Clichy, 2005), p. 133.
105. *Le Charentais*, 8 February 1888.
106. See 'Erfarhrung und Armult', in *Walter Benjamin: Ein Lesebuch*, ed. by Michael Opitz (Frankfurt am Main: Surkamp, 1999), pp. 618–23 (pp. 621–22).
107. Hans and Blanc, p. 41.
108. 'Explosion à la poudrière du Champs de Mars', *Cri du peuple*, 19 May 1871.
109. Hans and Blanc, p. 62.
110. Ibid., pp. 56–57.
111. *La Cloche*, 4 April 1871; 10 April 1871.
112. Ibid., 28 March 1871.
113. Ibid., quoted in Fournier, p. 96.
114. Ibid., 6 April 1871.
115. Ibid., 21 March 1871.
116. Ibid., 12 April 1871.
117. Hans and Blanc, pp. 91, 96.
118. *La Cloche*, 13 June 1871.
119. Georges Bell, *Paris incendié: Histoire de la Commune de 1871* (Paris: n. pub., 1872), p. 154.
120. Steckel, pp. 46–47.
121. *La Cloche*, 12 June 1871.
122. On 21 March, 11 April, 21 May, twice on 22 May, and three times on 23 May.
123. Goncourt, *Journal*, II, p. 439 [*Paris under Siege*, pp. 291–92]; II, p. 446 [p. 302]; II, p. 439 [p. 291].

124. Fournier, p. 198.
125. *La Cloche*, 3 June 1871.
126. H. de Bleignerie, *Paris incendié 1871. Album historique contenant: I. Historique, par H. de Bleignerie; II. Notice sur les monuments, les rues incendiées, par E. Dangin; III. Vingt photographies artistiques des plus remarquables ruines de Paris* (Paris: A. Jarry, 1871), n. pag.
127. Dabot, p. 245.
128. Alcohol and the Commune have been discussed at some length by Susanna Barrows in 'After the Commune: Alcoholism, Temperance, and Literature in the Early Third Republic', in *Consciousness and Class Experience in Nineteenth-Century Europe*, ed. by John M. Merriman (New York: Holmes and Meier, 1979), pp. 205–18.
129. Paul de Saint-Victor, *Barbares et Bandits: La Prusse et la Commune* (Paris: Michel Lévy, 1871), p. 249.
130. *La Cloche*, 9 April 1871.
131. Vallès, p. 79.
132. Huysmans, *Pierrot Sceptique*, in *Œuvres complètes*, V, pp. 113, 124–25, 104.
133. Alfred Franklin, *Les Ruines de Paris en 4875* (Paris: Librairie de l'Echo de la Sorbonne, 1875), pp. 84, 93, 98.
134. Sigmund Freud, *Beyond the Pleasure Principle*, in *Standard Edition of the Complete Pscychological Works of Sigmund Freud*, trans. and ed. by James Strachey, 24 vols (London: Hogarth Press, 1955), XVIII, pp. 7–69.
135. These include: the Boulevard Haussmann becoming the Boulevard Victor Hugo and the Avenue de l'Impératrice becoming the Avenue Ulrich in September 1870 (*La Vie parisienne*, 8 June 1872, p. 362); the Rue de Berlin becoming the Rue de Richard Wallace (*La Cloche*, 7 March 1871); the Rue d'Allemagne becoming the Rue de la Revanche (*La Cloche*, 9 March 1871); the Avenue de l'Empereur becoming the Avenue des Lacs; the Avenue Ulrich (ex-Avenue de l'Impératrice) becoming the Avenue des Bois-de-Bologne; and the Avenue du Prince-Jérôme becoming the Avenue de Phalsbourg (*L'État*, 5 January 1873).
136. On the one-month anniversary of the *semaine sanglante*, *La Cloche* reported the successful repair of a photographer's gallery on the Boulevard Richard-Lenoir, of the ruins of several houses on the Rue Rampon, and of the Magasin du Pauvre-Jacques (23 June 1871). Within the next year, the same newspaper (now entitled *L'État*) advertised the reopening of the Bon Marché after repairs and an extension (29 April 1872); it noted that buildings had been reconstructed and trees replanted on the Rue Royale (2 May 1872); it reported the plans for a new Théâtre Porte Saint-Martin after the fires (18 May 1872); and it recorded the rapid progress of repair work on the Arc de Triomphe and the Colonne de Juillet (26 May 1872).
137. *La Vie parisienne*, 8 June 1872.
138. Hans and Blanc, pp. 8, 18.
139. Henri Bergson, *Matière et mémoire*, in *Œuvres*, ed. by André Robinet (Paris: Presses Universitaires de France, 1963), pp. 161–382 (p. 183).
140. *La Vie parisienne*, 14 October 1871, p. 967.
141. Ibid., 8 July 1871, p. 747.
142. Zola, 'Lettres parisiennes', *La Cloche*, 22 May 1872.
143. Colette E. Wilson, *Paris and the Commune 1871–1878: The Politics of Forgetting* (Manchester: Manchester University Press, 2007).

CHAPTER 2

❖

Shopping for Harmony: Glass, Sound, and the Exhibition Effect in Zola's *Au Bonheur des Dames*

> On avait enfin atteint le grand but poursuivi depuis si longtemps: celui de faire de Paris un objet de luxe et de curiosité plutôt que d'usage, une *ville d'exposition*, placée sous verre, hôtellerie du monde, objet d'admiration et d'envie pour les étrangers, impossible à ses inhabitants.
>
> [After a long pursuit, the great objective had finally been achieved: that of making Paris into an object of luxury and curiosity rather than being practical, an *exhibition city*, kept beneath glass, providing hospitality to the world, an objet of admiration and envy for foreigners, and impossible for its inhabitants]
>
> Victor Fournel, *Paris nouveau et Paris future*[1]

Zola's department store, Au Bonheur des Dames, is a dazzling exhibition of all that is glamorous in modern, Second Empire shopping. Women race to purchase the latest novelty in this majestic store, be it silk, lace, or garter ribbons. Zola paints a world filled with material objects as the very embodiment of modern fashion and consumerism; yet these objects could never gain their full importance without the physical characteristics of the shop itself, and without its carefully orchestrated architecture and décor. The department store is characterized by an abundance of glass: glass roof, glass windows, glass doors, glass lift, endless mirrors and two-way mirrors, glass display cabinets, drinking glasses, and perfume bottles. Zola takes the reader of 1883 back to the resplendent Second Empire of the 1860s, when glass architecture and accessories first took their glittering place in mainstream culture. In this world of glass, the ingenious entrepreneur and owner of Au Bonheur des Dames, Octave Mouret, places the visual at the centre of his commercial strategy.[2]

Given the context of material culture in the second half of the nineteenth century (explored in the previous chapter), it is hardly surprising that Mouret privileges the eye. The saturation of glass at Au Bonheur des Dames entails nothing especially surprising for this era of Haussmannization and of the burgeoning mass production of mirrors and window panes. However, Zola's representation of glass is particular in its retrospective gaze, being written after the *année terrible* at a time when the easy fantasies of Second-Empire commodity culture had been shaken. By taking the reader back to the 1860s, glass gains a doubly symbolic presence; first, as a symbol of the fantasmagoric commodity culture of Louis-Napoleon's new Paris (to both the characters and the reader); and second, as a symbol evoking the terrible crises which befell that culture (to the reader alone).

Department stores had been directly embroiled in these recent conflicts — a fact which the reader of the 1880s was unlikely to have forgotten. Shopping and the role of the department store in feminine life was inevitably altered during the *année terrible*; a writer for the women's magazine *La Mode nouvelle et Miroir parisien* commented that

> il est bien changé, Paris; cette ville qui était, hier encore, [...] la promenade favorite de la fashion des cinq parties du monde [...] est devenu un camp [...]. La population masculine porte l'uniforme de la garde nationale; quant aux femmes, [...] aucune d'elles ne songe à sa toilette; nous avons usé cet hiver nos vieilles robes, nos vieux manteaux et nos vieux chapeaux.[3]

> [Paris has changed so much; this city which, even yesterday, [...] was the favoured destination for fashion from the four corners of the globe, [...] has become an encampment [...]. The male population wears National Guard uniform; as for the women, [...] none of them think about their clothing; we have used our old dresses this winter, our old coats and our old hats.]

If women did buy new clothing, even at the beginning of these crises it tended to be modest, black dress with none of the flamboyance and colour which had been the stock in trade of the new department stores: the *Vie parisienne* reported that 'la toilette des femmes a changé de caractère du jour au lendemain. Plus de couleurs voyantes, plus de formes exentriques, plus d'ornements tapageurs — du brun, du gris, du noir de préférence' ['women's clothing changed its character overnight. No more lively colours, no more eccentric shapes, no more flashy ornamentation — brown, grey, black by preference'][4] — which must have had an impact upon sales strategies and sales figures in the department stores.

Not only was the commercial side of operations altered, but many department stores were entangled in the fighting. The Bon Marché provided the Gouvernement de la Défense Nationale with funds to forge a canon to fight the Prussians (to be christened 'Le Bon Marché').[5] During the Commune, the Pygmalion and the Magasins du Louvre were surrounded by Federal forces who conscripted all male staff between seventeen and thirty-five.[6] Fires razed the Magasin de nouveautés du Cherche-Midi, the Tapis rouge, and the Pygmalion, and damaged the Rue du Bac end of the Bon Marché[7] — events which Zola echoes indirectly in his novel with the devastating fire at Mouret's rival store, Aux Quatre Saisons, in Chapter 14.

The World of the Window Display

The visual and vision have considerable import in the *Rougon-Macquart* series, and are very often reliant upon an interplay of mirrors and windows. Naomi Schor sees Zola's window as a locus of observation, on the borders between constraint and liberation. Vision through windows is not passive, Schor writes, but always seems to augur change; in *La Fortune des Rougon* [*The Fortune of the Rougons*] (1871), for instance, Félicité's covetous gaze seems actively to precipitate the death of M. Peirotte.[8] Such emphasis on the visual, Schor contends, also reverberates at the textual level for, 'while [Zola is] deeply aware of the pitfalls of observation, [...] [it] can lead to the creation of a work of art which alone can transcend the anguish of enclosure and perhaps even bring about revolutionary change'.[9] Ilona Chessid, likewise, has highlighted the important narratorial role of the window as one of the key thresholds where transgressive desires are contained, expressed, or unleashed throughout the *Rougon-Macquart*, linking physical windows with Zola's concept of literary veils and screens.[10] Philip Walker notes the frequency of both literal and metaphorical appearances of mirrors and windows in Zola's fiction, arguing that their presence creates a narrative universe and a reading experience that is both vision-focused and visionary, dominated by and defined by the eye.[11] This emphasis on sight and vision is taken up by Brian Nelson in his discussion of Renée's downfall in *La Curée* [*The Kill*] (1871). His argument revolves around the importance of eyes, sight, and the interchange of gazes — a series of sightlines which Nelson notes are only possible because of the copious mirrors and windows throughout the novel.[12] Sight not only influences relations between characters, but also between individuals and the city, as Christopher Prendergast observes in his study of Zola's Parisian cityscapes. Prendergast defends Zola's five grand panoramas of Paris in *Une Page d'amour* [*A Love Episode*],[13] remarking that Zola's characters often view the city from a distance in order to conceptualize and homogenize the heterogeneous proliferation of urban modernity.[14]

All of these studies build a convincing picture of Zola's sensitivity to the narratological and symbolic potential of glass for his literature — particularly windows and mirrors. Yet for all the apparent power of glass and glass spaces in Zola's writing in general, a critical reading of *Au Bonheur des Dames* [*The Ladies' Paradise*] reveals that, in this novel, such power does not manifest itself entirely as one might expect. Contrary to the title, there is little in Zola's heavily-glazed department store that offers any kind of *bonheur* to the majority of its female shoppers.[15] They are manipulated into purchases they often cannot afford, they are driven to kleptomania by temptations they cannot withstand — this is the milieu Zola claims ironically to be a ladies' paradise. And yet there is no doubt that the ladies return again and again to the store. In this novel, Zola draws on the reader's memories of commercial and exhibition fever in the Second Empire, and places them alongside memories of the destruction of glass and glass culture during the *année terrible*; a contrast which problematizes the beguiling aura cast by glass over the products of consumerism. From this material viewpoint, whilst the visual clearly has considerable power in the department store — as I discuss in the first part of this chapter — it becomes questionable whether it is really Mouret's visual seductions alone which give the ladies so much pleasure. Zola's reader is invited to consider whether it is the visual world that we should locate at the heart of the narrative — or whether there is more to the sensory experience of Au Bonheur des Dames and *Au Bonheur des Dames* than initially meets the eye.

Octave Mouret uses glass intentionally and unremittingly to choreograph the visual landscape of his commercial project.[16] His scopic seduction of the shopper begins as soon as the female passer-by encounters the shop window — and this seduction is by no means a passive one. As Lynn Penrod has observed, the shop windows at Au Bonheur des Dames *actively* attempt to transform the passer-by into a shopper.[17] The eye of the lady of leisure is drawn mesmerically by the windows, which — in the narrative world of 1864 — have none of the negative associations of the *année terrible*. Rather, they are lively and fascinating, like three-dimensional versions of the popular panorama entertainments. Large plate-glass windows such as these prefigure the cinema screen in their ability to enthral, holding the viewer at a physical distance from what she sees, yet striving to capture her psychologically. This brings to mind Laura Mulvey's work on the psychological seductions of the cinematic screen. It could be said of the shop window as well as of the cinema that, 'quite apart from the extraneous similarities between screen [or shop window] and mirror (the framing of the human form in its surroundings, for instance), the cinema [or shop window] has structures of fascination strong enough to allow temporary loss of ego while simultaneously reinforcing it'.[18] Moreover, unlike the cinema screen, the window display does not turn off and break the illusion with a blank screen at the end of the film. Colourful images behind the glass screen may enthral the passer-by for as long as she desires to look at them, particularly once they are artificially lit at night-time. Moreover, Rachel Bowlby has noted that this kind of clear, visual display of real products is the most seductive of advertisements, as 'to see the thing itself — that is more likely to create desire in people's minds. People sometimes say "Oh, that is only an advertisement" but they never say "Oh, that is only a window display".'[19] This combination of seductions awakens the shopper's desire to enter the store where she may see and enjoy more.

Mouret's department store windows also make it possible for the passer-by to admire a twofold reflection of her own image. Behind one of the plate glass windows at Au Bonheur des Dames stands a mannequin of which Zola writes: 'la gorge ronde [...] gonflait l'étoffe, les hanches fortes exagéraient la finesse de la taille, la tête absente était remplacée par une grande étiquette, piquée avec une épingle dans le molleton rouge du col' ['the bosoms swelled out the material, the wide hips exaggerated the narrow waist, and the missing head was replaced by a large price tag with a pin stuck through it into the red bunting around the collar'] (*ABD*, 392/6). As the lady gazes at this display, she may well imagine the headless mannequin being completed with the image of her own head. Glass facilitates this visual play on two levels: first, the window pane produces a translucent reflection of the passer-by, overlaying the mannequin with an ethereal double of the self — not fully solidified, but seductively close. Secondly, the store incorporates an ever-increasing number of two-way mirrors, the 'glaces sans tain'. The dressmaking department has '[des] glaces sans tain [qui] donnaient sur la rue de la Michodière' ['plate-glass windows facing the Rue de la Michodière'] (*ABD*, 436/50). Piles of stock are visible 'par les glaces sans tain' ['through the plate-glass windows'] (*ABD*, 611/233). When the new façade is revealed, large sections are built entirely 'en glaces sans tain, dans les châssis de fer, rien que des glaces' ['from plate glass in a framework of metal — nothing but glass'] (*ABD*, 762/390). These two-way mirrors harness the bright light outside to render the glass at the back of the window display reflective when viewed from the street, but transparent when viewed from inside. Thus reflected, the passer-by observes not an ethereal image but a crisp, clear double of herself, over there, already inside the store.

These two-way mirrors also enhance the seductiveness of the window by concealing the shop beyond. Here, glass in the 1860s already manifests the powerful effect which Baudrillard would ascribe to this 'model material' a century later. Baudrillard suggests that

> un matériau résume ce concept d'ambiance, où on peut voir comme une fonction moderne universelle de l'environnement: le VERRE. C'est, selon la publicité, le 'matériau de l'avenir', qui sera 'transparent', comme chacun sait: le verre est donc à la fois le matériau et l'idéal à atteindre, la fin et le moyen. [...] À la fois proximité et distance, intimité et refus de l'intimité, communication et non-communication. [...] Une vitrine, c'est féerie et frustration, c'est la stratégie même de la publicité. [...] Le verre offre des possibilités de communication accélérée entre l'intérieur et l'extérieur, mais simultanément il institue une césure invisible et matériau, qui empêche que cette communication devienne une ouverture réelle sur le monde.[20]
>
> [one material sums up the idea of atmosphere and may be seen to embody a universal function in the modern environment: GLASS. It is, according to advertising, 'the material of the future' — a future which, as we all know, will be 'transparent'. Thus glass is both the material chosen and the ideal to be achieved, the ends and the means. [...] It is at once proximity and distance, intimacy and the refusal of intimacy, communication and non-communication. [...] The shop window is at once magical and frustrating — the epitome of an advertising strategy. [...] Glass offers faster communication between inside and outside, yet at the same time it creates an invisible caesura which prevents such communication from becoming a real opening onto the outside world at all.]

The passer-by, after initially feeling drawn into the store eyes-first by the intimacy and communication of the window display, finally finds herself drawn physically feet-first into the store by what the window keeps at a distance and *refuses* to communicate. It is notable that some of the store's publicity images testify to the seductive potential of obstructed sight; these images show nothing of the inside of the store, and depict only the glass surface of the roof panelling, with 'les galeries couvertes, leurs cours vitrées où l'on devinait les halls, tout l'infini de ce lac de verre et de zinc luisant au soleil' ['the covered galleries and their courtyards with glass roofs through which the halls could be guessed at, an endless lake of glass and zinc shining in the sunshine'] (*ABD*, 763/392 — translation adapted).[21] This play of the seen and the unseen aims to harness the fascination and frustration of glass to enrapture the passer-by, tempting her into the store to buy.

Just as the physical shop window teases the passer-by with a play of visible and invisible, so too the narrative structure teases us as readers as we try to complete a mental image of the shop beyond the window display. For example, Zola's lengthy, almost 'overflowing' description of the windows serves as a textual veil to prevent the reader from imagining the shop within. To take the lace display:

> [U]ne grande écharpe en dentelle de Bruges, d'un prix considérable, élargissait un voile d'autel, deux ailes déployées, d'une blancheur rousse; des volants de point d'Alençon se trouvaient jetés en guirlandes; puis, c'était, à pleines mains, un ruissellement de toutes les dentelles, les malines, les valenciennes, les applications de Bruxelles, les points de Venise, comme une tombée de neige. (*ABD*, 392)

> [A long scarf worked in Bruges lace, and costing a considerable amount, was spread out like an alter cloth, its two reddish-white wings unfurled; flounces of Alençon lace were strewn like garlands; then there was a cascade of every kind of lace — Mechlin, Valenciennes, Brussels appliqué, Venetian rose-point — streaming down like a snowfall (6)][22]

The reader is faced with a sentence whose end is deferred repeatedly by semi-colons and commas, and which loops together clauses like the threads of the lace it describes. The text presents swathes of signifiers, focusing the mind's eye on the complexities of the immediate foreground. Simultaneously, the continual shifting between a number of apparently arbitrary metaphors for the different varieties of lace — from altar cloths, to wings, to garlands, to snow — obliges the reader to concentrate intently on imagining the window display if they hope to create a precise mental image of it, so leaving the shop behind the glass temporarily out of (mental) focus. Both the shopper and reader, then, are drawn to Au Bonheur des Dames and *Au Bonheur des Dames* by this teasing preview of unseen splendour.

Old Glass, New Glass

Whilst the glass of Au Bonheur des Dames itself is able to manipulate the shopper (and reader) visually, a significant contributor to its impact stems from its visual juxtaposition with the *petit commerce*. The periodic efforts of the *petits commerçants* to modernize their own shop frontages make the reader increasingly aware of the centrality of the window in creating the modern commercial dreamworld. This effort always revolves around a modernization of the window and window display. In Robineau's head-to-head struggle with Au Bonheur des Dames, 'il soignait son étalage, entassait à ses vitrines des piles énormes de la fameuse soie' ['he also took great pains over his display, heaping up huge piles of the famous silk in his windows'] (*ABD*, 576/196). Bourras attempts to modernize the façade of his shop, but as the inevitability of defeat looms, it is his new glazing that becomes one of the first signs of his failure — 'les glaces, l'enseigne dorée, tout craquait, se salissait déjà, offrait cette décrépitude rapide et lamentable du faux luxe, badigeonné sur des ruines' ['the mirrors, the gilded signboard, were all cracking and collecting dirt already, presenting a picture of the rapid and depressing decay of sham luxury plastered on top of ruins'] (*ABD*, 741/368).

As with the narration of the lace window, punctuation is used to juxtapose the old and new commerce and to create an experience for the reader analogous to the visual experience of the shopper. Zola's descriptions gradually unveil Mouret's window displays, and although the reader may at first be overwhelmed by the deluge of imagery, the depiction of these windows is nonetheless neatly structured by a rhythmic parade of semi-colons. Just like the visual merchandising of the window, the sentences are built to dazzle but control simultaneously. For example:

> D'abord, ils [Denise et ses frères] furent séduits par un arrangement compliqué: en haut, des parapluies, posés obliquement, semblaient mettre un toit de cabane rustique; dessous, des bas de soie, pendus à des tringles, montraient des profils arrondis de mollets, les uns semés de bouquets de roses, les autres de toutes

nuances, les noirs à jours, les rouges à coins brodés, les chairs dont le grain satiné avait la douceur d'une peau de blonde; enfin, sur le drap de l'étagère, des gants étaient jetés symétriquement, avec leurs doigts allongés, leur paume étroite de vierge byzantine, cette grâce raidie et comme adolescente des chiffons de femme qui n'ont pas été portés. (*ABD*, 391)

[First they were attracted by a complicated arrangement: at the top, umbrellas, placed obliquely, seemed to form a roof of some rustic hut; beneath, suspended from rods and displaying the rounded outline of calves, were silk stockings, some strewn with bunches of roses, others of every hue, black net, red with embroidered corners, flesh-coloured ones with a satiny texture which had the softness of a blonde woman's skin; lastly, on the backcloth of the shelves, gloves were symmetrically arranged, their fingers elongated, their palms as delicate as those of a Byzantine virgin, with the stiff, seemingly adolescent grace of women's clothes which have never been worn (5 — punctuation adapted)]

In complete contrast, the description of the Vieil Elbeuf is not only briefer, but, more importantly, is utterly lacking in structuring, rationalizing punctuation. Baudu's façade manifests itself to the reader in phrases scattered with commas that lend little coherence to the imagery. The sentences seem to lack direction and merely drift to a close:

Ces fenêtres, carrées, sans persiennes, étaient simplement garnies d'une rampe de fer, deux barres en croix. Mais, dans cette nudité, ce qui frappa surtout Denise, dont les yeux restaient pleins des clairs étalages du *Bonheur des Dames*, ce fut la boutique du rez-de-chaussée, écrasée de plafond, surmontée d'un entresol très bas, aux baies de prison, en demi-lune. Une boiserie, de la couleur de l'enseigne, d'un vert bouteille que le temps avait nuancé d'ocre et de bitume, ménageait, à droite et à gauche, deux vitrines profondes, noires, poussiéreuses, où l'on distinguait vaguement des pièces d'étoffe entassées. La porte, ouverte, semblaient donner sur les ténèbres humides d'une cave. (*ABD*, 393)

[These windows, square, without shutters, were decorated merely with an iron railing, two crossed bars. But what Denise found most striking among all this bareness, her eyes still full of the bright displays at the Ladies' Paradise, was the shop on the ground floor, crushed by a low ceiling, topped by a very low mezzanine floor, with prison-like half-moon shaped windows. To the right and left, woodwork of the same colour as the signboard, bottle-green, shaded by time with ochre and pitch, surrounded two deep-set windows, black, dusty, in which the heaped-up goods could hardly be seen. The door, ajar, seemed to lead into the dark gloom of a cellar (7 — translation adapted).]

Text depicting the Vieil Elbeuf fails completely to seduce the mind's eye, just as its windows fail to seduce the shopper's eye. It provides no panning description of an array of entrancing colours and images — rather, it emphasizes repeatedly the blackness of the windows with the signifiers 'prison', 'bitume', 'noires', 'ténèbres', and 'cave'. Shopper and reader alike are faced with a dull and unenticing image.

For the reader of the 1880s, unlike the purified sheen of the department store's windows, these dark, dusty, crumbling windows also carry associations with the dark days of suffering, black-outs, and destruction during the long winter of the Prussian siege, and the buildings blackened by fires during the Commune — a period during which, as noted above, women did *not* indulge in frivolous, frenetic shopping. The choice of black silk for Robineau's doomed attempt at competition is by no means accidental, but reflects those melancholic fashion choices for feminine apparel during the *année terrible*. Darkened windows were at the centre of Gautier's mournful evocation of the Parisian ruins in June 1871: 'Hier soir le temps était bien sombre. Il pleuvait. Je passai devant les ruines de l'Hôtel de Ville; j'en contemplai la masse noire, et par les fenêtres et les arcades j'apercevais le ciel comme à travers les ossements d'un squelette' ['Yesterday evening the weather was sombre. It was raining. I passed in front of the ruins of the Hôtel de Ville; I contemplated its black mass, and through the windows and the arcades I saw the sky as if through the bones of a skeleton'].[23] A special edition of the *Vie parisienne* recounted during the siege that 'il n'y a d'éclairé que les fenêtres des ambulances qui se détachent sur ce fond de ténèbres avec l'éclat sinistre de bâtiments incendiés' ['nothing was lit but the windows of the ambulance stations, standing out against the shadowy backdrop with the sinister glare of burning buildings'].[24] Indeed, Zola's emphatic contrast between the windows of the dark old and the light new commerce also effects a deliberate *projection* of the blackness and destruction associated with the *année terrible* away from the department store windows and onto the *petit commerce*. This is perhaps why Zola has relocated his department store, so clearly calqued upon the Bon Marché, to the 2ᵉ arrondissement; Au Bonheur des Dames stands on streets which were beyond the reach of the Prussian shelling, and which formed an island of relative tranquility during the Versaillais invasion of Paris, sheltered from the ravaging fires which damaged Boucicaut's store, and at least two streets removed from the Communard barricades on the Rue de la Chaussée d'Antin or the Versaillais push along the Rue de Gramont.

Through both its structure and its imagery, the text encourages readers to turn away from these troubling visions of the *petit commerce* in order to focus their attention on the principal visual and literary spectacle at Au Bonheur des Dames. Faced with Baudu's dark windows, the experiences of the passer-by (and the reader) pre-empt those of Walter Benjamin and Louis Aragon in the arcades — the old shop windows sit in awkward juxtaposition with the new department store, unseductive, enigmatic, even hideous in their coffin-like appearance and their inability to partake in the illusions of commodity culture.[25] Potentially, of course, the proximity of the *petit commerce* to Au Bonheur des Dames could disabuse the shopper, revealing the illusions fabricated by the department store by metonymic association. However, this juxtaposition of old and new glass — physically within the street scene and linguistically within the narrative — also highlights that both Mouret and Zola differ in a fundamental way from the *petit commerce*; unlike their predecessors, they have the ability to understand and to exploit the symbolic potential of glass.

The visual effects made possible by glass are not only influential when the passer-by or shopper stands in close proximity to these vitreous surfaces; rather, Mouret uses glass to liberate light throughout the store and the surrounding streets. Light augments the impact of his visual merchandising in comparison to the *petit commerce* — which is in turn placed in the department store's shadow, 'assombrie, gagnée davantage par la somnolence de la ruine' ['gloomier, more overcome by the somnolence of ruin'] (*ABD*, 588/209). The brightness of Au Bonheur des Dames carries associations of clarity and cleanliness, despite the dustiness of the Parisian streets and of the building works that beleaguer the quartier's *petit commerce*. This is all the more remarkable as department stores were criticized in the nineteenth century for their poor ventilation and accumulation of dust, leading to shop workers suffering one of the highest rates of tuberculosis in Paris.[26] 'The presence of light itself,' Christopher Prendergast suggests, 'both natural and artificial [...] came to be seen as one of the most precious commodities in the city'[27] — and Mouret shows every intention of investing in this commodity to sell his commodities. The power of light seems so intertwined with the power of Au Bonheur des Dames that everything to do with the store becomes illuminated. Even the light emitted from the window displays at Au Bonheur des Dames has its strategic place in this vast visual machine; it places the passer-by in the spotlight, turning the encounter with the window into the first act of the shopping melodrama, and compelling the shopper to enter the store to complete the play. As a German company selling illuminated advertising boards reminded their clients succinctly in the 1920s, 'Licht lockt Leute' ['Light Lures People']; the brilliance of the window panes may lure not only the eye, but also the psychological — and subsequently physical — being of the passer-by until she is compelled to cross the threshold.[28]

Moreover, glass in Mouret's scopic system goes beyond the window display outside the store. Repeated descriptions of sun rays as they shine obliquely through the vast windows into the store emphasize the importance of glass within Mouret's visual merchandizing strategy. During the first *mise en vente*, 'au blanc, un angle de soleil, entré par la vitrine de la rue Neuve-Saint-Augustin, était comme une flèche d'or dans de la neige' ['in the linen department, a ray of sunlight coming through the windows on the Rue Neuve-Saint-Augustin was like a golden arrow in the snow'] (*ABD*, 492/109); at the end of the working day, when 'les rayons du soleil à son coucher entraient obliquement par les larges baies de la façade, éclairaient de biais les vitrages des halls; et, dans cette clarté d'un rouge d'incendie, montaient, pareilles à une vapeur d'or, les poussières' ['the rays of the setting sun were entering obliquely through the wide bays at the front of the shop, lighting up from the side the glazed roofs of the halls; in this fiery brightness, the thick dust, raised from the morning onwards by the trampling crowd, was floating upwards, like a golden vapour'] (*ABD*, 642/265); and, as the inventory comes to a close, 'le soleil luisait encore, un blond soleil d'été, dont le reflet d'or tombait par les vitrages des halls' ['the sun was shining, a pale summer sun, the golden reflection of which was coming through the hall windows'] (*ABD*, 676/300). The threefold repetition of 'd'or' alongside the various kinds of window suggests the direct transition from light as commodity to light as income; the air seems to be decked with gold in honour of the brimming cash registers.

Indeed, gold — or more precisely, gilding on glass — becomes a replacement sun as 'les vitres niellées d'or et les rosaces d'or semblaient un coup de soleil, luisant sur les Alpes de la grande exposition de blanc' ['the glass inlaid with gold, and the golden roses were like a burst of sunshine shining on the Alps of the great exhibition of white'] (*ABD*, 770/399). This golden glass seems to emit rays of light around the store, creating its own, self-contained solar system. Furthermore, given the use of the imperfect tense in describing these illuminations, light and frenzied shopping gain an air of timelessness and permanency that augurs well for the future of Mouret's coffers.[29] Pre-destiny seems to play a role here for commerce, as light-play and word-play combine in the homonymy of *rayon* (shop department) and *rayon* (ray of light).

Glass is positioned by Mouret with the intention of channelling the shopper's eyes and body in accordance with each of his principal sales novelties. His large-scale use of glass fully realizes Graeme Gilloch's contention (with reference to Benjamin) that 'architecture and action shape each other; they interpenetrate'.[30] Just as the glass of the window captures the shopper's attention outside the store with its play of display and concealment, so the glass roofing and panelling within the store captures the shopper's attention, and gives her the impression that she is an active part of that interplay. The glass surfaces all around her suggest that she has entered the world of the magical window display, which she is now at liberty to explore.

The layers of internal glass walls within this 'window world' constantly renew scenes of display and concealment, offering only a select set of items to the eye, and/or offering items to the eye but not to the touch. In Chapter 2, for example, we see that Mouret's architecture seeks to use glass to shape the shopper's actions; the 'cour intérieure qu'on avait vitrée' ['inner courtyard covered with a glass roof'] (*ABD*, 431/45 — see Figure 2.1) draws the shopper towards the silk department where the 'Paris Bonheur' silk is the day's main loss-leader. The roof of this department is glazed, the better to draw the clientele towards the silks. It implies that there may be concealed delights to be discovered within, just as there are beyond the window display. Before the second sale day in Chapter 9, more areas are glazed, reflecting Mouret's conviction in the success of this strategy. Several glass galleries now radiate out before the eye: 'une large galerie allait de bout en bout, flanquée à droite et à gauche de deux galeries plus étroites, la galerie Monsigny et la galerie Michodière. On avait vitré les cours, transformées en halls' ['a wide gallery ran from one end of the shop to the other, flanked on the right and left by two narrower galleries, the Monsigny Gallery and the Michodière Gallery. The courtyards had been glazed over and transformed into halls'] (*ABD*, 611/233). Now the quasi-magnetic attraction of glass may confuse the shopper by pulling her towards several areas of the shop floor at once, using glass walls to channel her footsteps without giving the impression of constriction that an opaque wall would. Ultimately, after the grand extension unveiled during the third and final sale day in Chapter 14, the entire entrance hall has become 'un hall aux glaces claires' ['the entrance hall, with bright mirrors'] (*ABD*, 768/397); finally, the shop window — with all its seductive potential — and the entire shop are virtually contiguous.

Even the smallest vitreous objects are situated to perpetuate the glittering, mesmeric effect of glass in Au Bonheur des Dames. There is such a proliferation of small glass objects that any line of sight will inevitably have glass in it somewhere. Hundreds of drinking glasses and bottles are aligned in the buffet, and it is ensured that they attract the attention of the viewer by catching the light each time they are turned over and over as the waiters, 'continuellement, essuyaient et emplissaient les

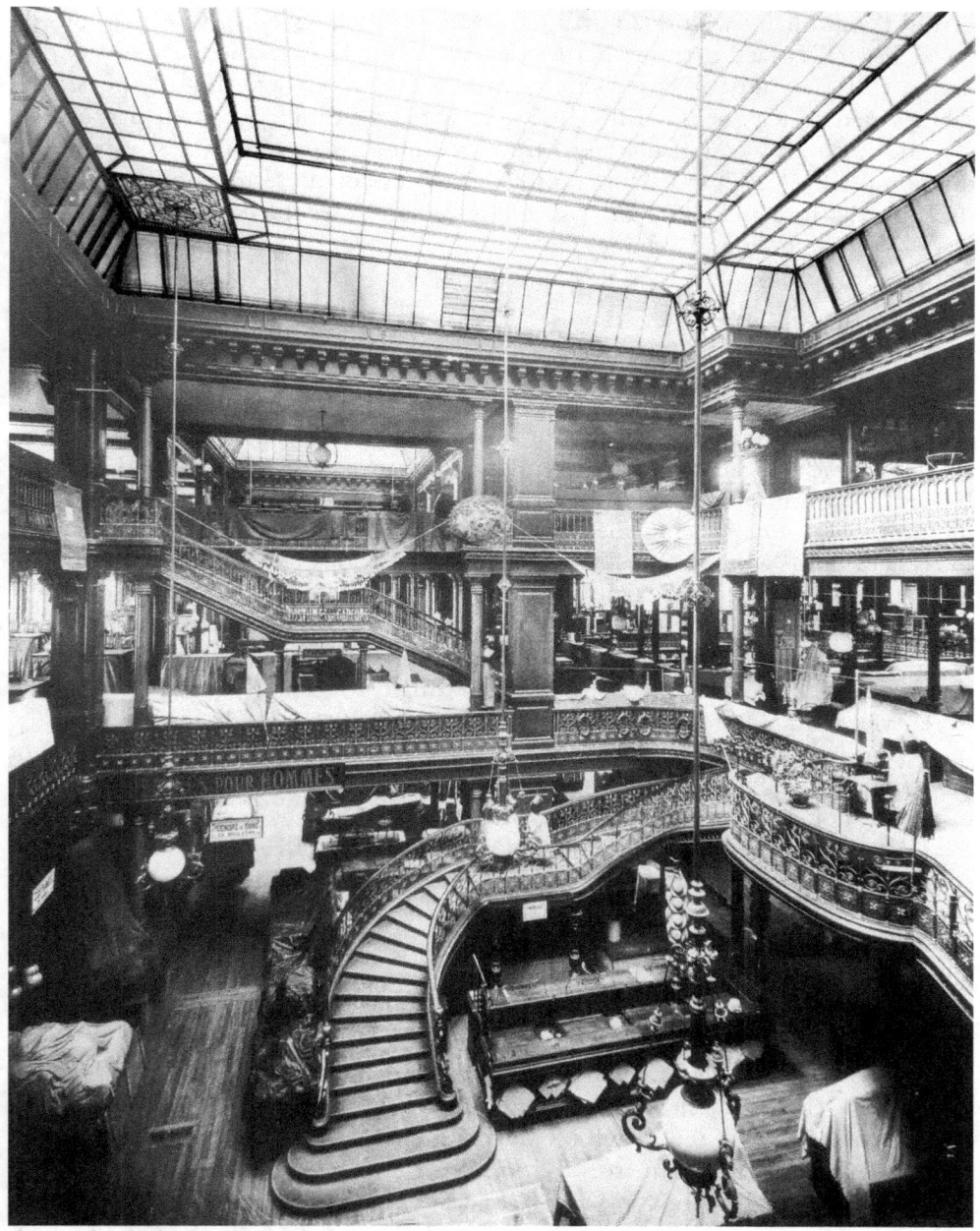

FIG. 2.1. The grand staircase of the Bon Marché below glazed roof panelling, around 1900, photographed by Albert Chevojon (1865-1925).

verres' ['continually wiping and filling glasses'] (*ABD*, 623/245). Glass 'flacons de poche' ['pocket-sized perfume bottles'] (*ABD*, 788/418) from the perfume counter ensure that glass and all its seduction can be seen everywhere the lady goes. The subtle visual strategy behind filling the store with a superfluity of small glass objects is made apparent when glass bottles are stored on glass shelves in glass cabinets in the perfumerie (*ABD*, 788/418). This cabinet is essentially a miniature version of the gigantic store and all its glazing, and it demonstrates the enchanting power of glass as both exhibit and exhibitor.

Flaws in the Visual

Whilst, thus far, there is little reason to question the effectiveness of Mouret's visual strategies, when glass takes the form of the looking-glass at Au Bonheur des Dames it reveals that the relationship between female shopper and the visual is in fact more complex. Like the glass windows and glass roof-panels, mirrors too are ubiquitous. Indeed, their omnipresence is exacerbated for the reader by the fact that 'la glace' signifies a high-quality glass sheet rather than a finished product, and is thus used to refer to both 'window panes' and 'mirrors' at various points in this novel. The frequency with which this signifier appears in *Au Bonheur des Dames* floods the reader's mental reconstruction of the shop with images of glass surfaces, which may be imagined as transparent, or reflective, or both.

At one level, the strategic deployment of mirrors is simply used to render the store ever more impressive to the eye, multiplying and brightening the visual splendour. In psychological terms also, Mouret's decision to install an abundance of mirrors to attract business seems theoretically sound. The pervasive mirrors should in theory nourish the female shopper's narcissistic fantasies, enchanting her with the reflection of her own 'new you', and providing her with a fresh and (unusually) complete image of her selfhood. Flattering the consumer with praise of her beauty and aesthetic grandeur, Rachel Bowlby suggests, can create an advertisement of her (new) Self to herself, promoting a new identity that she will seek both to purchase and consume.[31] It certainly seems logical that such an inviting reflection would compel the shopper to buy whichever fashionable articles have temporarily permitted her to enjoy this sense of wholeness.

Furthermore, Lacanian theory proposes that, whilst no woman can be a subject in the patriarchal symbolic, she may participate in the illusions of identity belonging to the imaginary — the order of identification with images and the visual.[32] Mouret's mass dispersal of mirrors should therefore provide the necessary images so that each lady can create a comforting concept of the self. This logic is not unique to Mouret, but is discernable in a number of advertisements from the period which place the mirror at the heart of all female happiness. An 1871 advertisement for *Veloutine Fay* rice powder, for example, rewrote Sleeping Beauty in such a way that mirrors, feminine self-assurance, and beauty are made inseparable:

> Quand la Belle-au-Bois-Dormant se réveilla, au bout de cent ans, avec toute sa cour, elle se retrouva aussi jeune qu'au premier jour de son sommeil, dit la légende. Il y eut un instant d'anxiété terrible parmi les dames de la cour en

rouvrant les yeux; leur premier cri fut: Une glace! vite, une glace! Et un sourire de satisfaction fut le résultat de cet examen.³³

[When Sleeping Beauty woke up, at the end of a hundred years, with all her court, she found herself as young as the day she fell asleep, so says the legend. One moment of terrible anxiety spread among the ladies of the court when they opened their eyes; their first cry was: A mirror! Quickly, a mirror! And a smile of satisfaction was the result of this inspection.]

With such assumptions rooted firmly in popular culture, it is thus hardly surprising that Mouret feels impelled to multiply the number of mirrors with each refurbishment.

However, the mirror's theoretical ability to please the shoppers is challenged by the fundamental flaw inherent in any attempt to use narcissism to mesmerize the individual. Always entailed in narcissism is a troubling and alienating element. Although there is 'self-centredness and self-love' on the one hand, there is also the 'partial *abandoning of the self* in favour of the external object of reflection' on the other.³⁴ The very nature of the ego-construction process that may give the individual shopper a sense of uniqueness and wholeness may also, if the immersion in the imaginary is anything other than entirely complete, reveal to her that her real body is a site of absence. The specular image with which she identifies is 'over there', located in the mirror or counterpart; it is alienated from her real body and may therefore provoke an identity crisis. Isobel Armstrong has remarked that 'no one owns a reflection. In the glazed urban phantasmagoria reflections are random and arbitrary, mirages of the body in public space. They cannot be controlled as in a personal mirror'.³⁵ This contrast may be extended from public windows/personal mirrors, to public *mirrors*/personal mirrors in Au Bonheur des Dames. And, for the *année terrible* generation, this goes further still. The memory of melted, fragmented, and shattered mirrors means that this alienation is likely to affect not just the one but the many; it implies not just a fragmentation of the individual body, but of the body politic. For all these reasons, despite the theoretical benefits of the looking-glass for Mouret's commerce, there are in fact very few satisfying or productive mirror encounters for Zola's shoppers. None of the central group of ladies is ever seduced into making purchases by seeing an ego-affirming image in Mouret's mirrors. Even Mme Marty, the most voracious shopper, hardly gives her reflection a glance but focuses on viewing and touching the products themselves.

Mme Desforges, whose mirror encounters are described in the most detail, is not merely indifferent but actively distressed by the sight of her reflection. As she contemplates dejectedly whether 'elle vieillissait donc, qu'on la trompait pour la première fille venue?' ['was she growing old then, if he was unfaithful to her with the first girl who passed by?'], her face rather than the fashion items she wears comes into focus in the looking-glass: 'la glace reflétait le rayon entier, avec sa turbulence; mais elle ne voyait que sa face pâle' ['the mirror reflected the whole department, with its endless commotion; but she saw nothing but her own pale face'] (*ABD*, 634/256). As discomforting as this mirror experience may be, Mme Desforges finds herself compelled to look repeatedly, and 'ses regards, continuellement, retournaient à la glace, en face d'elle. Maintenant, elle s'y regardait près de Denise, elle établissait des comparaisons' ['she kept glancing at the mirror opposite her. Now that she could see herself in it next to Denise, she began to make comparisons'] (*ABD*, 634/257). Indeed, this attack on the self at the mirror is further emphasized here by the use of free indirect discourse, which weakens the uniqueness of the character by disindividuating Henriette's thoughts into the externalized narrative voice.

The fact that Mme Desforges not only looks at Denise with despair, but specifically observes her via the looking-glass, signals the failure of Mouret's attempt to incorporate a narcissistic panacea into his visual dreamworld. As David Bell argues in his discussion of *La Curée*, 'the narcissistic ego must appropriate the exterior world, and organize it into a speculative system. It must deny the alien nature of the exterior world, its irreducible alterity'.[36] Saccard may achieve this while he dominates Paris from the Montmartre restaurant, and Renée may appropriate Paris to the point that the streets seem mere extensions of her mansion hallways (*LC*, 389, 496), but Mme Desforges consistently fails to appropriate her visual surroundings in this mirror-laden department store. She is unable to deny the unsettling nature of the world around her, and thus she cannot construct her narcissistic ego.

This failure demonstrates Lacan's contention that a comforting self-image can be produced 'only in so far as our attitude offers the subject the pure mirror of an unruffled surface'.[37] No matter how smooth the physical glass surfaces in Mouret's store, Henriette's jealousy and fear of ageing 'ruffles' the imago and makes narcissistic comfort impossible. This is aggravated further by the mannequins populating the shop floor at Au Bonheur des Dames. Whilst their fragmented bodies, torsos, and stocking-clad legs may appear to represent woman as a mindless, passive, eroticized object to the reader (particularly the masculine reader), to the female shopper these representations of the female body are allied with her mirror reflection. At first, the mirror and mannequin seem to transmit conflicting messages: the mirrors tell the shopper that she will feel as complete as this reflected image if she buys the item she is trying on; the mannequins tell the shopper that she will be as fragmented as they are if she follows their example and dons the item they are modelling. The mannequins undermine the illusions of wholeness in the mirror image; they encourage the shopper to be more reserved and resistant to Mouret's visual seductions rather than letting herself be ravished passively. This is borne out by the fact that the majority of mirror reflections in this novel are not of whole bodies but amputated forms, such as 'des moitiés d'épaules et de bras' ['bits of shoulders and arms'] (*ABD*, 627/250). Far from Barbara Vinken's assertion that 'the department store is [...] a place where the secret vices of women are shamelessly bared in public, as they expose themselves without veil in the glaring, hot artificial light. Ravished, [...] they touch everything and let themselves, pale with desire, be raped', at no point does the reader witness any of Zola's shoppers literally wandering around 'without veil' or being raped.[38] They are utterly indifferent to Mignot's caresses as he fits them for gloves. They never undertake any act that is inherently erotic in itself if we discount the eroticism imposed by the narrative and/or Mouret's desire to assert his masculinity and authority.

Furthermore, the mirror's inability to seduce the shopper does not situate the mirror as the opposite of the seductive window but, rather, draws our attention to the inherent fallibility in *all* attempts to use the visual to manipulate women. Instead of the glass surroundings producing a utopian space, they highlight that in a crystalline city anything that is flawed or tainted is rejected. In this respect, glass fosters an inhospitable atmosphere of inadequacy and exclusion. Even the windows are not universally seductive. Although the leisured, upper-bourgeois lady is enticed by the window display, those who are busy or less wealthy hurry past at the beginning of Chapters 4 and 9 (*ABD*, 470/86; 611/233). Even the lower-bourgeois women who enter the shop on the first sale day show no signs that they feel they belong there, or that they appreciate the store's scopic fascinations; the speed and sense of purpose with which they plan and execute their purchases reveal that they retain control over their own thoughts and actions (*ABD*, 470/86). For the window to tantalize the passer-by, she must feel that her reflection in the window is an adequate companion to the personifications of wealth and leisure staged by the mannequins of the window display.

Within this conflict at the mirror, there lingers the fundamental incompatibility of the supply of fashion and the supply of narcissism. Fashion, being a socially defined phenomenon, incorporates the fashionable woman into an interpersonal domain. Fashion draws the shopper into a sphere where, as Bell remarks, 'the freedom of the individual subject is effectively negated [...] because that commodity has been designated as desirable by others'.[39] In addition, the nineteenth-century woman had a very particular experience of dress, as she not only wore but was also moulded physically and socially by corsets, bustles, hoops, and petticoats. Clothes became a text which was read by men and which led her body beneath to be read by men; clothes functioned as key signifiers in the social narrative of a woman's wealth (or her male relatives' wealth), and, moreover, of her morality, her sexuality, and of the assumed mental and physical inferiority of her gender. It is significant in this context that all of the central group of ladies are well beyond the age which the nineteenth century would have defined as 'young'; at thirty years old or more, their value in a society that saw women as important in so far as they were beautiful and fertile was waning, and so the mirrors remind them — in this milieu where everything it marked with its price — that their worth is constantly diminishing.

Reading a woman's identity from her clothes is so engrained in society that women perform this reading, pre-emptively, for themselves. Even young girls of only nine or ten try to read their own image with other people's eyes; one young shopper in Denise's children's department, 'ayant aux épaules un paletot de drap, l'étudiait devant la glace, se tournait, la mine absorbée, les yeux luisants du besoin de plaire' ['when trying on a cloth coat would study it in front of a looking-glass, turning round with an absorbed look, her eyes shining with the desire to please'] (*ABD*, 727/354). This incorporation of an external, male eye was taken for granted in contemporary culture. One toy shop exhibit at the 1867 World Fair included a tableau of dolls arranged to depict 'une jeune femme [qui] donne un coup d'œil à sa toilette devant une glace, et son regard inquiet sollicite le suffrage d'un jeune homme qui l'examine' ['a young woman looking over her outfit in front of the mirror, and her concerned glance seeking the approval of a young man who is studying her'] — a lesson about the status quo that all girls needed to learn as young as possible.[40] This episode also recalls the Bon Marché's 1882 catalogue, in which an etching shows a young girl modelling the 'Mignon' corset for eleven to fifteen-year-olds whilst looking at her reflection in a hand mirror, and the 1885 catalogue which uses a similar image to advertise the 'corset bébé' for six to nine-year-olds. In marked contrast are the images for men's and boys' clothing; in the first catalogues for male customers in the early 1880s, the Bon Marché depicted either no glass objects at all or men using binoculars or glasses to observe the world around them but never themselves.[41] Elisabeth Bronfen has argued (in reference to Edith Wharton's tragic Lily Bart) that a woman being regarded and read by the men around her 'can never be narcissistically whole because she always also includes the masculine gaze that makes her other than herself'.[42] So, like Wharton's Lily, if the female shopper were to seek to create a desirable, narcissistic self-image in the mirrors at Au Bonheur des Dames, she would inevitably be hounded by the otherness within her own fashionable image, and by the incorporation of the other within her own gaze.

Failed narcissism comes to the fore in the episode surrounding the silk waterfall display. This scene presents a curious disconnect between the female shoppers' perception of the display, and the interpretations of that experience through the filter of patriarchal expectations. The narrative voice would have us believe that the women mistake the fabric for a pool of water, and that they see and are seduced by their reflections to an extent that never occurs around any of the genuinely reflective surfaces in this novel; we are told that 'des femmes, pâles de désirs, se penchaient comme pour se voir, [...] restaient debout, avec la peur sourde d'être prises dans le débordement [...] avec l'irrésistible envie de s'y jeter et de s'y perdre' ['women pale with desire were leaning over as if to look at themselves, [...] standing there, filled with the secret fear of being caught up in the overflow [...] with an irresistible desire to throw themselves into it and be lost'] (*ABD*, 487/104). Yet Mme Desforges and Mme Bourdelais seem to find this 'envie [...] de s'y perdre' just as resistible as the enticements of the mirrors; they merely give the fabric pool an appreciative 'coup d'œil' before praising instead the Oriental carpets in the entrance hall. The nameless women filling the area around the waterfall display are by no means whipped into a sudden frenzy of acquisitive desire after looking into the pool's depths 'comme pour se voir' — rather, '[elles] regardaient les étoffes, les tâtaient, stationnaient là des heures, *sans se décider*' ['the crowd of ladies who were looking at the materials and feeling them, remaining there for hours, *without making up their minds*'] (*ABD*, 488/105 — my emphasis). Even Mme Marty does not buy anything from the silk department (*ABD*, 489/105). Those who do buy purchase predominantly the 'Paris-Bonheur' silk, which is a loss-leader for the store. Self-control is clearly in evidence here, not self-abandonment to narcissistic seduction.

These problematizations of the mirror and of reflections reveal Mouret's misconception that he could gain and maintain total control of his shoppers through the visual. It becomes clear that Mouret's manipulation of feminine actions, which at first appears absolute, is in fact far from complete. The turning-point confrontation between Henriette, Denise, and Mouret in Henriette's boudoir makes it clear that

Mouret is not the all-powerful manipulator of glass — and particularly of the mirror — that he had thought. Zola juxtaposes Henriette's boudoir with the *confections* department, complete with an equally plush red carpet and with '[une] armoire à trois corps, aux larges glaces' ['a three-door wardrobe with broad looking-glasses on each door'] (*ABD*, 692/317) similar to the store's 'hautes armoires de chêne sculpté, des glaces tenant la largeur des panneaux' ['tall cupboards of carved oak, mirrors filling the whole width of the panels'] (*ABD*, 633/256). Where a distinction is made is that in the boudoir, 'comme la fenêtre donnait sur la cour, il y faisait déjà sombre' ['as the window overlooked the courtyard, it was already dark there'] (*ABD*, 692/317). The lack of light through the window pane removes the golden sheen of splendour and commercial success, and brings the raw, disturbing potential of the mirror to the surface.

In this dim and tense atmosphere, the mirror never reflects either of the two women directly; instead, 'les glaces de l'armoire reflétaient de larges pans de clarté vive sur les tentures de soie rouge, où dansaient *les ombres* des deux femmes' ['the wardrobe mirrors reflected broad patches of bright light on the red silk hangings, on which the *shadows* of the two women were dancing'] (*ABD*, 694/319 — my emphasis). These dancing shadows seem to come from a place prior to the formation of the ego, negating any illusions of stable identity. When Denise departs and Henriette's battle is finally lost, Henriette is no longer reflected even as a shadow in the mirror: 'les reflets des glaces n'étaient plus traversés d'ombres dansantes, la pièce semblait nue, tombée à une tristesse lourde' ['dancing shadows were no longer passing across the reflections in the mirrors; the room seemed bare and had taken on an oppressive sadness'] (*ABD*, 696/321). Far from the mirror being an ally for bolstering the self, Henriette's distress enacts the mirror's capacity to provoke identity crises for Mouret's female clientele.

Notably, when a more susceptible male character, M. Boutarel, has an hysterical outburst, it takes place in an area of the store which features a particularly high concentration of glass; in the changing room area, where looking-glass walls add an additional layer of glass to the windows, mirrors, and roof panels throughout the store. In this vitreous setting, M. Boutarel exhibits behaviour typically associated with the emotional woman rather than the rational man, and he is far from finding any satisfaction in the physical proximity of hundreds of female bodies as one might expect from a red-blooded male. Rather, as his wife uses the changing room, he screams that he wants her to come out of there, wants to know what they are doing to her, and refuses to allow her to undress without him present (*ABD*, 780/409). What is it that he fears they are doing behind the closed mirror-doors? The complete lack of interest inscribed on the bored faces of the other patient husbands leaves little suggestion that they are getting any titillation from the peepshow-like glimpses of 'dames en chemise et en jupon, le cou nu, les bras nus, des grasses dont la chair blanchissait, des maigres au ton de vieil ivoire' ['ladies in their chemises and petticoats, with bare necks and arms, of fat women whose flesh was fading, and of thin women the colour of old ivory'] (*ABD*, 780/409). Instead, we see that the emotional M. Boutarel shares enough feminine traits to be sensitive to the challenges posed to the ego by this dense concentration of mirrors.

With the unsettling images of the mirror in mind, the progressive increase in the number of looking-glasses at the department store brings no guarantee of positive results for either Mouret's clientele or his commerce. Yet having established that mirrors afford no pleasure to the female shoppers — moreover, that they may provoke identity crises — it seems curious that Zola depicts Mouret adding still more reflective surfaces to his already heavily-glazed store. We might deduce from this a deliberate attempt to cause the women upset; mirrors are located throughout the fictional store not for feminine pleasure at all, but as a reflection of *masculine* anxieties. This goes further than just Mouret striving to take control over individual women like Henriette or Denise. Mouret's desire to trouble his clientele can be read as a broader allegory for patriarchal society's desire to bring any person that embodies the dangerous, irrational, and chaotic under its control — particularly in the wake of the Commune. Alongside the dramatization of, specifically, a conflict of the sexes,[43] I contend that Zola uses sex and gender *allegorically* to dramatize the conflict between dominant patriarchy — rational, controlled, ordered — and its marginal other — irrational, chaotic, effeminate/feminine. In *Au Bonheur des Dames*, masculinity and femininity respectively are compelling metaphors for these two opposing forces; indeed, virility was a popular metaphor for national strength during the Franco-Prussian War and bombardment, whereas descending into effeminacy was the epitome of the nation's worst fears.[44] Femininity, having so often been associated with hysteria throughout patriarchal history, is an effective shorthand for the dangers of unbridled desire in both men and women — a pertinent concern for the reader of the early Third Republic. So, perhaps the mirror's failure to give the feminine characters confidence and a sense of identity is precisely the objective. Significantly, none of the mirrors ever present Mouret, Paul, M. de Boves, or the Baron Hartmann with a distressing reflection; any potential challenges to these masculine egos are carefully ignored. Additionally, no male clothing mannequins seem to adorn the shop floor, even after the establishment of a men's clothing department — thus avoiding any contemplation of male bodily fragmentation, in spite of the implications in the masculine gender of the word 'le mannequin'.

This reading is sustained by the fact that Zola chooses to invert the gender balance from Rachilde's department store novel, *Monsieur de la Nouveauté* (1880). In Rachilde's novel, it is a *man* who is seduced by the mirrors, windows, and fabrics of the department store. Indeed, there are many passages in Rachilde's first novel from which Zola seems to have drawn inspiration — often to the point of near-plagiarism. For example, in Rachilde's text it is Louis and not a female shopper who is seduced by the window display, which is narrated from his point of view in this strangely familiar passage:

> Des glaces splendides descendaient des sandales du grand roi [sur l'enseigne du magasin] jusqu'aux chaussures des passants. [...] Derrière! Un entassement, un fouillis, un superbe désordre d'étoffes multicolores, de rubaris aux nuances arc-en-ciel, de passementeries scintillantes, poudrées de perles, piquées de points de feu, d'argent, d'acier. Des flots de dentelles neigeuses, des voiles pareils à ceux de la nuit, des costumes se tenant droits! De loin, en oubliant le mannequin qui était dessous, on aurait juré que ces pauvres élégantes avaient perdu la tête se

voyant enjuponnées de la sorte. Puis des châles, qui s'étageaient sur des marches invisibles comme les tapis d'une mosquée. Des soieries en cascades, en roues, en vagues! Tout un étalage de lingerie, cousue de faveurs; brodée... noyée de dentelles et affectant des poses provocantes.[45]

[Splendid mirrors stretched downwards from the sandals of the great king [on the shop sign] to the shoes of the passer-by. [...] Behind that! A heap, a jumble, a superb disorder of multicoloured fabrics, rabari prints in all the colours of the rainbow, sparkling trimmings, dusted with pearls, pricked with points of fire, silver, steal. Floods of snowy lace, veils like the night sky, whole outfits standing tall! From a distance, forgetting the mannequin beneath, you could have sworn that these poor, elegant ladies had lost their heads on seeing themselves so dressed up. Then the shawls, laying upon invisible steps like the carpet of a mosque. Silks in waterfalls, in wheels, in waves! A whole display of lingerie, sewn with favours; embroidered... submerged in lace and placed in provocative poses.]

This reversal by Zola reveals a keen anxiety about the gradual feminization of Parisian men in the *fin de siècle*, and the fear of the irrational hysteria that this could unleash — and by 1883 had unleashed — within the urban crowd.

The Exhibition Effect

This allegorical recasting of chaos, violence, and irrational desire into a squabble over buttons and bows may, at first glance, appear a naïve attempt by a bourgeois author to brush the real causes of class conflict under a narrative carpet, making it seem arbitrary or entertaining, and not worthy of serious concern for the bourgeois reader. However, Zola's fictional rewriting of the flaws in the fabric of French society does not so much aim to hide the problem, but instead to re-present it in a different form. The importance of social conflict to this novel is illuminated when we compare *Au Bonheur des Dames* with Zola's other Parisian retail novel, *Le Ventre de Paris* [*The Belly of Paris*] (1873) — and particularly when we compare the play on glass in each novel. Although the narrative events of *Le Ventre* are set prior to the Commune, its situation around Les Halles and the Boulevard Montmartre — a Communard stronghold — evokes the events of the Commune constantly for the contemporaneous reader, just two years after the *semaine sanglante*. Glass in *Le Ventre* is almost unilaterally associated with revolution, violence, and distress. Even the enchanting lexicon of Florent's first vision of Les Halles as 'une suite de palais, énormes et réguliers, d'une légèreté de cristal' ['a series of enormous, symmetrically built palaces, light and airy as crystal'] (*VP*, 609/8) is tempered by the physical agony of his hunger, his disorientation faced with the newly-Haussmannized neighbourhood, and his sense of unease at the glass market building, 'cette vision colossale et fragile' ['this huge but seemingly fragile sight'] (*VP*, 609/8). The vitreous fragility and the ethereal appearance of Les Halles underlines Florent's own fragile and necessarily fleeting situation in Paris, and glass will be a constant marker of his gradual downfall.

There are a number of clear parallels between the narratives of the commercial worlds of Les Halles and Au Bonheur des Dames. Like the department store, Les

Halles too resembles a miniature, enclosed city under glass, with 'ses promenades et ses routes, ses places et ses carrefours, [une ville] mise tout entière sous un hangar, un jour de pluie, par quelque caprice gigantesque' ['its walks and streets, squares and intersections, all suddenly placed under a huge roof one rainy day by the whim of some gigantic power'] (*VP*, 621/20). Denise and Deloche gaze in rêverie over the glass rooftops of Au Bonheur des Dames (*ABD*, 716–17/344), and Florent gazes in rêverie from his bedroom window over the glass rooftops of Les Halles (*VP*, 808). *Le Ventre* even mentions a new department store being established alongside the marketplace, where, 'au milieu des vitrines vides du grand magasin de nouveautés, des commis bien mis [...] faisaient l'étalage' ['in the empty windows of the big drapery shop, smart-looking assistants [...] were preparing their displays'] (*VP*, 628/27).

However, unlike in *Au Bonheur des Dames*, glass is also prominently associated with alcohol in *Le Ventre*, drawing many parallels with the one substantially-glazed building in *L'Assommoir* [*The Assommoir*] (1877) — Père Colombe's bar. Although Lebigre and Colombe's bars propose to cater for a slightly different class of clientele, there are distinct similarities between the emphatic presence of glass in the two. In *Le Ventre*,

> les glaces claires laissaient voir la salle, ornée de guirlandes de feuillages, de pampres et de grappes, sur un fond vert tendre. [...] L'armée des verres, rangée par bandes, occupait les deux côtés: les petits verres pour l'eau-de-vie, les gobelets épais pour les canons, les coupes pour les fruits, les verres à absinthe, les chopes, les grands verres à pied, tous renversés, le cul en l'air, reflétant dans leur pâleur les luisants du comptoir. [...] Sur l'une, les bocaux de fruits, les cerises, les prunes, les pêches, mettaient leurs taches assombries; sur l'autre, entre des paquets de biscuits symétriques, des fioles claires, vert tendre, rouge tendre, jaune tendre, faisaient rêver à des liqueurs inconnues. (*VP*, 706)

> [through the clear glass windows you could see the interior, decorated with garlands of leaves, vine branches, and grapes, painted on the pale green walls. [...] Arranged in groups on both sides, stood the army of glasses: little glasses for brandy, thick tumblers for draught wine, cup glasses for brandied fruit, absinthe glasses, beer mugs and tall goblets all turned upside down and reflecting the glitter of the counter. [...] On one of them, jars of preserved fruit, cherries, plums, and peaches, stood out darkly; on the other, between neatly arranged packets of biscuits, were flasks of bright green, red, and yellow, suggesting mysterious liqueurs (98–99)]

The lexicon is strikingly similar in *L'Assommoir*:

> le comptoir énorme, avec ses files de verres, sa fontaine et ses mesures d'étain, s'allongeait à gauche en entrant [...]. Plus haut, sur des étagères, des bouteilles de liqueurs, des bocaux de fruits, toutes sortes de fioles en bon ordre, cachaient les murs, reflétaient dans la glace, derrière le comptoir, leurs taches vives, vert pomme, or pâle, laque tendre. Mais la curiosité de la maison était, au fond, de l'autre côté d'une barrière de chêne, dans une cour vitrée, l'appareil à distiller que les consommateurs voyaient fonctionner. (*A*, 404)

> [the enormous counter with its rows of glasses, its water vat, and its pewter measures stretched along to the left of the entrance. [...] Higher up were shelves

displaying bottles of liqueur, jars of brandied fruit, and carefully arranged flasks of all kinds; they concealed the walls, reflecting their vibrant splashes of apple green, pale gold and soft reddish-brown in the mirror behind the counter. But the real attraction of the place, standing beyond an oak balustrade in the glassed-in rear courtyard, was the still, which the customers could see working (34)]

Both of these vitreous environments become linked with the violence and supposed depravity of the working classes. Although Florent and Denise both have humanitarian aspirations for the Parisian working classes, Florent's plans are developed in Lebrigre's private glass-screened *cabinet*, surrounded by the glass fittings of the bar, with glasses of alcohol in hand. Given the revolutionary plotline, the social class of the participants, and the publication so shortly after the *année terrible*, this could not help but align the characters in Le Ventre with the destructive violence of the Commune.

This link between Florent and the Commune is highlighted by Zola's choice of metaphors for Denise and Florent's respective perceptions of the glass rooftops. Whilst Denise sees the glass as a vast lake (*ABD*, 716/344), a natural metaphor, in *Le Ventre* the sight of the glass in the rooftops of the Halles reminds Lisa of '*les bouteilles de liqueur, devant la glace de monsieur Lebigre*' ['*the liqueur bottles* on the shelf in front of M. Lebigre's mirror'] (*VP*, 808/194). Indeed, when Lisa enters Florent's bedroom (which overlooks the Halles) and sees all his revolutionary insignia, 'elle vit ces hommes, avec toutes ces étoffes rouges, passer devant sa charcuterie, *envoyer des balles dans les glaces et dans les marbres*' ['she saw all these men with their red badges running past the charcuterie, *firing bullets into the marble and the mirrors*'] (*VP*, 814/199 — my emphases). While this is partly a free indirect discourse expression of Lisa's sense of betrayal and malice, Zola's choice for Lisa to imagine, specifically, the shattering of *mirrors* clearly recalls the destructive acts of the Commune for the 1873 reader. Given the lack of time elapsed between the events of 1871 and this novel, glass in *Le Ventre* leads the reader to focus on their recent past and its sociopolitical errors, rather than being able to look towards the future. The only solace that can be provided by the working-class passions in *Le Ventre* is the comforting conceptualization of the events as inevitable; of many of the revolutionaries as pitiable; and of narrative closure with Florent's arrest.

Although twelve years have elapsed since the Commune, *Au Bonheur des Dames* still contains clear references to the events of this troubled period. Many of the staff — as the novel's representatives of the lower classes — evoke wide-spread accounts from the Commune era. The unattractiveness and varying degrees of promiscuity among the female staff recollect the stereotypes attached to the *pétroleuses*. For example, accounts from the trial of two prominent Commune women, Zélie Grandel and Marguerite Guindaire, were quick to condemn the women with a damning combination of ugliness, promiscuity, and, in the case of Marguerite, the past profession of *confectionneuse*. The *Cloche* (a newspaper for which Zola occasionally wrote) reported that 'les deux femmes sont loin d'être belles; Zélie, la maîtresse de François, est encore moins bien que la cantinière du 66e; laquelle déclare avoir exercé la profession de confectionneuse avant d'être au bataillon' ['the two women are far from beautiful; Zélie, François's mistress, is even less good-looking than the canteen girl of the 66th regiment; who declares that she used to be a dress-shop assistant before joining the batallion'].[46] The aggressive pursuit of wealth by both sexes at Au Bonheur des Dames evokes the violent Communard lootings of public buildings and houses of politicians (most notably Thiers) in Paris. Indeed, the erasure of the boundaries between men and women at the department store as 'la bataille continuelle de l'argent [...] avait effacé les sexes' ['the constant battle for money had [...] already wiped out the difference between the sexes'] (*ABD*, 516/134) and the gender-swapping Monsieur et Madame Lhomme (with Mme Aurélie's military appearance and M. Lhomme's 'castrated' arm) recall stories of Fury-like wives who took their husbands' masculine forenames and wore their clothes during the Commune. *La Vie parisienne* depicted a woman who is much like a (even more) caricatured version of Mme Aurélie:

> Figurez-vous une grande femme solidement charpentée, avec des muscles apparents, de gros membres: nulle délicatesse. Un front crânement bombé, des lèvres charnues avec des tons violacés à force d'être rouges, le teint brun et des moustaches! [...] Chez elle c'étaient des mains de travailleur et d'homme d'action, courtes, fortes, larges [...]; rien de féminin; chez l'autre [son mari], elles étaient molles, blafardes et trop longues. [...] Elle avait pris son nom [à son mari], le nom d'Isodore, et le faisait connaître.[47]

> [Imagine a big woman, solidly built, with visibly-defined muscles, large limbs: no delicacy. A proudly rounded forehead, fleshy lips with purplish tinges from being so reddened, a brown complexion and a moustache! [...] She had the hands of a worker and a man of action, short, strong, wide [...]; nothing feminine; he [her husband] had limp hands, pasty and too long. [...] She had taken his name, the name Isodore, and let everybody know it.]

From the male staff, Mignot, who tries (unsuccessfully) to seduce all his clientele, is nonetheless depicted in an effeminate manner with his 'jolie figure poupine' ['his pretty baby face'] and 'de tendres inflexions à sa voix' ['voice full of tender inflections'] which demonstrate no traces of vigorous, virile courtship (*ABD*, 484/100). The general tendency towards connivance and malice rather than fair, up-front debate associates the majority of the staff with the irrational and chaotic at society's margins.

These references to the Commune continue in marked lexical choices. Numerous events are described as a 'débâcle' — which would of course become the title for Zola's novel of the *année terrible*. We find 'la débâcle de marchandise' ['decimation of his merchandise'] and 'la débâcle de leurs casiers' ['the chaos of their counters'] as the various departments are sacked by a voracious crowd (*ABD*, 422/37, 423/37, 642/265, 676/300). M. Marty mourns 'la débâcle de ses appointements' ['the decimation of his hard-earned salary'] as his good honest hard work is attacked by his wife's irrational shopping habits (*ABD*, 467/83). Bourras contemplates 'la débâcle de son commerce' ['the decimation of his commerce'] as the war between new and old commerce advances (*ABD*, 571/191 — translation adapted). War and revolutionary violence are pointedly evoked by the 'grande révolution des nouveautés' ['the great revolution in drapery'] (*ABD*, 459/75), the 'champ de bataille encore chaud du massacre des tissus' ['a battlefield still hot from the massacre of materials'] (*ABD*, 500/116), and during the sale day when 'la rue était barrée, ainsi qu'en temps d'émeute' ['the street was barricaded as if there were a riot'] (*ABD*, 617/240). Denise uses language very much like that employed by Jean in *La Débâcle* [*The Debacle*] [1892] when she concedes that 'toute révolution voulait des martyrs, on ne marchait en avant que sur des morts' ['every revolution demanded its victims, progress can only march forward over the dead'], and that 'cela était bon, qu'il fallait ce fumier de misères à la santé du Paris de demain' ['she was even aware that it was a good thing: this manure of distress was necessary to the health of the Paris of the future'] (*ABD*, 748/375–76).

Imagery of fire and ruins also runs through the novel: for example, Mouret envisions displays 'flambants des couleurs les plus ardentes, [...] [il] allumait cet incendie d'étoffes' ['blazing with the most flamboyant colours [...] lighting this conflagration of materials'] (*ABD*, 434/48); the light in Au Bonheur des Dames takes on flame-like qualities, with 'cette clarté d'un rouge d'incendie' ['this fiery brightness'] and a haze which 'découpait sur un fond de flammes les escaliers' ['making the staircases [...] stand out against a background of flames'] (*ABD*, 642/265); on hearing that his shop has gone bankrupt, Robineau says that 'il m'a semblé que des flammes dansaient, comme si les murs avaient brûlé...' ['I seemed to see flames dancing as if the walls were burning...'] (*ABD*, 752/380). Importantly, the vision of glass being broken or glowing with reflected flames is incorporated into the narrative: the shop is described as 'une braise vive, où brûlaient maintenant les étalages [...], des glaces resplendissaient' ['the displays [...] were now burning in live embers. The mirrors were resplendent'] (*ABD*, 642/265). Outside Robineau's shop as he lies injured, 'des ouvrières, échappées d'un atelier, menaçaient d'enfoncer les glaces des vitrines, pour mieux voir' ['some girls who had left their workroom were in danger of breaking the glass of the shop-windows in their attempt to get a better view'] (*ABD*, 752/380).

In many ways, then, the *année terrible* lingers in *Au Bonheur des Dames* on a localized scale, as the events of the Franco-Prussian War and, especially, the Commune are deliberately evoked by Zola's narrative. Yet it is crucial to note that the use of qualifiers cleanses these memories of much of their traumatic impact here; it is not a debacle but a 'débâcle *de marchandise*', not a revolution but a 'révolution *des nouveautés*', not an actual period of social unrest but '*ainsi qu'*en temps d'émeute'. As Peter Starr observes in his study of the Commune, Zola makes a deliberate choice to evoke the confusion of the Commune through commercial upheaval as opposed to violent revolt; shopping and glass architecture become foils for discussing past troubles.[48] It is perhaps the commercial context of Zola's novel which allows many of the references to the Commune to remain ambiguous. Heidi Brevik-Zender remarks upon a number of problematic evocations of the *semaine sanglante*: the frequent references to victory in an atmosphere evoking a dark episode of recent history; the gory delight in slaughter of the Communards which is implied by the red fabric stuffed in the necks of beheaded mannequins; and 'the ambivalence about who is fighting whom, the questionable outcome of this sartorially described conflict, and the location in which it occurs'.[49] Indeed, this minimized version of destructive violence is in marked contrast with the conflict between the Gras and the Maigre in the 9ᵉ arrondissement in *Le Ventre* that has genuine potential for social unrest, or indeed across Montsou in *Germinal* which breaks out into physical violence.

Zola's deliberate reductionism of chaos and conflict in *Au Bonheur des Dames* is highlighted by the adoption of a rhetoric of exhibition and display. The unfettered desires, unleashed violence, abundant anguish, and attacks upon Zola's cherished Republican values, all associated with the Commune, are safely contained within the store like a vast, anaesthetizing, glass display cabinet. Anne Green has remarked that at the World Fairs, 'items displayed in the exhibition cases and listed in the catalogues were detached from their own environment. New and depersonalized, they were presented without history or troubling context'.[50] Zola transposes not just the rhetoric of exhibition (as Green identifies in a variety of texts from the 1860s), but also the material context of exhibition, and the effect this context had upon the reception of objects and events. Brevik-Zender focuses on staircases within the store as an exhibition spaces, places where the novel may display symbolic fabric choices, female bodies, physical struggle, and the barricades.[51] I would take this trajectory further, and suggest that the entire store is a space for displaying and exhibiting the past. The glass casing of the department store produces what we might call an 'exhibition effect'; any object placed in the context of exhibition, including conflict-in-miniature, is glossed with a sheen of education and curiosity — and, crucially, it is extracted from the threatening reality of the city street. Furthermore, since the lower-class representatives in this novel are placed *inside* the glass box rather than outside in the street like Armstrong's London window-breakers, the risk of glass being shattered is quashed.[52] In the same way that natives imported from colonial lands were a pleasant, often titillating novelty at the World Fairs but a menacing presence when roaming free in the city, so conflict housed within the glass retail palace is cleansed of any active threat of violence.

This exhibition effect allows *Au Bonheur des Dames* to represent social conflict in such a way that the more conservative readers might find themselves able to begin contemplating the topic; it eases them in, and so avoids an immediate rejection of the very idea of any compromise which might loosen the ruling power's stringent control over its margins. The exhibition effect provides a means of mooting the possibility that an outlet for the frustrations of the 'feminine' — that is to say, irrational, passionate, or otherwise marginal and non-conformist — may be to everybody's advantage. The visual world of the heavily-glazed department store, as we have seen, clearly aspires towards absolute subjugation at the start of the novel. However, the female shoppers, rather than being engulfed in what Susan Harrow has described as 'the maw of Mouret's department store' (a term, indeed, that indicates the near-hellish lack of *bonheur* that would be on offer for women in Mouret's store were all his visual manipulations to engulf them), instead seek their own forms of pleasure and satisfaction within the controlled environment of Au Bonheur des Dames.[53] They find a way to express their passions by repurposing the materials provided by Mouret for his world of the eye, enjoying a moderate degree of freedom, and thus tempering their desire to simmer into full-blown revolt against their master.

From Sight to Sound

The extensive, dazzling displays at Au Bonheur may themselves be essentially visual creations, but they quickly become more important to the female shoppers as an impetus for verbal refrain. The ladies translate what they see into sound, and it is in this sonority that they find *bonheur*. When they repeatedly discuss the Salon Oriental in Chapter 4, it is in fact extremely unlikely that even at the height of the nineteenth-century mode for Orientalism all of these shoppers would be able to identify spontaneously one of sixteen regional varieties of Persian rug (*ABD*, 471/87–88). However, accurate or not, these carpets provide a pretext to exchange sounds, interwoven with exotic words — an exchange so enjoyable that they repeatedly return to the topic every time they meet during the sale. Indeed, although Rosalind Williams does not extend her observations to sound, this shift is the natural extension from her assertion that 'there can be no authentic democratization of luxury because by definition luxury is a form of consumption limited to a few. Modern society has instead introduced the proliferation of superfluity'.[54] If visual and commercial luxuriance were the focus of the shopper's *bonheur*, its inherent exclusiveness would render it impossible to satisfy. Sound, on the other hand, becomes a luxury precisely when it is *most* generalized and *most* superfluous.

Sound is exchanged and intensified in numerous ways in the store. Shop-work and staff gossip underwrite the soundscape of the store with a constant, background hum; chairs are dragged, lifts grind, and bolts of fabric thump upon cutting tables. Long before the crowd appears at the first sale day, it can already be heard inside the store: first with 'un lointain brouhaha' ['a distant hubbub'] (*ABD*, 478/95), then '[un] brouhaha grandissant de foule' ['the growing babble of the crowd'] (*ABD*, 482/99), before finally the women enter the store and 'le brouhaha augmentait, fait de tous les bruits, du piétinement continu, des mêmes phrases cent fois répétées autour des comptoirs' ['the hubbub was increasing, made up of all sorts of noises — the continuous trampling of feet, the same phrases repeated a hundred times at the counters'] (*ABD*, 492/109). On the second sale day, Mme Desforges quickly finds that her eyes tire of the spectacle, but is surprised to feel the full thrill and intensity of the crowds when she closes her eyes (*ABD*, 631/254). For Mme Marty, the zenith of the shop's pleasures is to be found in the exhilarating experience of palpable sound when sound vibrations become so strong as to be a physical as well as an aural experience. Even after she has burned away her vision ('elle s'était lentement brûlé la vue' ['her sight [...] gradually became scorched']), her pleasure continues as she immerses herself in the sounds of 'les appels enroués des vendeurs, dans le bruit d'or des caisses et le roulement des paquets tombant aux sous-sols' ['the hoarse shouts of the salesmen, in the noise of gold pouring into the cash registers and the rolling of packets falling into the cellars'], and she finally abandons what little remains of her self-control after feeling this sound duplicated in 'la vibration métallique des escaliers suspendus et des ponts volants' ['the metallic vibration of the hanging staircases and suspension bridges'] (*ABD*, 643–44/267) of which the 'limons de fer avaient sous les pieds un branle sensible, comme tremblant aux haleines de la foule' ['the iron supports were perceptibly moving underfoot, as if trembling at the breath of the crowd'] (*ABD*, 630/253).⁵⁵ Indeed, we might notice that this roar of the crowd on the final sale day becomes 'un bruit mourant de triomphe [...] dans cette *défaite* du maître' ['a dying sound of triumph, a discreet accompaniment to the master's *defeat*'] (*ABD*, 674/298 — my emphasis). Sound is clearly not under Mouret's control, and it is the product of and source of pleasure for the unruly crowd.

However, it is only the concentrated presence of glass at Au Bonheur des Dames that makes a complete immersion in the aural possible. Glass, because of its semi-crystalline structure, will resonate when exposed to vibrations at the right frequency. This is the case for glass musical instruments, such as Franklin's eighteenth-century Glass Armonica which would later be used by Mesmer; the 'glass harp' consisting of a series of wine glasses containing varying volumes of water; and the Verillon, defined in the 1874 *Grand Dictionnaire universel* as '[un] instrument de musique fait de touches de verre qu'on frappe avec des baguettes drapées' ['a musical instrument made from glass keys and struck by cloth-covered sticks'].

Zola's awareness of the resonant and amplificatory quality of glass is clear in *Le Ventre de Paris*. As the Halles fill with stallholders and shoppers, the reader is told that 'les carreaux bourdonnaient, les pavillons grondaient' ['the roof panes were buzzing, the markets were roaring' — translation adapted] (*VP*, 633/31). Zola writes that one enthusiastic seafood seller cried out '"La moule! la moule!" d'une clameur rauque et brisée, dont les toitures des Halles tremblaient' ['"Mussels! Mussels!" in such a raucous voice that the roof of the market shook'] (*VP*, 701/95). In the *cabinet* in Monsieur Lebigre's bar, 'les vitres dépolies vibraient comme des peaux de tambour' ['the frosted glass vibrated like the skin of a drum'] when a revolutionary debate became heated (*VP*, 708/140). Given the multiplicity of forms of glass in Mouret's shop, it would seem that the mysterious ringing and booming sounds which are attributed repeatedly to the store may well be caused by glass resonating with the noise of the crowd — especially since none of the wood, carpet, or fabrics in the shop, nor indeed any of the activities of commerce, have any natural capacity to make these sounds. Indeed, when Denise and Deloche gaze over the glass roofs, they listen as 'toute la maison vibrait du piétinement de la foule' ['the whole shop vibrating with the trampling of the crowd'] (*ABD*, 718/345). The intensity of noise in Au Bonheur des Dames suggests that the numerous external and internal windows and the endless sea of glass roof panels resonate and produce sound in the same way as those in *Le Ventre*, greatly intensifying the experience of, and pleasure in, this immersion in sound.

Thus the repeated return of women to the store is not due solely to Mouret's clever visual intoxications; rather, I would argue that the female shopper herself makes an active and self-interested decision to return there. Whilst Mouret invests heavily in publicity because 'il professait que la femme est sans force contre la réclame, qu'elle finit fatalement par aller au bruit' ['he declared that Woman was helpless against advertisements; in the end she inevitably went to see what all the noise was about'] (*ABD*, 613/235), the actual appeal of advertising is in fact in the literal 'bruit' within it; the 'appels de toutes sortes, [...] comme une monstrueuse trompette d'airain, qui, sans relâche, soufflait aux quatre coins de la terre le vacarme des grandes mises en vente' ['appeals of every kind [...] as if by a monstrous brass trumpet relentlessly amplifying the noise of the great sales to the four corners of the globe'] (*ABD*, 763/392). Such noise gives a sound-bite in advance of the unregulated soundscape to be found within the heavily-glazed store. Mouret does not seem to acknowledge this consciously, but does manifest an unconscious awareness of the appeal of sound as he recognizes the need for 'du bruit, de la foule, de la vie; car la vie, disait-il, attire la vie' ['noise, crowds, life; for life, he would say, attracts life'] (*ABD*, 613/235). And although Mouret's visual advertising does have a certain organizing influence on the passions of the female characters, it goes further than just being an invitation to shop for shopping's sake; it also announces a date on which women may congregate to create and enjoy an intense experience of sound, a temporary adventure into disorder. So, where Rachel Bowlby suggests that in Au Bonheur des Dames 'the pleasures of looking, *just looking*, [...] [are] the commodity for which money is paid',[56] I would contend that it is, moreover, the pleasures of listening, *just listening*, for which money is paid.

As the word spreads and ever-increasing numbers of women visit the store without being manipulated into it, Mouret loses a degree of his absolutist control. This is reflected in a series of evolving metaphors for the decreasing clarity of his eyes. Initially, like his clear glass windows, there is an air of transparency to 'ses yeux clairs' ['limpid eyes'] (*ABD*, 422/37). Elsewhere his eyes act like mirrors — as the gold piles up in his cash desks, his eyes assume '[la] couleur de vieil or' ['the colour of old gold'] (*ABD*, 417/31; 442/56). As the influx of products tumbles before him, his eyes reflect 'cette débâcle de marchandises qui tombait chez lui' ['this deluge of goods falling into his shop'] (*ABD*, 422/37). Yet as his personal crisis worsens, the reader sees that 'ses yeux avaient un peu du ravissement éperdu dont vacillaient à la longue les yeux des acheteuses' ['his eyes had something of the bewildered rapture which flickered in the end in the eyes of the customers'] (*ABD*, 632/254). His eyes are no longer glassy but glazed over as his domination of the crowd is tempered.

Importantly, this reliance upon glass for the sonorous delights of the ladies also begins to recuperate glass from the traumatic associations it held as a result of real, historical conflict between patriarchal 'rational' order and its chaotic other. As I discussed in Chapter 1, sound was associated with glass during the Prussian siege and the Commune; the sounds of shells and bullets whistling past windows, and the sound of windows and mirrors shaking or shattering as buildings were struck by munitions and shrapnel. Such traumatic, eruptive sounds are replaced at Au Bonheur des Dames by the sustained, resonant sound of the shop work and the crowds, made possible by the manifold *unbroken* glass surfaces in the department store. This novel uses glass to dramatize a compromise between control and chaos, the masculine and the feminine, those who have the power and those who would like to challenge it; it reveals that there is a space for freedom and pleasure within the framework of patriarchal authority.

★ ★ ★ ★ ★

The heralding of a female 'messiah' becomes a metaphor for the completion of the miniature conflict exhibited by the commercial world of Au Bonheur des Dames. Mouret's more feminine, emotional unpredictability and his masculine capacity for authority and control are complemented perfectly by Denise's combination of the sensible logic attributed to masculinity with the modest maternal instincts of femininity. Throughout the novel, Denise is inscribed within a discourse of reason: she has no interest in taking a lover because that would be 'déraisonnable' ['senseless'] (*ABD*, 565/185), and she always acts according to 'de la bonté et de la raison, un amour de la vérité et de la logique qui était toute sa force' ['kindness and good sense and a love of truth and logic which was her great strength'] (*ABD*, 730/357).

Imagining a space in which potentially insubordinate forces may find some freedom does not go so far as to suggest a gender revolution or support the cause of subversive groups that opposed the sanctioned, patriarchal authority. When Denise challenges Mouret's abuse of power against both staff and shoppers, it is no revolutionary upheaval but subtle change. She is not allied with one side against the other, but is systematically marked out as different from both the powerful and the underdogs — especially as her character type has no historical associations with the revolution and repression during the nineteenth century. Indeed, there is never any genuine pretence that Denise is even a *real* woman: her perfect combination of virgin-motherly, hardworking, honest, modest, and self-sacrificing practicality veers towards the implausible; a view confirmed by her rags-to-riches marriage.

In a feminist reading, the ending to this novel is no doubt disappointing, with the assimilation of a strong woman into a man's master-narrative; but in the context of the more allegorical reading I have elaborated here, that would perhaps miss the point. The key struggle here is not Denise's struggle, but that of a society with a grave internal division, vacillating uncontrollably between violent chaos and violent oppression. In contrast to other *Rougon-Macquart* novels in which a member of this family must be expelled to restore order (such as *La Faute de l'Abbé Mouret* [*The Sin of Father Mouret*] and *Germinal*), in *Au Bonheur des Dames* Denise is brought in from the outside to bring the hope of compromise that Parisian society had been unable to plumb from within its own depths.

Zola does not promise miracles, nor does he wish to dismantle pre-existing social values: he does not suggest that women should be given genuine independence, or that any other subordinate class should be given radical freedoms or equalities. However, there is a sense in this novel that both sides are being encouraged to work together towards a compromise rather than to continue as antagonists. Glass in this narrative is central in leading readers to this conclusion. Seductive Second Empire windows sit in uncomfortable juxtaposition with disconcerting mirrors and with distressing memories of fractured, damaged glass during 1870 and 1871. Yet with the introduction of glass into the sonorous as well as the visual experience shopping, it is revealed that the satisfaction of both factions may be found in the same place. Not every pleasure or desire of the subordinate classes need necessarily be destructive. No windows or mirrors are broken here, and as Mouret's autocratic control over the subversive crowd weakens, no disasters strike his commerce or modern society. On the contrary, both his commerce and his romantic affairs benefit. The 'débâcle' has been replaced with a mere 'débâcle de marchandise'; stringent, patriarchal authority has been moderated by accepting the need for some degree of freedom for those without the power in society; and absolute chaos has been avoided with the provision of an outlet for the passions of the crowd. Rulers, this suggests, should wield power with respect, and the ruled might be given a degree of freedom which allows them to express and satisfy their passions whilst abstaining from destructive violence. The whole shop becomes akin to a glass exhibition case, drawing on the pleasant associations of glass at World Fairs and in consumer culture to cast this microcosmic world in a positive light for the bourgeois reader — who inevitably has the most to lose by any form of compromise.

The exhibition effect contributes to the sense of inevitability surrounding this dénouement; after all, the purpose of exhibition was to present everything in a positive way, glazing over any unpleasantness and shedding an optimistic light upon anything that might be distressing. In the glass exhibition case of the department store, the release of pent-up energies is performed in an unthreatening context and on an unthreatening scale, and so the narrative can turn its attention to frivolous thoughts of love and marriage in a way that would be improbable in times of revolution. Revolution here, as Baudrillard would say a century later of France in 1968, is a living concept: 'L'exigence révolutionnaire est vivante, mais faute de s'actualiser dans la pratique, elle se consomme dans l'idée de la Révolution. En tant qu'idée, la Révolution est en effet éternelle, et elle sera éternellement consommable au même titre que n'importe quelle autre idée' ['revolution is a living demand, but so long as it is not actualized in practice it will be consumed as the idea of Revolution. As an idea the Revolution is indeed eternal, and must needs remain eternally consumable just like any other idea'].[57] Zola's glassworld creates a space in which it is conceivable for reason and chaos to work together for a middle ground which would benefit the future of French society, rather than either class seeking the erasure of the other — a future *au bonheur de tous*.

Notes to Chapter 2

1. Victor Fournel, *Paris nouveau et Paris futur* (Paris: Jacques Lecoffre, 1865), p. 241.
2. The visual has largely dominated discussions of *Au Bonheur des Dames*. Representative examples include Brian Nelson's discussion of the sexualization of the female shopper/staff member as visual object ('Zola and the Counter Revolution', *Australian Journal of French Studies*, 30:2 (1993), 233–40); Susie Hennessy's examination of the female shopper's response to the visual presence of consumer merchandise ('Consumption and Desire in *Au Bonheur des Dames*', *The French Review*, 81:4 (2008), 696–706); Eleanor Salatto's exploration of identity formation in the shop's specular universe ('Shopping for an "I": Zola's *The Ladies' Paradise* and the Spectacle of Identity', in *L'Ecriture du féminin chez Zola et dans la fiction naturaliste*, ed. by Anna Gural-Migdal (New York and Bern: Peter Lang, 2003), pp. 449–70); and Rachel Bowlby's account of the pleasures of the scopic (*Just Looking: Consumer Culture in Dreiser, Gissing and Zola* (London and New York: Methuen, 1985)).
3. *La Mode nouvelle et Miroir parisien*, March 1871, p. 2.
4. *La Vie parisienne*, 27 August 1870, p. 694.
5. *Journal officiel de la République française*, 27 October 1870, p. 1665.
6. *La Cloche*, 7 April 1871.
7. *La Cloche*, 6 June 1871 and 7 April 1871.
8. Naomi Schor, *Zola's Crowds* (Baltimore, MD and London: Johns Hopkins Press, 1969), p. 41.
9. Ibid., p. 51.
10. Ilona Chessid, *Thresholds of Desire: Authority and Transgression in the* Rougon-Macquart (New York: Peter Lang, 1993).

11. Philip Walker, 'The Mirror, the Window and the Eye in Zola's Fiction', *Yale French Studies*, 42 (1969), 52–67 (p. 52).
12. Brian Nelson, 'Speculation and Dissipation: A Reading of Zola's *La Curée*', *Essays in French Literature*, 14 (1977), 1–33 (p. 14).
13. In 'Du Roman', Zola addressed criticism of these five panoramas, which a number of contemporary critics saw as repetitious superfluity (in *Le Roman expérimental*, ed. by François-Marie Mourad (Paris: Flammarion, 2006), pp. 203–64 (p. 226)).
14. Christopher Prendergast, *Paris and the Nineteenth Century* (Oxford and Cambridge, MA: Blackwell, 1999), p. 44.
15. To clarify, Au Bonheur des Dames will refer to the fictional shop, and *Au Bonheur des Dames* will refer to Zola's novel.
16. Scholarship on *Au Bonheur des Dames* focuses frequently on Mouret's visual manipulations of the female shoppers. The most notable of such arguments is Rosalind Williams's *Dream Worlds*, in which she asserts: 'Seeking a pleasurable escape from the workaday world, they find it in a deceptive dream world which is no dream at all but a sales pitch in disguise' (p. 65).
17. Lynn Penrod, 'Shopaholic Space: From Zola's *Au Bonheur des Dames* to The Gap', in *New Approaches to Zola: Selected Papers from the 2002 Cambridge Centenary Colloquium*, ed. by Hannah Thompson (London: The Emile Zola Society, 2003), pp. 21–30 (p. 28).
18. Laura Mulvey, *Visual and Other Pleasures* (Basingstoke: Palgrave Macmillan, 1989 [2009 second ed.]), p. 18.
19. Rachel Bowlby, *Carried Away: the Invention of Modern Shopping* (London: Faber and Faber, 2000), p. 60.
20. Baudrillard, pp. 57–59.
21. This brings to mind etchings used in publicity for the Bon Marché, and of the *palais* at the 1878 World Exhibition.
22. Figures in parentheses refer to page numbers of published translations as listed in the preliminary notes to this book.
23. *La Cloche*, 10 June 1871.
24. *La Vie parisienne pendant la guerre*, September 1871, p. 14.
25. See Walter Benjamin, *The Arcades Project*, pp. 871–72; Louis Aragon, *Le Paysan de Paris* (Paris: Gallimard, 1926), p. 19, p. 42.
26. Rather than tuberculosis being associated with the department store in *Au Bonheur des Dames*, it is instead associated symbolically with the expiring *petit commerce* — Robineau's sales assistant suffers from the disease as another symptom of the dying commercial sector (*ABD*, 572/192). See Michael Miller, *The Bon Marché: Bourgeois Culture and the Department Store, 1869–1920* (Princeton, NJ: Princeton University Press, 1981), p. 94.
27. Prendergast, *Paris and the Nineteenth Century*, p. 31.
28. The German Regi Company's poster continues: 'Wo Licht ist, sammeln sich die Menschen. Im Schein des Lichtes wirst du leichter ihre Gunst gewinnen. Lichtbestrahlt sprechen unsere Tafeln zu den Massen in den Hallen der Schwebebahn. Sprechen? Eindringlich, laut, unwiderstehlich ist diese stumme Sprache des Lichts' ['Where there is light, there people gather. Under the shining light, goodwill is easier to win. Light illuminates and enunciates the billboard's message for the crowds at the tram station. Enunciates? Yes, penetrating, loud, irresistible — that is the mute voice of light']. Quoted in Janet Ward's discussion of light in German mid-war advertising, *Weimar Surfaces: Urban Visual Culture in 1920s Germany* (Berkeley, CA: University of California Press, 2001), p. 129, my translation.
29. Indeed, the imperfect tense here emphasizes that this is something of an already-fulfilled prophecy — the time elapsed between the fictional commercial events taking place within the novel (based on real events at the Bon Marché department store during the Second Empire), and the real-life success of the Bon Marché in the intervening years preceding the novel's publication in 1883, already suggest the efficacy of the merchandising strategies of Boucicaut/Mouret's commercial giant.
30. Gilloch, p. 6.
31. Rachel Bowlby, *Shopping with Freud* (London and New York: Routledge, 1993), p. 16.
32. See, for example, Jacques Lacan, *The Seminar. Book II*, ed. by Jacques-Alain Miller, trans. by John Forrester (New York: Norton, 1988), p. 262.

33. 'Veloutine Fay', *La Mode nouvelle et Miroir parisien*, October 1871, p. 251.
34. Cornel Sandvoss, *Fans: The Mirror of Consumption* (Cambridge: Polity Press, 2005), p. 114 — my emphasis.
35. Armstrong, p. 8.
36. David Bell, *Models of Power: Politics and Economics in Zola's* Rougon-Macquart (Lincoln, NE: University of Nebraska Press, 1988), p. 61.
37. Jacques Lacan, *Ecrits: A Selection*, trans. by Alan Sheridan (London: Tavistock, 1977), p. 15.
38. Barbara Vinken, 'Temples of Delight: Consuming Consumption in Emile Zola's *Au Bonheur des Dames*', in *Spectacles of Realism: Body, Gender, Genre*, ed. by Margaret Cohen and Christopher Prendergast (Minneapolis, MN: University of Minnesota Press, 1995), pp. 247–67 (p. 257).
39. Bell, *Models of Power*, p. 112.
40. *L'Exposition universelle de 1867 illustrée*, I, n. pag.
41. *Au Bon Marché, Vêtements pour Hommes et Jeunes Garçons*, Winter 1884–85 and Summer 1885.
42. Elisabeth Bronfen, *Over Her Dead Body: Death, Femininity and the Aesthetic* (Manchester: Manchester University Press, 1992), p. 282.
43. This has been usefully discussed in studies elsewhere: for example, Vaneed K. Ramazani traces the creation and destruction in the novel in terms of male and female bodies ('Gender, War, and the Department Store: Zola's *Au Bonheur des Dames*', *Substance*, 113 (2007), 126–46); Françoise Jaouen distinguishes between the masculine shop and the masculized machine — the former as a de-sexualized idol to the female shoppers, and the latter as a sexualized partner with whom the women seek satisfaction ('Le Bonheur des Dames ou la Machine du Célibataire', *Qui Parle*, 2:1 (1988), 98–112); and Véronique Cnockaert works through the layers of desire and relations in the novel — the narcissistic feminine rivalry, the identification of the Self in the Collective, and the community relationship in which the individual shopper identifies with the crowd ('Intimité publique. L'exemple d'*Au Bonheur des Dames*', *Les Cahiers naturalistes*, 83 (2009), 205–12).
44. For example, the *Journal officiel de la République* declared that 'la population de Paris, par son calme, par la virilité de son attitude, continue de se montrer à la hauteur de la tâche qui lui incombe' (7 September 1870). In this there is an assumption that certain behaviours are inherent to each of the sexes — this is not to suggest that this elision is an ontological fact, but that it is an assumption of fact made by the patriarchal society in which Zola wrote and in which his first readers would have gained their understanding of sex and gender.
45. Rachilde, *Monsieur de la Nouveauté* (Paris: E. Dentu, 1880), pp. 123–24.
46. *La Cloche*, 9 January 1872.
47. *La Vie parisienne*, 16 September 1871, p. 895.
48. Peter Starr, *Commemorating Trauma: The Paris Commune and its Cultural Aftermath* (New York: Fordham University Press, 2006), p. 149.
49. Heidi Brevik-Zender, *Fashioning Spaces: Mode and Modernity in Late Nineteenth-Century Paris* (Toronto: University of Toronto Press, 2015), pp. 49–51.
50. Green, p. 16.
51. Brevik-Zender, Chapter 1.
52. See Armstrong, Part I: Chapter 3.
53. Susan Harrow, *Zola, The Body Modern: Pressures and Prospects of Representation* (London: Legenda, 2010), p. 58.
54. Williams, p. 102.
55. I have discussed elsewhere the use of verbal refrains in creating the aural and in immersing the women in a soundscape where they go beyond the signification of words to enjoy words as pure sounds ('Symphonic Shopping: From Masculine Visuality to Feminine Aurality in Zola's *Au Bonheur des Dames*', *Dix-Neuf*, 18:3 (November 2014), 259–71).
56. Bowlby, *Just Looking*, p. 6.
57. Baudrillard, p. 281.

CHAPTER 3

Breakdowns and Breaking Glass: Glass and Identity Crises in Maupassant's Short Stories

> Miroir douloureux, miroir brûlant, miroir vivant, miroir horrible, qui fait souffrir toutes les tortures!
> [Woeful, searing, living, frightful glass, the cause of all our agonies.]
> GUY DE MAUPASSANT, 'La Morte'[1]

Guy de Maupassant's symbolic use of glass in the wake of the Franco-Prussian War and the Paris Commune could not be more different from that of Emile Zola. Far from any desire to conciliate or comfort, Maupassant deliberately channels the traumatic symbolism of glass into his short stories. He seems to foreground glass for its negative associations in late nineteenth-century society: glass is used as a murder weapon, as a means of gaining destructive feminine agency, and as a way of attacking subjectivity. It is a material incapable of evoking purely pleasurable connotations. There are no carefree days at the exhibition, or attractive but merely decorative cut-glass bibelots. Maupassant's mirrors, windows, and glass objects are distinctly contrary; they refuse reflections, become obscure, and shatter. They refuse to follow in the age-old speculum tradition, according to which mirrors should provide a reflection of personal flaws only to help banish them. This speculum genre was still very much alive in morality guides and conduct books in the Second Empire and Third Republic, especially for women and children: for example, a booklet was published by A. Maugars providing lessons in conduct for children, called *Miroir de l'enfance* [*The Mirror of Childhood*];[2] Alexis Dalès's pamphlet entitled *Miroir de la femme parfaite* [*Mirror of the Perfect Woman*] offered last-minute spiritual and behavioural tips for brides-to-be;[3] and M. l'Abbé Petit's religious pocket book named *Petit Miroir du dix-neuvième siècle* [*Little Mirror of the Nineteenth Century*] likened itself to the pocket-mirror, able to give a quick and handy reflection of the soul.[4] However, when Maupassant's characters gaze anxiously into mirrors and glass surfaces, self-help and comfort are conspicuously absent.

In Maupassant's short stories, glass demonstrates frequently that the psyche is fundamentally weak and permanently at risk of immanent destruction. This is dramatized through a number of scenarios: the erotic encounter, the fetishistic fantasy, the daily glance into a mirror, and the shattering of drinking glasses. This chapter explores the role of glass in each of these to consider, within the narrative, how Maupassant's characters relate to glass objects and, at the diegetic level, how this disconcerting aesthetic might shape the text and affect the reader. In a handful of Maupassant's stories, female protagonists suffer similar psychological travails to their male counterparts (although this is generally sparked by some kind of crisis of maternity), but in a striking majority of cases, crises of self are at their most serious when experienced by men. Patriarchy grants the masculine self a dominant position in society, giving him unrealistic expectations about the strength of his ego — the widespread objectification of women never fully permits this illusion of wholeness for members of the fairer sex. Consequently, when the flaws in the male character's selfhood become apparent, he is afflicted by a devastating psychological breakdown.

This was a particularly poignant topic, given that the psychological stability of individual men was the foundation for the collective stability of patriarchal society. As Mark S. Micale argues convincingly, it is for this reason that medical cases in nineteenth-century Parisian asylums were wilfully misinterpreted in order to continue defining hysteria as a purely feminine problem.[5] Yet in Maupassant's texts, glass objects of all kinds are used to exacerbate rather than attenuate the challenges which society posed to the male self. This was, after all, a time in which gender identity, class identity, and national identity were distinctly fragile. Plebiscites, universal suffrage, and education reforms by Victor Duruy and Jules Ferry undermined ideas of innate class merit. Virility was called into question for the *fin de siècle* generation by persistently low birth rates and rampant syphilis. The inherent superiority of the male gender was challenged by the growing women's suffrage movement, and by Darwin's discovery that fœtuses only develop their sex several weeks into their development.

With the events of the *année terrible*, these concerns were intensified. The Franco-Prussian War had dealt a severe blow to national pride that could only be partially compensated for by the violence of *révanchiste* sentiment. Whilst the *Journal officiel* no doubt meant to be encouraging with its declaration that 'nous sommes les victimes innocentes, mais viriles, de fautes que nous n'avons pas commises' ['we are the innocent but virile victims of errors that we did not commit'], the gendered lexicon — the feminine noun 'victime' and its two accompanying feminine adjectives — casts masculinity and virility into doubt.[6] During both the Franco-Prussian War and the Commune, the profusion of gender-crossing physiologies and caricatures may have been ostensibly comic, but it nonetheless revealed the permeable borders of masculinity. Four Commune women — Rétiffe, Marchais, Papavoine, and Suétens — were reported to 'ne fai[re] pas le plus grand honneur au sexe auquel elles appartiennent. Volontiers elles en abdiquaient la grâce, la timidité, le prestige, et ne s'attachaient depuis longtemps qu'à faire des œuvres viriles' ['not to do the greatest of honours to their sex. They voluntarily abdicated grace, shyness, prestige, and for some time had endeavoured to undertake only virile tasks']. Indeed, it is noticeable that in this account, unusually, these women are not given a marital status as either Mademoiselle or Madame, but are referred to by surname alone.[7] A woodcut of a group of imprisoned *pétroleuses* depicts all the women as ugly and brutish with rather masculine faces, including one woman in a sailor suit — the only vaguely pretty woman among them is clearly a prostitute.[8] In her discussion of Commune caricature, Hannah Thompson asserts that 'it is as if the shock of war — or, more precisely, the trauma of defeat — has the power to separate biological sex from the gender attributes usually associated with that sex'.[9] As the nation was wrought by crises, so was masculinity.

The psychological turn of Maupassant's works infuses his writing with a sense of the impossibility of certainty, knowledge, or truth; there is nothing here of the neat, resolute cataloguing and conceptualization offered by early works of Realism. What often initially *appear* to be comforting, Realist narratives are subtly woven with anxiety and uncertainty. Rather than strengthening masculine identity, its weaknesses are underwritten. Writing and glass, together, break down the self in these short stories as Maupassant crafts an aesthetic of anxiety for his reader — and unlike the memories of the recent social conflicts which could be blamed upon someone else, Maupassant's reader must accept and engage with this aesthetic of anxiety if he is to appreciate the significance of the writing.[10]

Breakdowns at the Mirror

Glass is the material par excellence of the psychological crisis for Maupassant's beleaguered characters. On two occasions, this manifests itself in violence against other people using glass as a murder weapon. The maddened protagonists of 'Moiron' (1887) and 'La Confession' ['The Confession'] (1883) hide glass in sweets and cakes so that it will puncture the wall of their victim's digestive tract — in the former, in retribution against God for the death of the protagonist's son; in the latter, in a fit of sexual and sororal jealousy at an older sister's engagement. Such murderous violence does not dominate Maupassant's thematization of glass objects, but it lingers in the reader's mind, lending a foreboding aura to other evocations of glass in tales of horror and insanity. Indeed, the *fait divers* style of these two short stories is striking, inviting the 1880s reader to make the connection between fictional tale and journalistic reports, rather than to dismiss them as gory hyperbole. Newspapers often carried real-life accounts of glass being used in bloody assaults: for example, the *Revue parisienne* recounted a disgruntled bar owner smashing a broken bottle over the head of a soldier in Lyon;[11] *L'État* described a fight in which a (supposedly) German waiter smashed a glass into the temple of his French colleague;[12] and the paranoid asylum patient Jean Bétinat internalized the danger of glass and insisted that his sister-in-law was trying to kill him with ground-up glass.[13]

More often, glass is not a weapon used by the mad, but madness strikes the protagonist in front of the looking-glass — as we might expect from our post-psychoanalytic vantage point. According to psychoanalysis, mirrors are expected to provide a panacea which tricks the conscious mind into overlooking the fragmentation of the subject. Instead, the mirror should allow the viewer to imagine the image of a complete self. Mirrors are allied with the ego and the imaginary, that 'order of mirror-images, identifications and reciprocities',[14] to foster the narcissistic self-love needed for a happy level of sanity. However, in Maupassant's stories a streak of aggression is often directed towards the specular image. The comforting, narcissistic process is rendered ineffectual, and as a consequence scenes of sadism, self-mutilation, madness, and fetishism ensue.

Sometimes women are afflicted by crises at the mirror, usually when they have betrayed feminine decorum with an illegitimate pregnancy or in their failure to supply motherly love. The woman pregnant with an illegitimate child in 'L'Enfant' ['The Child'] (1883) becomes so distressed at the sight of her expanding waistline in the mirror that she tries to cut the foetus out with a kitchen knife, guiding her incision by using her reflection in the looking-glass (CN, I.981/I.394). Rose in 'Histoire d'une fille de ferme' ['Story of a Farm Girl'] (1881) also stares anxiously and compulsively at her reflection in the mirror as her illegitimate pregnancy advances (CN, I.225/I.83). The eponymous Madame Hermet (1887) looks obsessively into a hand-mirror as she sits in her asylum cell, driven mad by guilt after having refused to comfort her dying child for fear of catching smallpox. This guilt manifests itself in the mirror, as she gazes at her reflection and hallucinates that she is hideously scarred (CN, II.874/III.594). In 'Yvette' (1884), the adolescent Yvette decides to commit suicide, and she stares, harrowed, at her reflection, imagining her face with the rotting features of a corpse (CN, II.234/II.275). However, in each of these cases there is little compassion for women's plight in an oppressive patriarchal society; the voyeuristic, fascinated descriptions of self-mutilation and madness suggest a desire to project concerns about the integrity of the *masculine* self onto another target.

There is a significantly more sympathetic tone applied to Robert's suffering at the mirror in 'Suicides' (1880); after struggling for several years against the burning desire to slit his throat each time he looked into his shaving mirror, he finally decides to shoot himself. In 'Promenade' ['A Walk'] (1884), M. Leras's depression is encapsulated by the ageing of the reflection he sees each day in his office mirror; he watches mortality run its course without life ever seeming worthwhile, and ultimately he commits suicide by hanging. In both versions of 'Le Horla' (1886 and 1887), the narrator suffers a mental breakdown after looking into the mirror and finding his reflection totally absent. Characters such as these seldom progress beyond the stage where the developing ego 'invests the specular image of itself or another with all the hostility directed towards its own lack of satisfaction, the very motivation for internalizing the image in the first place'.[15] For these partially-formed identities, they cannot deny the lack of wholeness inherent in the self when confronted with the looking-glass.

Prior to the narrative events of 'Fini' ['Finis'] (1885), the protagonist Lormerin had smiled at his reflection with satisfaction every day for some forty years of his life, in the firm belief that 'il était vraiment encore bel homme' ['he was still quite a fine-looking man'] (CN, II.513/III.794).[16] The operation of the imaginary required to underwrite this belief is so strong that it seeps beyond his reported speech into free indirect discourse; such indicators as the 'vraiment' here reveal that he is constantly, unconsciously at work to shore up his vulnerable sense of selfhood. Furthermore, the narrative emphasizes that this glance into the mirror has become ritualized; he gives 'un dernier regard' ['a parting glance'] of many into his dressing mirror (CN, II.513/III.794), and it is 'd'instinct' ['instinctively'] that he contemplates his reflection head-to-toe on receiving his erstwhile mistress's dinner invitation (*CN*, II.515/III.797). Yet this apparently unperturbed narcissism does not, of course, go long unchallenged. In contrast to his mirror image, it is the presence of a photographic image that instigates his psychological downfall, 'son propre portrait, une vieille photographie déteinte, datant de ses jours triomphants, pendue au mur dans un cadre coquet de soie ancienne' ['his own portrait, an old, faded photograph dating from the days of his triumph, hanging on the wall in a dainty old brocade frame'] (*CN*, II.516/III.797). Although Lormerin's eye is first drawn to his photograph by a narcissistic impulse — making it 'la première chose qu'il vit en entrant' ['the first thing he saw on entering'] — the emphasis on the age of the image, its faded colours, and its old brocade frame soon highlights the undeniable disparity between his imagined, youthful body image and his actual aged appearance.

This conflicted pairing of the mirror and the photographic lens situates glass at the heart of both Lormerin's illusions and his disillusionment. The glass lens and glass plate of the camera freeze a precise moment in time. In one sense, this could be considered immortalizing as it creates a durable image of youth, yet that static moment also becomes increasingly distinct from the owner's ageing appearance. Of course, this realization was not unique to Maupassant, and was one that would have struck a chord with most of his readers. One magazine commented that:

> La photographie est à la fois le portrait de notre figure et celui de notre prétention. [...] Elle vous jette brutalement votre âge au nez. Quel homme de cinquante ans, de soixante, si vous voulez, pour peu qu'il soit sincère, ne s'est pas dit tout bas, en face de sa photographie: 'Bonté du ciel! Que je suis vieux! Comment! toutes ces rides-là, c'est à moi!'[17]
>
> [Photographs are at once the portrait of our appearance and of our pretentions. [...] They brutally throw your age in your face. What man of fifty years old, of sixty if you will, however insincere, has not said quietly to himself when faced with his photograph: 'Sweet heavens! How old I am! How can all those wrinkles belong to me!']

For the first generation who had had the chance to be photographed throughout their adult lives, photography for the fifty-somethings of the 1880s became, in Susan Sontag's words, an 'inventory of mortality'.[18] This is compounded for Lormerin, because instead of internalizing his image at the mirror (as narcissism dictates), he has been internalizing the photographs of his youth. Jules Henrivaux places these two reflections of the self side by side in his 1883 reference work on glass. He writes:

> Puisque l'homme était organisé de manière à tout voir sans se voir lui-même, quel présent que cette feuille de verre sur une feuille de métal, qui ne fixe pas seulement, comme la plaque du photographe, l'image humaine, immobile et grisâtre, mais la lui rend, aussi bien que celle de la nature, avec la couleur, le mouvement, la changeante expression, l'ombre, la lumière, la perspective, aussi souvent qu'elle se présente![19]
>
> [Since man was put together in such a way as to see everything without seeing himself, what a gift is this sheet of glass on a sheet of metal, which does not

only fix the human image like the photographic plate, immobile, greyish, but which also returns it to the viewer as nature intended, with its colour, movement, changing expression, shadow, light, perspective, just as often as it presents itself!]

Subsequently, as Lormerin aged, he confounded the real image in the mirror with his internalized, mental photograph of his younger days; he projects the image internalized from his photograph onto the mirror, combining the living colour of his reflection with the frozen youth of the snapshot. Indeed, it is notable that although a number of the objects in his apartment are described, no photographs seem to be present, thus strategically avoiding any unwanted reminders of the illusion under which he has been operating. For many years, this brings Lormerin extremely positive results — until at last he is confronted with the presence of the real and emphatically withered photograph in its faded frame.

This first trickle of realization from his real photograph is soon exacerbated by Lise — perhaps deliberately, given his callous failure to make any contact after her husband forced her to leave Paris all those years ago. In the past, Lormerin had enjoyed a position of dominant masculinity over Lise's feminine weakness, finding in her eyes and her romantic tears something 'bête et charmant' ['foolish and charming'] (*CN*, II.515/III.796). But Lise's eyes, redoubled in her daughter Renée's face, seem to look at Lormerin from not one but two positions. It is as though he has strayed unwittingly into a circus house of mirrors, and now her eyes are 'charmant' in the literal sense of bewitching. They rob him of his self-mastery. Far from the confidence with which he looks into the mirror, now his vision is troubled by the two women's matching gazes, and his scopic mastery is shaken by 'une idée fixe dans l'esprit, une idée malade de dément' ['obsessed by an idea, the diseased idea of a madman'] (*CN*, II.517/III.799). He finds himself visually outnumbered, unable to engage two identical sets of eyes at once, and incapable of gaining control over the scene taking place.

In his desperation, Lormerin attempts to fall back on his old narcissistic habits in the hope that he can regain a sense of mastery of both himself and the situation. In the absence of a mirror in Lise's salon, he seeks his reflection as a subject by seeing his lover as object — but this quickly backfires as it is not in the mother's eyes but in 'l'œil clair de la jeune fille [qu'] il retrouvait ses souvenirs' ['the girl's bright eyes which revealed the past to him'] (*CN*, II.518/III.799). In these two remarkably similar women, past and present clash. Lise and Renée illustrate physically the irresolvable division between then and now, old and young — and they demonstrate the void of time between Lormerin's own past and his present. His photographic image correlates with the daughter (as the 'living portrait' of her mother's youth), and thus his current physical image must correlate with Lise (as the mirror-image of passed time and of their advanced years). His illusory usage of the mirror now becomes all too apparent.

Once Lormerin becomes aware of his self-deception, no glass objects can bring him any further comfort: neither the mirror, nor the magnifying glass (with which he tries to work out whether letters are from friend or foe before opening them), nor the photographic lens. After this traumatic dinner party, his habitual narcissistic self-affirmation fails catastrophically and he is no longer capable of denying reality or mortality. In contrast with the confident glance at himself 'de la tête aux pieds' at the opening of the story, when Lormerin next passes before his large dressing mirror the image he sees shakes him 'de la tête aux pieds'. For the first time, he sees the reflection of an old man in the mirror — and he completely fails to identify with this 'homme mûr à cheveux gris' ['man of mature years with grey hair']. Suddenly his sense of self falls apart and he crumbles, 'accablé, en face de lui-même, en face de sa lamentable image, en murmurant: "Fini Lormerin!"' ['he sat down opposite his reflection, crushed at the sight of his wretched appearance, murmuring: "Finis, Lormerin!"' (*CN*, II.518/III.800).

This harrowing episode illustrates that glass may have as many dangers as benefits for the modern man in search of an ego boost. And for Lormerin, the situation is even more precarious than for the regular narcissist. Instead of the conventional process, where the body is elided with its reflected image, Lormerin has sought to *deny* the relationship between his body and the ageing man in his reflection, and to elide his body instead with the photograph of his youth. When he finally recognizes his delusion, the effects on his psyche are catastrophic; instead of his self splitting once as it enters the symbolic (like every subject), Lormerin already has a split self. Consequently, when it splits again, it is fragmented beyond redemption. There is no possibility of explaining this tale away or providing it with one of Maupassant's frequent, conceptualizing frame narratives. In a flash, without narratable sequel, Lormerin is simply, utterly 'fini'.

Breaking down Love

Challenges to Maupassant's male characters are often triggered by their desiring relationships with women — from those men who keep the greatest possible distance from real female bodies, to those who seek the most intimate familiarity with them. Fetishism, at one extreme, reveals just how fragile the masculine self can be in Maupassant's short stories. Theoretically speaking, fetishism is an attempt to displace an individual's fears about his own fragile selfhood onto an external object, a signifying fragment.[20] Of course, Maupassant's many tales of fetishism do not all involve glass,[21] but when glass is involved the sense of psychological fragility is intensified. The literal fragility of glass as a material, and the metaphorical associations with social fragility after the *année terrible* both exacerbate the atmosphere of vulnerability.

In 'Un cas de divorce' ['A Divorce Case'] (1886), Mme Chassel gives evidence to a divorce court, inculpating her husband for his extreme fetishism for flowers. She reads out perverse extracts from his diary, in which he records his passionate obsession with the inhabitants of his hothouse: 'je passe mes jours et mes nuits dans les serres où je les cache [les fleurs] ainsi que les femmes des harems' ['I pass my days and my nights in the greenhouses where I hide them [the flowers] like women in harems'] (*CN*, II.781/III.443). Whenever his desire is particularly inflamed by one favoured orchid, he takes it deeper into his glass harem, removing it from the communal *serre* for some time alone 'dans un mignon cabinet de verre' ['a darling little glass retreat'] (*CN*, II.783/III.444). The nineteenth-century reader could not miss the analogy here with the *cabinet particulier*, that much-loved locus of the Parisian erotic encounter. M. Chassel's *cabinet de verre* saturates his surroundings with glass even more than would be expected in the familiar *cabinet particulier*, which is rarely depicted without large mirrors, windows, and frosted glass panels. The increase in glass runs in parallel with the added degree of perversion. The reader is clearly led to see glass as a signifier of perverse, even nefarious sexuality.

When male characters make misguided attempts at fetishizing vitreous objects — or bodies seen via vitreous objects — the tenuous nature of fetishistic illusions is laid bare. Such is the case in 'Rencontre' ['A Meeting'] (1884). A large mirror is mounted beside the Princess's bed, where the Baron d'Etraille, taking a quiet moment away from a ball, muses that 'la glace regardait la couche, sa complice. On eût dit qu'elle avait des souvenirs [...] et qu'on allait voir passer sur sa face unie et vide ces formes charmantes qu'ont les hanches nues des femmes, et les gestes doux des bras quand ils enlacent' ['a huge looking-glass, [...] seemed to look at the bed, which was its accomplice. One might fancy that it felt memories, [...] that across its smooth, empty surface one might see pass the lovely lines of women's naked bodies, the soft movements of embracing arms'] (*CN*, I.1231/I.705). The Baron fantasizes about fragments of the female body — thighs, intertwining arms — on the feminine bed in the feminine mirror.

Yet the main impact of the Baron's tendency to fragment and objectify is, inevitably, on his own psyche. By enjoying his fetishistic fantasy of isolated but living body parts indirectly via the looking-glass, the mirror becomes the site of the fragment, not the whole; it is henceforth rendered useless in the narcissistic process. Notably, mirrors never provide the Baron with the sight of his own, complete bodily image in 'Rencontre'. Rather, when he glances into the mirror again, instead of reflecting the Baron, it shows him a disembodied reflection of his *wife's* lips as she kisses the Marquis de Cervigné. The drapes bordering the mirror cast a shadow over the rest of their features, leaving their lips detached from their bodies and isolated in a striking, proto-cinematic freeze frame (*CN*, I.1231/I.705). Perhaps, the reader wonders, the disembodied thighs and arms of the Baron's earlier reverie were in fact those of his wife all along, in the twilight between fetishistic fantasy and reality. At this moment, one identity crisis piles upon another: the mirror shows him his wife in the process of cuckolding him; the mirror reveals that his identity as the dominant, desiring subject in the marital relationship was only ever an illusion; and the mirror now refuses the Baron a comforting reflection of his own wholeness to compensate for any of this.

It is worthy of note that Maupassant's most self-confessedly fetishistic character, the narrator of 'La Chevelure' ['A Woman's Hair'] (1884), systematically avoids having glass objects around him. Although his entire existence is driven by a love of material objects, he takes no part in the general superfluity of glass in Maupassant's writing. There is a striking absence of the normal vases, drinking glasses, glass bottles, mirrors, windows, shop fronts, lamps and lamp shades, monocles, spectacles, or magnifying glasses; by shunning glass objects, the diarist evades their connotations of clarity, fragility, and crisis. However, whilst his diary in the embedded narrative may scrupulously avoid all mention of glass, the opening frame narrative almost immediately depicts a window high above the fetishist-madman in the asylum (*CN*, II.107/II.205). The glass is high above him, out of his control but ever present, filtering light and enlightenment into the protagonist's cell. Glass haunts the diarist, in spite of all his attempts to avoid it, and foreshadows the tale behind his psychological collapse that we are to discover in the embedded narrative.

The presence of glass comes to augur crisis in Maupassant's short stories; when glass is there, the reader learns to anticipate the rupturing of some underlying psychological weakness. This is exacerbated by the fact that glass often seems to collaborate with female characters in Maupassant's writing. As patriarchal society's most convenient other, women have the most frequent opportunities to contest the stability of the masculine subject — and in such situations, glass proves to be their ally. This is a collaboration rooted in the popular culture of nineteenth-century patriarchy, where women were supposed to be insatiably vain and thus incapable of functioning without their looking-glass. Indeed, the mirror was considered so much a part of the eternal feminine that the 'Tout Paris' display at the Musée Grévin in 1882 contained, 'devant un psyché, une amazone excentrique, la PARISIENNE EN 1982' ['standing before a cheval mirror, an eccentric amazon, the PARISIENNE IN 1982'].[22] Even a century into the future, women would surely still spend most of their time admiring themselves in the looking-glass. However, in the aftermath of the *année terrible* when glass is already associated with the weaknesses at the heart of patriarchal society, this collaboration between glass and women becomes a troubling one.

In 'La Morte' ['The Dead Woman'] (1887), the male lover's sense of self is built upon seeing his reflection in the eyes of his beloved, using her as a mirror.[23] This in itself is not unconventional; however, this system falls apart after her death, and he is suddenly forced into a conscious awareness of the illusion upon which he has built his sense of selfhood. Robbed by death of his beloved-as-mirror, he breaks down, specifically, in front of her mirror. After the funeral, he returns to their apartment and stares frantically into her full-length hallway mirror, 'qu'elle avait fait poser là pour se voir, des pieds à la tête, chaque jour, en sortant' ['which she had had placed there so that every day before she went out she could see herself from head to foot']. He scrutinizes the glass in the vain hope that '[le miroir] avait dû garder aussi son image' ['it must have caught and held the image of her'] (*CN*, II.940/III.578). Rather than trying to affirm his selfhood using his own reflection, he searches — fruitlessly — for her eyes in the mirror so that they may in turn reflect him as they had always done before.

The vital narcissistic role that had been fulfilled by his beloved-as-mirror is underlined when his subconscious overcompensates, attempting to transfer his feelings of love as well as his need for a reflection onto the actual, physical mirror — he declares, 'il me sembla que j'aimais cette glace' ['I thought that I loved this glass'] (*CN*, II.940/III.579). But its coldness to the touch serves as a chill reminder that both women and glass only ever provide a fragile affirmation of selfhood. He laments that he ever relied on his now-impossible reflection in his beloved's eyes, and curses the mirror for its failure to retain her reflection in turn: 'miroir douloureux, miroir brûlant, miroir vivant, miroir horrible, qui fait souffrir toutes les tortures! Heureux les hommes dont le cœur, comme une glace où glissent et s'effacent les reflets, oublie tout ce qu'il a contenu' ['Woeful, searing, living, frightful glass, the cause of all our agonies. Happy the man whose heart, like a glass across whose surface reflections glide and vanish, forgets all that it has held'] (*CN*, II.940/III.579). Finally, he suffers his psychological breakdown during a traumatic night in the graveyard, and he hallucinates that the dead are rising around him. During this nightmarish scene, he reads on his mistress's tomb: 'Étant sortie un jour pour tromper son amant, elle eut froid sous la pluie, et mourut' ['Going out one day to deceive her lover, she caught cold in the rain, and died'] (*CN*, II.943/III.582). Whether she was unfaithful in life or only in his hallucination, now that the mirror has lost her reflection — and he has lost his reflection in her eyes — he loses grip upon his psychological stability.

In the short story 'Imprudence' ['Indiscretion'] (1885), the collaboration between glass and women is manifested as an explicit analogy between feminine sexual desire and glass objects. The link between glass and feminine desire is no innovation here; rather, Maupassant invokes a considerable intertextual network for the reader of his short stories. It is hard to read of any greenhouse, conservatory, or winter garden after Zola's *La Curée* (1871) without recalling Renée and Maxime's perverse, quasi-incestuous encounters. 'Paris as a hothouse' was used widely as a metaphor for the sexualization of the city's inhabitants, particularly in terms of the enflamed sexual appetites of young women. Edmond de Goncourt, on describing Chérie's adolescence in Paris (1884), writes that 'l'effervescente atmosphère des salons [...] avivent et précipitent la formation de la germe, ainsi que la tiédeur humide d'une serre chaude pousse la floraison d'une fleur' ['the effervescent atmosphere of the salons [...] kindles and precipitates the germination of the seed, just as the humid warmth of the conservatory speeds up the blooming of flowers'].[24] Paul Bonnetain even applies this metaphor to infants, with a boy of six and girl of three in this description of a street scene:

> [Le garçon] empoigna [la fille], la baisa sur le cou, sous les oreilles, sur la nuque, puis sur la poitrine, et ses deux mains tiraient sur le corsage, descendaient l'étoffe, tandis que ses lèvres tentaient de se couler plus bas, cherchaient les seins à venir. Innocent, ce petit libertin; instinctive, sa recherche; mais Paris et sa civilisation de serre chaude sont dans cette caresse enfantine qui me fit rêver.[25]

> [[The boy] grabbed [the girl], kissed her on the neck, under the ears, on the nape of her neck, then on the chest, and his two hands tugged at her bodice, pulling down the fabric, while his lips tried to slide lower, searching for the breasts yet to come. Innocent, this little libertine; instinctive, his search; but Paris and its hothouse civilization are there in this childish caress which left me dreaming.]

The familiar nature of this analogy between glass and (particularly female) sexuality allows Maupassant to project existing erotic connotations onto a variety of other glass spaces and glass objects — auguring that the situation will rarely end well for the men involved.

In the *cabinet particulier* of the Parisian café in 'Imprudence' there hangs '[une] grande glace ternie par des milliers de noms tracés au diamant' ['a large mirror marked all over by thousands of names traced on it by diamonds'] (*CN*, II.550/ II.598). This sizeable, heavily-engraved mirror overlooks Henriette and her husband Paul as she spices up their marital sex life by role-playing at being her husband's mistress. The fact that there is a mirror here is in essence entirely unremarkable. Flaubert's Frédéric tries to seduce Rosanette in a mirrored *cabinet* in *L'Education sentimentale* (Part II, Chapter 4). Renée and Maxime consummate their liaison for the first time in a very similar *cabinet* at the Café Riche in *La Curée* (*LC*, 448). Indeed, looking-glasses were such a standard feature of the *cabinet particulier* and so consistently associated with sexual activity that one comic guidebook to Paris from 1878 advised:

> Quelle que soit la femme que vous conduisiez dans les cabinets particuliers, empêchez-la d'écrire son nom sur la glace à l'aide d'un diamant. D'abord parce que si elle n'a pas de diamant elle vous en fera acheter un sous forme de bague ou de pendants d'oreilles, ensuite parce que, pendant la période de l'exposition universelle, les restaurateurs sont décidés à porter sur l'addition, tout comme un simple parfait, la glace qui aura la moindre rayure.[26]

> [No matter what woman you take into a private *cabinet*, stop her from inscribing her name on the mirror with a diamond. First, because if she does not have a diamond, she will make you buy her one on a ring or earring; then, because, throughout the World Fair, restaurant owners have decided to charge to the bill, like a simple parfait, any mirror which has the slightest scratch.]

What is unusual in 'Imprudence' is the shear density of signatures borne by the mirror. There is no possibility of Henriette and Paul getting specular pleasure from watching their own sexual encounter in the mirror; their reflections are obscured entirely by etched names. This looking-glass banalizes and de-personalizes sex — the etchings act as an effective metonyms for the thousands of encounters that have taken place there before. Whilst male sexual profligacy was rarely condemned at this time, we immediately suspect things will soon go awry for Paul when his wife finds this arousing. She puts into words what the scratched names on the mirror imply about her husband's bachelor sex-life, she asks a flood of questions about his sexual experiences, and she clearly gets a thrill from all this dirty talk.[27]

Not only are the names paired metonymically with their owners' liaisons, but the narrative links the mirror metonymically to all the other glass objects in the room. This Mirror of Promiscuity seems to project its erotic associations outwards until every glass object has sexual connotations. For example, Paul makes an explicit analogy between having multiple sexual partners and drinking from the glasses on the table, from which multiple lips have drunk (with obvious euphemistic play on lips and fluidity in reference to the female body, *CN*, II.552/II.600). Additionally, throughout their verbal foreplay, Henriette is never portrayed without her champagne glass in hand. The glass and the woman are physically separated only for the briefest of moments during the 'étreinte emportée' ['passionate embrace'] between husband and wife; as soon as the deed is done, Henriette picks up her glass again and the reader is soon told that '[elle] tenait de nouveau un verre plein entre ses doigts' ['she was holding another full glass between her fingers'] (*CN*, II.553–54/ II.601). She then gazes into the looking-glass, and muses that having multiple sexual partners 'doit être amusant tout de même!' ['Must be very amusing, all the same'] (*CN*, II.554/602). There is pleasure to be found for Henriette in the vicarious associations between herself and all the promiscuous women who have made their marks on the mirror. She cannot see her real reflection in its un-reflective surface, but she can glimpse a fantasized reflection of herself as a free, sexually active subject in its inscriptions. The mirror's lingering presence throughout reflects that all women — even respectable wives and objects of romantic affection — may harbour repressed erotic desires. In doing so, it reflects the potential threat posed to the husband or lover's subjectivity if these feminine desires are acted upon.

In 'Le Signe' ['The Sign'] (1886 — *CN*, II.725/III.104), this threat is manifested when the Marquise de Rennedon cuckolds her husband — admittedly, not through a deliberate endeavour, but through a series of misguided observations from windows and in mirrors. As she gazes aimlessly from her apartment window, the Marquise notices a prostitute at the window opposite who effects a particular gesture to invite business her way. The Marquise is intrigued; she goes over to her mirror to see if she, a lady, can carry off this subtle but lubricious gesture; and she is impressed by her attempt. So, she again mimics the same gesture, this time not before the reflective mirror but through the transparent window pane to the street below — not for the interpretation of her own eyes, but for those of any passing man. However, this cycle of window-mirror-window then escapes her control somewhat. Any man who sees and comprehends such a gesture might reasonably expect one thing, and just such an individual storms into her apartment to claim it. Without these liminal glass spaces, the Marquise would not have been tempted into this misadventure which precipitated the transgression of her marital fidelity; and, we suspect, the transgression of rather enjoying it.

So strong is this collaboration between glass and the feminine that a disconcerting aura of femininity seeps into the glass in 'Lettre d'un fou' ['Letter of a Madman'][28] (1885) without any actual woman ever being present. After a number of strange occurrences in his room, the male narrator stares, terrified, as his reflection disappears from his mirror. At that very moment, the text designates the mirror as 'elle', choosing the noun 'la glace' rather than 'le miroir', *throughout the period of his reflection's absence*:

> On y voyait comme en plein jour, et je ne me vis pas dans la glace! Elle était vide, claire, pleine de lumière. Je n'étais pas dedans, et j'étais en face, cependant. Je la regardais avec des yeux affolés. Je n'osais pas aller vers elle, sentant bien qu'il était entre nous, lui, l'Invisible, et qu'il me cachait. Oh! comme j'eus peur! Et voilà que je commençai à m'apercevoir dans une brume au fond du miroir, dans une brume comme à travers de l'eau; et il me semblait que cette eau glissait de gauche à droite, lentement, me rendant plus précis de seconde en seconde. C'était comme la fin d'une éclipse. Ce qui me cachait n'avait pas de contours, mais une sorte de transparence opaque s'éclaircissant peu à peu (*CN*, II.466).
>
> [It was as clear as day, but I could not see myself in the mirror! It was clear, bright, full of light. I wasn't reflected in it, but I was standing opposite it. I stared at it with maddened eyes. I didn't dare go towards it, feeling sure that he

was between us, him, the Invisible, who was hiding me. Oh, how I was afraid! And then I started to glimpse myself in a mist deep in the mirror, in a mist as though through water; and this water seemed to me to slide from left to right, slowly, allowing my reflection to sharpen second by second. It was like the end of an eclipse. The thing hiding me had no edges, but was a kind of opaque transparency, becoming clearer by degrees]

Notably, it is as the mirror becomes feminine that the masculine 'Invisible' finally reveals itself. His confident masculine ego seems to become detached here, when the feminine mirror refuses to satisfy his need to see his specular image. Without his ego, the void behind his sense of selfhood is rendered (in)visible. The haunting 'Invisible' apparition is a manifestation of the hidden illusions on which he has built his sense of self. Once aware of this illusion, however invisible it may be, his scopic image disappears and only the feminized 'glace' can remain.

Breaking Glasses

For Maupassant's male characters, then, the frequent collaboration between glass and unruly femininity already loads glass with troubling associations. All the more so for a generation who had so recently seen their two principal enemies — the Prussians and the Communards — being mocked for their inability to maintain their gender positions.[29] The fear of active feminine desire is epitomized in Maupassant's 'Le Lit 29' ['Bed No. 29'] (1884) by Captain Epivent's repulsion at his erstwhile mistress as she dies of syphilis after the Franco-Prussian War. Hannah Thompson indicates perceptively that this repulsion is not only due to the advanced stage of the disease but, moreover, because she represents a seemingly impossible or 'unnatural' combination of the feminine and masculine; she used her feminine seductiveness to wage war on the Prussians by aggressively infecting as many soldiers as possible with the pox.[30]

Occasionally, Maupassant writes what seems at first to be an uncharacteristically jovial, bawdy story of glass and eroticism in which a male character finally gets his wicked way. This is the case in 'La Serre' ['The Greenhouse'] (1883). M. and Mme Lerebour have long-since ceased to have marital relations; but when the husband discovers that their maid Céleste and her lover meet for assignations in the greenhouse, he and his wife discover a novel and considerable pleasure in voyeurism — to such an extent that the conjugal bed is put back into use. Not only does glass conveniently allow them to watch the busy couple without being so easily heard or observed, it also has an important tactile role. Maupassant specifically remarks that the Lerebours press themselves up against the glass and against each other simultaneously during these bouts of voyeurism ('blottis l'un près de l'autre contre le vitrage' ['huddled close together against the panes'] (*CN*, I.860/III.713)). Glass functions almost like a sex toy here, and without the stimulus of the greenhouse none of this titillation would be possible. This essentially light-hearted story in which a hen-pecked husband finally gets satisfaction does not initially seem to challenge masculinity. However, when it is glass, a material so easily broken, which is the difference between confirming or not confirming his masculinity, M.

Lerebour's virile selfhood is surely never far away from shattering. If men use glass to construct their subjectivity, then that subjectivity will by nature be extremely fragile. Indeed, with a patronym like 'Lerebour', the backward logic of relying on glass to sustain his masculinity is highlighted — in a way which Huysmans would echo in the title of *À rebours* the following year.

When the worst comes to the worst — in heterosexual relationships as in the *année terrible* — shattering glass marks out the most traumatic moments in Maupassant's narratives. The eponymous tale of M. Parent (1885) dramatizes one man's disillusionment from romantic love and mutual attraction, and his story demonstrates that these make woefully unreliable building blocks for subjectivity. After several years of marriage, the devoted M. Parent remains oblivious to the fact that his cruel wife has been cuckolding him all along — but on one fateful day this knowledge is forced upon him by his housekeeper. M. Parent emphatically rejects these allegations, but as the argument with the housekeeper escalates:

> elle ajouta: Il suffit de regarder le petit pour reconnaître le père, pardi! c'est tout le portrait de M. Limousin. Il n'y a qu'à regarder ses yeux et son front. [...]
> D'un effort désespéré [Parent] la lança dans la pièce voisine. Elle tomba sur la table servie dont *les verres s'abattirent et se cassèrent*. (*CN*, II.586–87, my emphasis)

> ['You've only to look at the little one to recognise the father', she added. 'Why, Lord-a-Mercy, he's the living image of Monsieur Limousin. You've only to look at his eyes and his forehead. [...]'
> With a desperate effort he flung her into the next room. She fell upon the table set for dinner, and *the glasses tumbled and smashed* (II.657–58, my emphasis)]

As the servant shouts repeatedly 'il verra! il verra si j'ai menti... Que monsieur essaie... il verra!' ['He will see!... he will see if I have lied!... Let Monsieur try... he will see'] (*CN*, II.587/II.658), the future tense of the verb *voir* provides a partial homonym to highlight the association between shattering glass and shattered illusions. It is only when glass breaks that M. Parent can no longer deny that his whole existence and identity are based on lies. He is not a husband possessing a loving wife, and Parent is not a parent after all; his very name is rendered meaningless.

Notably, the broken drinking glasses in this scene are followed by a long string of *unbroken* glasses from which Parent compulsively drinks away his lonely years in a Parisian brasserie. It is not only the alcohol they hold which he seeks in the hope of drowning his sorrows; he is also drawn to the unshattered glasses themselves, attempting to replace the shattered glasses of that fateful day with the unbroken glass of 'un carafon d'eau-de-vie', 'trois ou quatre petits verres', 'le bock', and 'son [verre d'] absinthe' ['decanter of brandy', 'three or four glasses', 'the bock', and 'his absinthe']. That this has a therapeutic effect for M. Parent is made clear by its ritualization; he goes to the brasserie and orders this succession of glasses of alcohol in the same order, every day, for some twenty years (*CN*, II.607/II.679–80). On the one day that he finally deviates from his routine and visits the Terrasse de Saint-Germain, he comes across his wife, her lover, and the young man that Parent once believed to be his son. At the very moment that he forms a plan to get his revenge, he orders a cognac — in addition to Dutch courage, this brings an intact glass before him to bolster his confidence (*CN*, II.613/II.689). Glass is far from just another prop to embellish a reality effect in this short story, but it may expose the fragile border between sanity and insanity for M. Parent.

In 'Le Port' ['In Port'] (1889), the shattering of glasses occurs at the moment of trauma *par excellence*; the recognition of incest, the pinnacle of all possible challenges to the virile, masculine subject. The sailor Célestin and the prostitute Françoise feel an affinity from the moment they meet, but rather than this blossoming into a story of humble romance, they discover too late that they have a rapport because they are siblings, estranged since their youth. At this instant of realization, 'tout à coup [Célestin] se leva, se mit à jurer d'une voix formidable en tapant sur la table un tel coup de poing que *les verres culbutés se brisèrent*' ['suddenly he leaped to his feet and began to swear in a dreadful voice, bringing his fist down on the table with such violence that *the overturned glasses broke to atoms*'] (*CN*, II.1133/III.576 — my emphasis). Here, what should have been a story in which Célestin's masculinity was confirmed through romantic fulfilment, instead becomes a scene of psychological devastation, with breaking glasses confirming and compounding the broken incest taboo.

Although glasses do not quite break in 'Un lâche' ['The Coward'] (1884), the 'beau Signoles' makes a similar attempt to use glasses therapeutically to compensate, in a play on the homonyms 'glace' (ice) and 'glace' (mirror), for a catastrophically unsuccessful flirtation over an ice-cream. In this tale, the hyper-masculine Signoles is known for his prowess with weapons, his *esprit*, and his dashing 'moustache brave et l'œil doux, ce qui plaît aux femmes' ['gallant moustache and an eloquent eye, attributes which women like'] (*CN*, I.1159/II.458). Yet for all his masculinity, Signoles's self-assured existence starts to unravel when he takes a female companion out for an ice-cream and she complains, rather coquettishly, that the admiring stare of another man 'me gâte ma glace' ['the creature is spoiling my ice'] (*CN*, I.1159/II.459). Out of pride, Signoles challenges the stranger to a duel, and from this spoiled *glace* a torrent of challenges to his emphatically masculine selfhood is unleashed — and which is manifested around a series of glass objects. He fears not appearing sufficiently brave and macho, but tries to take hold of his anxiety by taking hold of a series of drinking glasses. Immediately, before his fear begins to manifest itself in earnest, 'il but, coup sur coup, trois verres d'eau' ['[he] drank three glasses of water one after the other'] (*CN*, I.1161/II.460). Then, again, on becoming consciously afraid that he might be subconsciously afraid, 'il but encore un verre d'eau' ['he drank another glass of water'] (*CN*, I.1162/II.461). Kept awake by his growing anxiety, he gets up to drink again — but, finding no comfort in all these drinking glasses, he moves across to his looking-glass, in which 'il aperçut son visage reflété dans le verre poli, il se reconnut à peine' ['when he saw his face reflected in the polished glass, he scarcely recognised it'] (*CN*, I.1162/II.462). As he looks at his reflection, he contemplates in an eerily detached fashion that 'cette personne en face de moi, ce moi que je vois dans cette glace ne sera plus' ['this person facing me, this me I see in the mirror, will be no more'] (*CN*, I.1163/II.462). He feels alienated from his own idea of his identity; the traces of fear he sees in his reflection make him question whether his macho identity had been an illusion all along? It becomes imperative that he destroy this image of an emasculated, fearful Signoles — this double which utterly undermines what he has always believed to be his true self. The following day, he shoots himself in order to kill the cowardly other hiding within his macho self.

Breaking down the Reader

At the time Maupassant was writing, the symbolic associations persisting between glass and recent crises had the potential to foster anxiety for more than just his fictional characters. Maupassant's texts also gesture towards to fragility of the reader's own selfhood. There is something acutely unsettling for the reader in these short stories; concepts he believed to be empirical facts — masculine dominance, binary gender, even the simplicity and transparency of glass — are all destabilized, both within the stories and at the diegetic level. Maupassant's text are ridden with linguistic fluctuation, which questions the reader's purchase upon meaning, and challenges his very identity as reader.

First of all, it is with concern that the reader finds himself without a clear guide to lead him through the text. The *homme de lettres* in Maupassant's writing is defined by an unstable identity, and glass metaphors are used to establish his multifaceted, evasive character. The literary man is 'condamné à être toujours en toute occasion, *un reflet* de lui-même et un reflet des autres' ['condemned to be always, at every moment, *a reflection* of himself and a reflection of others'].[31] In 'Sur l'eau' ['Afloat'] (1876), the writer figure confesses that he is a split persona because 'je porte en moi cette seconde vue qui est en même temps la force et toute la misère des écrivains. [...] Je le regarde en moi-même, dans *le miroir de ma pensée*' ['I carry in myself this second sight which is at once the strength and all the misery of writers. [...] I see it in myself, in the *mirror of my thoughts*'].[32] Not just mirrors, but glass more generally becomes a key metaphor for the relationship between the writer figure and his reader: 'tout autour de lui devient *de verre*, les cœurs, les actes, les intentions secrètes, et il souffre d'un mal étrange, d'une sorte de dédoublement de l'esprit' ['everything around him becomes *glass* — hearts, actions, secret intentions — and he suffers from a strange pain, a sort of doubling-up of the mind'].[33] Far from Balzac's omniscient narrators, the authorial figure in Maupassant becomes more akin to Baudelaire's artistic modern man, 'un miroir aussi immense que cette foule' ['a mirror as immense as this crowd'].[34] Whether or not this applies to Maupassant's perception of his own real-life identity is not really relevant to the reader's reception of the texts; with an ironic play on the *types* so often used by Realism, Maupassant here establishes the writer *type* as transparent, brittle, or fragmented. So, at the very moment that we seem to have found one reliable constant within the texts, we are also defied by its polyvocality. Indeed, Maupassant has a predilection for framed narratives which have two explicit and often contradictory narrators both operating within the split *je* of an implied author.[35]

Moreover, this 'auteur de la vie moderne' does not merely avoid being objectified himself by deflecting the readers' gaze with the mirror of his thoughts; he may also confront the readers with distorted reflections of themselves. The refusal of a guiding hand through the text thus goes deeper. This is a refusal to provide the reader with a clear identity *as reader*. Evidence of this can be found in the various subject pronouns with unclear referents in Maupassant's short stories. The ambiguity of these pronouns leaves them open, and forces the reader into unwonted identification with fictional characters. For example, the reader as well as the fictional characters seems to be addressed by the familiar 'tu' in the frame narrative of 'L'Ami Patience' ['Our Friend Patience'] (1883); by the feminized 'vous' alongside the Baroness in the frame of 'L'Enfant' ['The Child'] (1883); and by the anonymous 'vous' at the end of 'Menuet' (1882). The reader becomes a character addressed by and thus preconceived by the narrative; he is seemingly stripped of his active, independent *logos* and is left, in the words of Roland Barthes, 'sans histoire, sans biographie, sans psychologie; il est seulement ce *quelqu'un* qui tient rassemblées dans un même champ toutes les traces dont est constitué l'écrit' ['without history, without biography, without psychology; he is just that *someone* who holds together in a single location all the traces which make up the text'].[36] Far from the act of reading proving a means of finding reassurance and certainty in these troubled times, Maupassant's narratives contrive to aggravate the reader's sense of insecurity. These short stories do not resemble Stendhal's 'miroir qui se promène sur une grande route' ['mirror in the roadway'] for the reader,[37] but, rather, they splinter an apparently approachable text into a confounding whirl of uncertain symbols and ideas. Angela Moger indicates in her discussion of Maupassant's narrative structure that 'meaning is a do-it-yourself project that incidentally and paradoxically removes the story from any condition of stasis';[38] meaning under Maupassant's direction loses fixity and may thus be rendered dubious even though the individual words and the generic style seem so very familiar.

The parallel between the distressing effect of glass and of Maupassant's texts for French readers is not merely coincidental. Maupassant carefully structures the narrative shape of a number of his stories to mimic the characteristics of the glass objects which they so often associate with crises. For example, the numerous frame narratives ape the structure of a window. I say window rather than mirror or picture frame, because the frame-narrative gives the reader the impression of 'seeing through' into a second narrative world beyond the first, rather than simply seeing a reflection of the first, or a static canvas. However, as John Moreau has pointed out, Maupassant does not use these frame narratives in the same way as canonical authors such as Boccacio, Chaucer, and Marguerite de Navarre, whose works 'tend to suggest a community of raconteurs linked metonymically to the social collectivity or nascent national group'.[39] Rather, Maupassant's textual windows *refuse* to create a community of storytellers, and are more akin to barriers than openings. The world of the narrative frame resembles the bourgeois domestic interior and the embedded narrative, the unsettling, unknowable city beyond to which the readers cannot fully relate.

This disconnect is especially striking in 'En voyage' ['On the Journey'] (1883), in which the embedded narrative appears to be a fairly conventional story of the fateful imperative of forbidden love — yet it is set in a deeply incongruous frame narrative about train passengers sharing horror stories. Furthermore, the closing half of the frame makes it impossible to decipher the frame-audience's interpretation. One of the fictional ladies begins to pronounce her thoughts about the love story, babbling that 'ces deux êtres-là ont été moins fous que vous ne croyez... Ils étaient... ils étaient...' ['those two people were not so crazy as you think. They were — they were — '] before her sobs overcome her and 'on changea de conversation pour la calmer, [donc] on ne sut pas ce qu'elle voulait dire' ['as we changed the conversation to calm her, we never knew what she had wished to say'] (*CN*, I.815/II.104). What *did* she want to say? And what did Maupassant want to say in choosing to frame the story in this way, when it could have been provided with a satisfying exegetic frame or, indeed, have stood alone as a short story in its own right? Is the problem here that the private world on the inside of the window frame and the public world beyond it can never fundamentally communicate? And if so, how are we, as readers, to gain any purchase upon these narratives at yet another remove? As Louis Forestier has rightly commented, 'tout se passe comme si, [...] après avoir imposé un récit à son lecteur, [Maupassant] imposait à ce dernier d'en reconstituer, à son gré, une autre version' ['everything happens as though, after having imposed a narrative on his reader, [Maupassant] then forces him to rebuild, according to his own will, another version'].[40] I do not read 'à son gré' here as indicative of a pleasingly liberated free will — rather, it reflects a discomfiting absence of guidance. Maupassant places the overwhelming burden of interpretation in the reader's hands.

Furthermore, the reader is never allowed to forget the presence of this narrative frame. The love story in 'En voyage' is recounted by one of the characters in the frame narrative, but as he had no personal involvement in the events of the embedded narrative it is couched in a detached third person. However, part way through the reader comes across an apparently throw-away interjection: 'le docteur se tut une seconde, puis reprit' ['the doctor was silent for a second, and then resumed'] (*CN*, I.814/II.102). This adds little to the plot of the embedded narrative, it tells the reader nothing about how the frame-audience reacts to the story, and it gives the reader no advice as to how he should react. All it achieves is to undo any illusion of transparency as we gaze through the window of the narrative; it frustrates our desire to enter into and engage with the embedded narrative. Such interjections block our path, like the glass panes which restrain the bourgeois women of Caillebotte's *Intérieur* and many of Berthe Morisot's paintings (as discussed in Chapter One). If text here mimics the window, then it is text which stands between us and our desire to fling ourselves out into the world of the embedded narrative — a leap which would destroy both the integrity of the text and the reader's relationship to it. Thus this reiteration of the presence of the frame in 'En voyage' strengths the barrier between reader and embedded narrative and refuses us passage; notably, in this case, it refuses passage into a world of romantic fantasy, and instead allows frustration and constraint to persist. Escapism, we learn from this, is by no means Maupassant's mission.

As well as borrowing the shape of the window for the shape of the narrative, Maupassant also makes the reader imitate the actions of his ill-fated male characters — particularly the repetitiveness of their behaviours and rituals. Many male characters who have breakdowns rely, prior to the moment of crisis, on looking repeatedly at their image in the looking-glass to confirm and reaffirm their identity.

Indeed, repetition is often seen by psychoanalysis as a side-effect of repressing traumatic memories beyond the reach of the conscious mind.[41] Such repetition is mimicked by Maupassant's texts. Across Maupassant's corpus of short stories, he has a tendency to use the same title for more than one tale,[42] and a number of plot segments appear in more than one story.[43] The reader therefore finds himself repeating the same acts of reading and interpretation on two or more occasions. However, just like the man at the mirror within the stories, the reader is left with a sense of uncertainty rather than affirmation when the double is revealed to be nearly what was expected, but not quite. The variations in length between versions, the presence or absence of narrative frames, and the contrast between acerbic or jovial tones in parallel tales all prompt the disconcerting question of whether the reader may have read wrongly the first time around.

'Lettre d'un fou' demonstrates just how unreliable repetition is as a means of repressing traumatic memories or knowledge. Repetition occurs at every level of this text. First, the narrator's daily life entails a number of ritualistic habits which one day, all of a sudden, cease to provide reassurance. The day begins like any other; he has all the same furniture in all the same places, and we are told that he looks into his mirror 'comme tous les jours' ['like every day'] (*CN*, II.465). Yet this ritualization turns against him when the 'haunting' events enter into his repetitious routine. The strange noise occurs repeatedly at 9:22pm three days in a row (*CN*, II.466), and the Invisible manifests itself, not by being coerced into being seen (which would leave the male character visually dominant), but by interrupting the narrator's routine glances in the mirror — leaving the narrator unseen. Secondly, there is repetition at an intertextual level. There is a parity here between this and other titles which announce the story of a madman: 'Fou?' ['Mad?'], 'Un fou?' ['A Madman?'], and the more affirmative 'Un fou' ['Madman'].[44] Additionally, there is intertextual repetition linking 'Lettre d'un fou' with other tales in which the protagonist tries to assuage their psychological anguish with repeated visits to the mirror — as we witness in 'Promenade', 'L'Enfant', 'Mme Hermet', both versions of 'Le Horla', 'Un lâche', 'Yvette', 'Monsieur Parent', 'Fini', and 'La Morte'.

Thirdly, as his breakdown approaches repetition filters into the narrator's use of language — notably, the repetition of the personal pronoun *je*. At the moment when the narrator's sanity and his hold on selfhood are at their most fragile, there is a sudden insistence on the pronoun *je*. In the page and a half it takes to narrate his crisis in front of the mirror, *je* appears forty-one times. This excessive repetition highlights the open, untenable nature of this signifier and of selfhood. It is simultaneously the most personal and most public of words; it paradoxically indicates 'my' uniqueness for every speaking subject. As the narrator's selfhood wavers, his *je* becomes increasingly generic through this extensive repetition, until his reflection in the mirror finally disappears. Then, *je* is robbed of its identity; it is reduced to a direct object pronoun when the narrative declares that 'il *me* cachait' ['he was hiding *me*'] (*CN*, I.466 — my emphasis). The narrator becomes what Genette terms 'un moi sans fond, un moi sans moi, soit à peu près le contraire de ce que l'on a coutume d'appeler un *sujet*' ['a self without foundation, a self without self, that is more or less the opposite of what we would conventionally call a *subject*'].[45]

Glass and text also join forces to augment the reader's anxiety, and parallels are established between glass objects and textual objects within the narratives. In 'Un lâche', Signoles's fear begins to take root when he is confronted by the lack of information and surplus of white space on the visiting card of his adversary. This is troubling in part because it echoes the pallor of Signoles's own distressingly white reflection in the mirror — 'il était pâle, certes, il était pâle, très pale' ['he was pale; yes, without doubt, he was pale, very pale'] (*CN*, I.1162/II.462). This interconnection between distressing glass and distressing text makes the reader examine his own experience of these stories, and to ask what the blanks on the page and the blanks in his understanding might imply for his own sense of selfhood.

Glass objects and distressing text are also elided in 'L'Ermite' ['The Hermit'] (1886). This is the story of a man who has accidentally committed incest with a daughter he never knew existed. He only becomes aware of what he has done when he finds his old glass daguerreotype among the glass objects littering her mantelpiece:

> Je m'avançai vers la cheminée afin d'y déposer le cadeau réglementaire, après avoir pris jour pour une seconde entrevue avec la fillette, qui demeurait au lit; je vis vaguement une pendule sous globe, deux vases de fleurs et deux photographies dont l'une très ancienne, une de ces épreuves sur verre appelées daguerreotypes. (*CN*, II.689)

> [I walked towards her mantel-shelf to deposit thereon the usual present. I had arranged a day for a second interview with the little wench, who was still lying in bed. I saw dimly under a glass case, two vases of flowers, and two photographs, one of which was very old, one of those negatives on glass called daguerrotypes. (II.779)]

This devastating realization leads not to the shattering of glasses, as in 'Le Port', but to the shattering of the text; thereafter, ellipses are scattered across this short story, particularly at all the key moments of psychological distress. For example, as the hermit begins to avow his deed ('Puis...je ne l'ai dit jamais à personne... jamais... et je voudrais savoir... une fois... ce qu'en pense un autre...' ['And besides... I have never told anyone... never... and I should like to know... just once... how it struck another person'], *CN*, II.687/II.777); as he discovers his photograph from yesteryear in her bedroom ('je me penchai, par hasard, vers ce portrait, et je demeurai interdit, trop surprise pour comprendre... C'était le mien, le premier de mes portraits...' ['I bent casually to look at this portrait, and I stood there paralysed, too surprised to understand... It was myself, my first portrait'], *CN*, II.689/II.779); as he acknowledges the act of incest to himself ('Ma fille!...' ['My daughter...'], *CN*, II.690/II.780); and as he retreats from society into his hermitage ('j'ai trouvé ce mont et je m'y suis arrêté... jusqu'à quand... je l'ignore!' ['I found this hill and stopped here... until when... I have no idea!', *CN*, II.691/II.781 — translation adapted). This juxtaposition of the set of glass objects on the mantelshelf and subsequent sets of ellipses draws an analogy between the troubling role of glass as material object and of ellipses as textual object for Maupassant. Like glass, an ellipsis is transparent; its presence is visible, but it seems to add nothing to its surroundings, and so destabilizes the text's readability with its lack of clear meaning.

This correlation between glass and text in Maupassant's aesthetic of anxiety is cemented in Maupassant's most famous tale of lost selfhood, 'Le Horla'. Philip Hadlock's comprehensive psychoanalytical study of 'Le Horla' (1886 version) discusses the ramifications of madness for both the narrative process and the individual masculine self.[46] Hadlock asserts that this identity crisis is the result of the male narrator being forced to choose between his specular image in the looking-glass — inscribed within the imaginary — and the language in which he writes in his diary — inscribed in the symbolic. Hadlock proposes that the narrator passes for one brief moment from the comforting delusions of the imaginary into the pure symbolic, and so experiences the madness of being utterly rent from his ego. Following this traumatic experience, the narrator seeks a less distressing relationship with the symbolic by placing himself in an asylum where there is no risk of being confronted with his specular image — or, rather, the lack thereof.

Whilst this argument is compelling, Hadlock passes over the role played by glass objects in this crisis. Hadlock states that Le Horla is a manifestation of the phallic, that which is 'always *already* known, and always *already* there as a precondition to and not a result of storytelling (and which has no referent)';[47] yet the empty mirror could just as easily evince the *never already* known beyond both the imaginary and the symbolic. The phallic has positive overtones as the ultimate super-signifier to which all language aspires, but Le Horla could equally be a manifestation of the negative absence of any possible signification. How, therefore, can the reader know whether the diarist is overcome by an absolute immersion into the symbolic (as Hadlock implies), or by absolute *exclusion* from it through a sudden revelation of — to pursue Hadlock's Lacanian terminology — the Real? Both the phallic and this 'anti-phallic' would inevitably manifest themselves by a similar degree of ineffability. However, as we have seen, glass and mirrors have little aptitude for fostering the imaginary in Maupassant's narrative universe. Thus I would contend that Le Horla is not a manifestation of the phallic blocking out the imaginary of the looking-glass, but that it is a manifestation of the lack *inherent in the looking-glass itself.* Therefore Hadlock's conclusion — that the narrator seeks refuge in the asylum to live in the symbolic without the anxieties of the specular image — needs attenuating. Rather than a choice between the imaginary realm of specular images and the symbolic realm of language, I see this retreat to the asylum as an attempt to avoid further contact with the Real which lurks within glass. The asylum in this narrative, unlike a number of others in Maupassant's short stories, remains a specifically glass-free environment.

The distress inflicted upon characters within the texts by glass, and the distress inflicted upon the reader by the glass-like qualities of the diegesis are drawn together in 'La Petite Roque' ['Little Roque'] (1885). Glass window panes are again at the centre of this narrative of trauma. Armstrong sees the 'hiatus of the window' as '*the* disputed space of the century' owing to the uneven power positions it establishes between subject and object.[48] Here, however, the Mayor finds that the fundamental dispute at the window is not one between two social classes — his sexual domination of the little peasant girl was almost effortless — but between the man and his own psyche. It is at the window pane that the Mayor must finally confront his repressed guilt. Indeed, the impulse for the repressed to return is so strong that the Mayor feels drawn to the window; first visually as 'la fenêtre sollicitait son regard' ['the window was tempting him to lift his eyes'], then physically as '[il] colla avidement sa face contre le vitre' ['avidly glued his forehead against the window'] (*CN*, II.642/II.641 — translation adapted). This attraction renews itself every night and, repeatedly, 'une force irrésistible le soulevait et le poussait à sa vitre' ['an irresistible force [...] thrust him to the window'] (*CN*, II.643/II.641). The Mayor finds that the window 'faisait une sorte de trou sombre attirant, redoutable' ['looked like a shadowy hole opening on to the darkened country-side; it fascinated and terrified him'] (*CN*, II.642–43/II.640). These horribly attractive panes evoke Kristeva's concept of the abject, which she describes as being that which is 'radicalement un exclu et me tire vers là où le sens s'effondre' ['radically excluded and which draws me towards that place where meaning collapses'];[49] the abject window both draws and repels, indicating that the Mayor's grip upon meaning, too, will finally collapse here at the window.

Moreover, 'La Petite Roque' explicitly links the sheet of glass with *the sheet of text*. During the Mayor's night horrors, the darkness of the window appears to him as 'encre luisante' ['gleaming ink'] (*CN*, II.642/II.639). This inkiness is indicative of unwritten, potential text; the ink seems to sit in the pane of glass as though it were waiting to be formed into letters, to be brought out of the abject, and to be conceptualized in language. This ink forms a stark contrast to the *clarté* of Petite Roque's 'ghost'. Indeed, her brightness apparently shining through the dark ink of the window parallels the role of the ellipses discussed above. The bright 'ghost' (as a manifestation of the Mayor's repressed guilt) shines brightly through the inky blackness; the ever-present blank sheet of paper (and its void of meaning) shines through from behind the ellipsis. The abject transmits the Mayor's fears into an anxiety of reading.

Although the 'encre luisante' metaphor seems to suggest that the Mayor might be able to transform his night horrors into text and thus make sense of them, the abject nature of the window renders this impossible. In the presence of the abject, textualization 'ne paraîtra soutenable qu'à la condition de se confronter sans cesse à cet ailleurs, poids repoussant et repoussé, fond de mémoire inaccessible et intime' ['seem[s] tenable only if it ceaselessly confronts that otherness, a burden both repellent and repelled, a deep well of memory that is unapproachable and intimate'].[50] If the Mayor were to try to textualize these events, then it would only result in a ceaseless confrontation with his guilt. This is certainly the case when the Mayor tries to expunge his terror by writing a confessional letter; although he ostensibly succeeds in translating the 'encre luisante' into physical writing and feels 'calme, [...] délivré, sauvé!' ['calm, liberated, saved!'] (*CN*, II.647/II.645), when day breaks it becomes clear that he was mistaken. Like a Purloined Letter, neither the blank page nor language is ever really his to possess or control,[51] as becomes apparent when the postman Médéric absolutely insists on delivering his letter to the magistrate. As the Mayor realizes the impossibility of regaining control, he finally resolves upon suicide — choosing, significantly, to break the window's hallucinatory force by opening it and jumping through the vacant space, defying its control of the aperture. Neither the apparently clear window nor the apparently simple short story are as transparent as they initially seem here. The reader is unavoidably reminded that, behind the ostensibly meaningful ink, there is a void of meaninglessness which is always ready to return.

★ ★ ★ ★ ★

Through Maupassant's consistently disconcerting play on mirrors, windows, photographs and photographic lenses, drinking glasses, and other glass objects in his short stories, glass, like Kristeva's abject, becomes 'un "quelque chose" que je ne reconnais pas comme chose. Un poid de non-sens qui n'a rien d'insignifiant et qui m'écrase' ['a "something" that I do not recognize as a thing. A weight of nonsense, which is far from insignificant, and which crushes me'].[52] I have suggested here that in Maupassant's texts, glass is balanced on the boundary between illusion and disillusionment. Glass, despite its apparent purity and transparency, carries with it distressing reminders of the fragile illusions from which the self, masculinity, and patriarchy are woven. And when text itself in many of Maupassant's horror stories becomes abject, the reader is implicated by extension, to pursue the Kristevan terminology, as the *deject*. For Kristeva, the deject (in French, 'le jeté' or 'l'égaré'), is the other necessary to the existence of the abject, the one '[qui] *erre*, au lieu de se reconnaître' ['who *strays* instead of finding himself'], the one for whom the abject is 'une *terre d'oubli* constamment remémorée [...] [où] la cendre de l'oubli fait maintenant paravent et réfléchit l'aversion, la répugnance' ['a *land of oblivion* that is constantly remembered [where] the ashes of oblivion now serve as a screen and reflect aversion, repugnance'].[53] We see these preoccupations in the experience of Maupassant's deject reader, who seeks a subject position but strays instead of finding one, and who is harassed by a text which reflects distressing, repressed memories of unknowable identity, gender, and reading positions; of uncertain boundaries, ellipses, and ambiguous meanings.

What can the reader possibly gain from this unsettling, vexatious experience of reading? What could possibly entice him to persist under such an assault on his sense of identity and on his mastery of language — especially when the often realist style of the writing seems at first to promise clear, reassuring conceptualization? It is, paradoxically, due to the external stresses on masculine, bourgeois identity in society after 1871 that Maupassant's attacks on the self could in fact be appealing. A *lisible* text, pleasurable in its 'pratique confortable de la lecture' ['comfortable style of reading'] may be reassuring for an ego which already has reasonably strong foundations — it may bolster a self whose illusions are already sufficiently intact that they may simply be augmented further.[54] But at a time when national identity, class identity, and gender identity were all being forcibly redefined, the illusions on which the masculine self had rested were becoming unreliable. In this context, Maupassant's glass-freighted and glass-mimicking texts encourage the reader to *accept* a radical abdication of selfhood. This is initially distressing, but may ultimately produce the most acute of cathartic pleasures. If the reader embraces this loss of selfhood, he may experience the 'jouissance [...] [dans] la perte abrupte de la socialité' ['*jouissance* in the abrupt loss of socialization'].[55] Kristeva suggests that the *jouissance* specific to abjection is defined by 'l'ambigu, le mixte' ['the ambiguous, the composite'];[56] thus, in throwing himself into Maupassant's ambiguous, composite literature, and in accepting a dejected readerly role, the reader may gain a rare glimpse of this kernel of exquisite *jouissance*. An odd sort of pleasure this may seem, but by embracing the troubling nature of Maupassant's aesthetics and facing its challenges, the reader may experience an intense catharsis which will take him beyond the harrowing uncertainties of the *année terrible* generation.

Notes to Chapter 3

1. 'La Morte', *CN*, II.940/III.579.
2. A. Maugars, *Miroir de l'enfance* (Paris: n. pub., 1851).
3. Alexis Dalès, *La Clé d'or des époux, ou les Vœux du poète, suivie du Miroir de la femme parfaite, poésies* (Paris: n. pub., 1861).
4. M. l'Abbé Petit, *Petit Miroir du dix-neuvième siècle* (La Rochelle: n. pub., 1862).
5. Mark S. Micale, *Hysterical Men: The Hidden History of Male Nervous Illness* (Cambridge, MA: Harvard University Press, 2008).
6. Speech by Jules Favre, reported in *Journal officiel de la République française*, 31 October 1870, p. 1673.
7. Bell, p. 203.
8. Ibid., p. 188.
9. Hannah Thompson, 'A Battle in the Feminine? The Gendered Body and the Franco-Prussian War', in *Visions/Revisions: Essays on Nineteenth-Century French Culture*, ed. by Nigel Harkness (Bern: Peter Lang, 2003), pp. 157–73 (pp. 157–58).
10. I suggest that it is specifically on the male reader who considers himself a subject that the affects of the texts discussed in this chapter have an impact. It is probable that those readers who were politically, socially, and linguistically disenfranchised to the status of object in patriarchy, such as women and homosexuals, would experience these texts differently. An analysis of these texts as experienced by objectified readers offers an interesting topic for future research; however, restrictions of space have led the present study to focus exclusively on the influence that these texts have upon the reading subject.
11. 'Quelques soldats, après avoir pris un très-modeste repas dans un restaurant situé sur le cours Charlemagne, à la sortie du tunnel, voulurent régler leur dépense; le propriétaire de l'établissement leur demanda environ 3 francs par tête. Les soldats ayant déclaré qu'ils ne se laisseraient pas rançonner ainsi, X... s'approcha de l'un d'eux et lui asséna sur la tête un coup de bouteille; puis, la bouteille s'étant brisée, il lui porta un second coup avec le tesson resté entre ses mains. La victime s'affaissa aussitôt, baignée dans son sang, et X... rentra chez lui pour aller se cacher dans une cave' ['Some soldiers, having eaten a very light meal at a restaurant on the Cours Charlemagne at the exit of the tunnel, wanted to settle their bill; the proprietor of the establishment asked for about 3 francs per head. After the soldiers had declared that they would not let themselves be held to ransom in that way, X... approached one of them and struck him a blow on the head with a bottle; then, the bottle having broken, he dealt him another blow with the shard which remained in his hands. The victim collapsed immediately, bathed in his own blood, and X... retreated into his house to hide in a cellar'] ('Nouvelles et fait divers', *La Revue parisienne*, 6 August 1870, p. 2).
12. 'Deux garçons de cet hôtel vivaient depuis longtemps en mauvaise intelligence. L'un d'eux, Froissardey, qui est Français, reprochait à l'autre, nommé Boëssler, d'être Allemand. [...] Hier soir [...] la discussion recommença. Elle prit même des proportions si vives, qu'un jeune garçon qui était avec eux crut devoir aller prévenir le patron, M. Stuttel, en le priant d'intervenir. M. Stuttel se rendit à la cuisine. Mais au moment où il arrivait, Froissardey se précipitait tout sanglant dans la rue au grand effroi des passants et des voisins. Boëssler venait de lui broyer un verre à pied sur la tempe droite. [...] Le verre — que nous avons vu à l'hôtel — était broyé en petit morceaux et couvert de sang. Ces débris ont été emportés, devant nous, par M. le

commissaire de police, comme pièces à conviction' ['Two waiters from this hotel had been on poor terms for some time. One of them, Froissardey, a Frenchman, reproached the other, named Boëssler, for being German. [...] Yesterday evening [...] the argument began again. It became so lively that a young waiter who was with them thought it necessary to alert the owner, Monsieur Stuttel, and to beg him to intervene. Monsieur Stuttel went to the kitchen. But at the moment he arrived, Froissardey lurched into the street, covered in blood, to the great horror of passers-by and the neighbours. Boëssler had just crushed a wine glass on his right temple. [...] The glass — which we saw at the hotel — was crushed into small pieces and covered in blood. These remnants were taken away, in front of us, to Monsieur the Chief of Police as evidence'] (*L'État*, 1 May 1873).

13. Du Saulle, *Le Délire des persécutions*, p. 206.
14. Jacques Lacan, *The Seminar. Book I*, ed. by Jacques-Alain Miller, trans. by John Forrester (New York: Norton, 1988), p. 92.
15. Elizabeth Grosz, *Jacques Lacan: A Feminist Introduction* (London and New York: Routledge, 1990), p. 41.
16. This brings to mind Flaubert's more satirical scene of male bourgeois vanity, as Bouvard admires himself in the looking-glass: 'Bouvard se considéra dans la glace. Ses pommettes gardaient leurs couleurs, ses cheveux frisaient comme autrefois, pas une dent n'avait bougé, et, à l'idée qu'il pouvait plaire, il eut un retour de jeunesse' ['Bouvard contemplated himself in the mirror. His cheeks had kept their colour, his hair still curled as it used to, not a single tooth had moved, and, at the idea that he might still be desirable, he had a resurgence of youthfulness'] (*Bouvard et Pécuchet*, in *Œuvres complètes*, V, p. 178).
17. 'Chronique du mois', *La Mode nouvelle et Miroir parisien*, December 1871, p. 291.
18. Susan Sontag, *On Photography* (London and New York: Penguin, 1977), p. 70.
19. Henrivaux, pp. 12–13.
20. Slavoj Žižek, 'The Fetish of the Party', in *Lacan, Politics, Aesthetics*, ed. by Willy Apollon and Richard Feldstein (Albany, NY: State University of New York Press, 1996), pp. 3–29 (p. 6).
21. As well as those tales discussed here, other tales of (inevitably unfortunate) fetishists include: 'Vieux objets' (1882), where an old lady remains miserable in the absence of her loved ones and attempts to replace them with an array of objects from her past; 'Pétition d'un Viveur malgré lui' (1882), in which a bitter and presumably impotent old man tries to soothe his desire for a love affair with a box of love tokens from the past; and 'Adieu' ['Farewell'] (1884), in which a young man adores a married lady and tries to compensate for her inaccessibility by worshipping her veil, her gloves, her dresses, and her hats — not unlike Flaubert's Frédéric in *L'Education sentimentale*.
22. *Catalogue-almanach du Musée Grévin* (Paris: n. pub., n.d. [1883?]), p. 19.
23. A masculine desire for woman on the basis of her role as a narcissistic mirror is hinted at further when women are found desirable for their 'soupçon de moustache' in 'Yvette' (*CN*, II.242/II.222) and in 'L'Inconnue' (*CN*, II.443/II.577). It makes the male reader conscious of the fact that, as Elizabeth and Edmond Wright state in their discussion of Žižek, '"masculine" and "feminine" are not the two species of the genus of man, but, rather, the two modes of the subject's failure to achieve the *full* identity of Man. "Man" and "woman" together do not form a whole, *since each of them is already itself a failed whole*' (*The Žižek Reader*, ed. by Elizabeth Wright and Edmond Wright (Oxford: Blackwell, 1999), p. 145).
24. Edmond de Goncourt, *Chérie*, ed. by Jean-Louis Cabanès and Philippe Hamon (Jaignes: La Chasse au Snark, 2002), p. 151.
25. Paul Bonnetain, 'Les Enfants', in *Les Types de Paris*, ed. by Jean-François Raffaëlli (Paris: Editions du Figaro, 1889), pp. 55–64 (pp. 62–63).
26. Huart and Draner, *Guide comique*, pp. 47–48.
27. In spite of judging that her husband's very active sex life before (only before?) their marriage is 'dégoûtant, quand on y pense... toutes ces femmes... nues... et toujours... toujours la même chose... Oh! que c'est dégoûtant tout de même, plus de cent femmes!' ['revolting, when you think of it... all those women... naked... and always the same thing. Oh, how revolting it is, all the same, more than a hundred women!'], she nonetheless goes on to ask far more questions than any apparently disgusted woman should. She asks about his previous partners' sexual

hygiene only to declare 'Oh! Tais-toi, tu me révoltes...' ['Oh, be quiet, you disgust me']. She asks whether he preferred prostitutes or other loose women and replies 'Oh! Que tu es sale!' ['Oh, what nasty tastes you have!']. She asks why he preferred prostitutes before she cries, 'Tu es abominable, sais-tu?' ['You really are detestable, you know'], and then she fires a rapid (and distinctly unrevolted) string of extremely curious questions about his experiences of various women's bodies (*CN*, II.552–53/II.599–600).

28. *The Complete Short Stories* does not include a translation of this short story, thus all translations of the text will be my own.
29. For example, *La Vie parisienne* published this physiologie of the Prussian soldier: 'Rien d'amusant à voir comme un officier allemand mettant sa coiffure devant quelque glace, ou donnant un pli à sa moustache devant la devanture d'un magasin... Cela dure un temps infini, et il y a dans le geste une telle confiance, une si adorable fatuité, une si grande assurance de succès inévitables, qu'il y a vraiment de quoi rire' ['Nothing is as amusing as seeing a German officer fixing his hairstyle in some mirror, or reshaping his moustache in a shop window... It takes an infinity, and there is something in that gesture of such confidence, of such adorable smugness, of such great certainty of inevitable successes, that it is really laughable'] ('Le chic allemand et le chic français', 29 July 1871, p. 786). A later edition pronounced a succinct judgment upon women active in politics (by implication, left-wing politics) such as Louise Michel, stating that 'la femme politique n'arrive guère à autre chose qu'à faire douter de son sexe' ['the political woman achieves hardly anything except rendering questionable her sex'] (11 November 1871, p. 1035).
30. Thompson, p. 169.
31. Guy de Maupassant, *Chroniques*, ed. by Hubert Juin, 3 vols (Paris: Union Générale d'Editions, 1980), II, p. 431.
32. Maupassant, *Sur l'eau; Blanc et Bleu; Livre du bord*, p. 80, my emphasis.
33. Maupassant, *Chroniques*, II, p. 132, my emphasis.
34. Charles Baudelaire, 'Le Peintre de la vie moderne', in *Œuvres complètes*, II, pp. 683–724 (p. 692).
35. Framed narratives with two disparate *je* include: 'Après', 'Auprès d'un mort', 'Un bandit corse', 'Un cas de divorce', 'Ce cochon de Morin', 'Clochette', 'L'Epave', 'L'Ermite', 'Le Fermier', 'Le Garde', 'Une lettre', 'Le Loup', 'Madame Baptiste', 'Madame Hermet', 'Madame Parisse', 'La Mère aux monstres', 'Mes vingt-cinq jours', 'Miss Harriet', 'Mohammed-Fripouille', 'Moiron', 'Mon Oncle Jules', 'Un normand', 'Nos anglais', 'L'Odysée d'une fille', 'L'Orient', 'Le Père', 'La Peur' (1882), 'La Peur' (1884), 'Sur l'eau', and 'Le Testament'.
36. Roland Barthes, 'La Mort de l'auteur', in *Œuvres complètes*, II, p. 495.
37. Stendhal, *Le Rouge et le Noir*, p. 414.
38. Angela Moger, 'Narrative Structure in Maupassant: Frames of Desire', *PMLA*, 100:3 (1985), 315–27 (p. 324).
39. John Moreau, 'Maupassant's Empty Frame: A New Look at "Boule de Suif"', *French Forum*, 34:2 (2009), 1–16 (p. 2).
40. In the notes to Maupassant, *Contes et nouvelles*, II, p. 1610.
41. It is a basic principle of Freudian psychoanalysis that a person repeats something because he has forgotten the origins of the compulsion, and that repetitive actions form the counterpoint of remembrance (see *Beyond the Pleasure Principle*, in *Standard Edition of the Complete Pscycrological Works of Sigmund Freud*, trans. and ed. by James Strachey, 24 vols (London: Hogarth Press, 1955), XVIII, p. 7).
42. Repeated titles include: 'Le Baptême' (*CN*, I.1144 and II.436); 'La Bécasse'/'Les Bécasses' (*CN*, I.666 and II.563); 'Clair de lune' (*CN*, I.473 and I.594); 'La Confession' (*CN*, I.1035, II.218, and II.371); 'L'Enfant' (*CN*, I.483 and I.981); 'En voyage' (*CN*, I.431 and I.810); 'L'Epave'/'Epaves' (*CN*, II.657 and I.324); 'L'Epingle'/'Les Epingles' (*CN*, II.519 and II.1011); 'Fou?'/'Un Fou?'/'Un Fou' (*CN*, I.522, II.308, and II.540); 'Le Père' (*CN*, I.1071 and II.975); 'La Peur' (*CN*, I.600 and II.198); 'Rencontre' (*CN*, I.440 and I.1231); 'Souvenir'/'Souvenir'/'Souvenirs' (*CN*, I.362, II.120, and I.1251); 'Une Soirée' (*CN*, I.987 and II.895).
43. Parallel narratives include: 'L'Aveugle'/'Le Gueux' (*CN*, I.402 and I.1225); 'Yveline Samoris'/'Yvette' (*CN*, I.684 and II.234); 'Un million'/'L'Héritage' (*CN*, I.614 and II.3); 'Le Père Mongilet'/elements of 'Les Dimanches d'un bourgeois de Paris' (*CN*, II.467 and I.122); 'Pétition

d'un viveur malgré lui'/'Une Passion' (*CN*, I.342 and I.515); 'Le Horla'(1886 version)/'Le Horla'(1887 version) (*CN*, II.822 and II.913); 'Le Legs' (*CN*, II.341/ Part II, Chapter 4 in *Bel-Ami* (in *Romans*, ed. by Louis Forestier (Paris: Gallimard, 1987), pp. 423–32)).

44. 'Fou?' exemplifies the failure of repetition at the linguistic level. The word 'fou' itself is repeated to the point of exhaustion in this tale. The narrator asks 'Suis-je *fou*? Ou seulement jaloux? Je n'en sais rien mais j'ai souffert horriblement. J'ai accompli un acte de *folie*, de *folie* furieuse', 'Je ne suis pas *fou*' (I.522); 'je *fus* jaloux avec frénésie; mais je ne suis pas *fou*, non, certes, non' (I.523); 'Suis-je *fou*? — Non', 'Je ne suis pas *fou*. Je le jure, je ne suis pas *fou*!'; 'Dites-moi, suis-je *fou*?' (I.524) ['Am I mad? Or just jealous? I have no idea, but I have suffered horribly. I have carried out an act of madness, of delirious madness'; 'I am not mad'; 'I was frenetically jealous; but I am not mad, no, certainly, no'; 'Am I mad? –No, I am not mad. I swear it, I am not mad!'; 'Tell me, am I mad?' (*CN*, I.526 — my emphases and translation throughout). This is exacerbated by the phonetically and/or semantically linked words in this passage — *folie, furieuse, fus, frénésie*. Obsessive and excessive repetition empties the word 'fou' of all sense — which, given that it signifies 'madness', always gestured towards non-sense.
45. Gérard Genette, *Figures II* (Paris: Seuil, 1969), p. 14.
46. Philip Hadlock, 'Telling Madness and Masculinity in Maupassant's "Le Horla"', *L'Esprit Créateur*, 43:3 (2003), 47–56.
47. Ibid., p. 53.
48. Armstrong, p. 7.
49. Julia Kristeva, *Pouvoirs de l'horreur: Essai sur l'abjection* (Paris: Seuil, 1980), p. 9.
50. Ibid., p. 14, my emphasis.
51. Man's inability to possess text is reflected in the strange capacity of texts to outlive their writers in Maupassant's texts, surviving the ravages of time (for example, the letters from the past which drive Robert to kill himself in 'Suicides') and, in the case of 'Lettre trouvée sur un noyé' ['Letter found on a drowned man'], even surviving lengthy immersion in water (although the Seine drowns its writer, the suicide note found on the body remains perfectly — if implausibly — legible).
52. Kristeva, *Pouvoirs de l'horreur*, p. 10.
53. Ibid., pp. 15–16.
54. Roland Barthes, *Le Plaisir du texte*, in *Œuvres complètes*, II, p. 1501.
55. Ibid., p. 1503.
56. Kristeva, *Pouvoirs de l'horreur*, p. 12.

CHAPTER 4

The Ideal Naturalist? Glass, Popular Culture, and Naturalism in Huysmans's *À rebours*

> Les goûts, les habitudes, les mœurs de l'homme se trahissent dans la maison qu'il se fait.
>
> [A man's tastes, habits, and customs are all betrayed by the home he makes for himself]
>
> VIOLLET-LE-DUC, *Habitations modernes* [*Modern Dwellings*]¹

The ultimate Decadent novel: this is the epithet most often applied to *À rebours* (1884).² Yet the concept of Decadence entails an inherent paradox. Whilst a period of Decadence is considered quintessentially, even threateningly modern to those contemporaneous with it, Decadence also entails a *rejection* of dominant social trends. Decadence is parasitic upon the mainstream; without the concept of the banal norm, there would be nothing from which Decadence could carve out its counter-culture, and Huysmans's *À rebours* is no exception. It is in constant conversation with the norms of popular culture — and particularly material culture — in order to forge its own particular aesthetic. Glass, as one of the materials par excellence of nineteenth-century mainstream society, is integral to this aesthetic operation, and it often plays a key narrative, symbolic, and stylistic role in this novel. It is never passive or transparent, as it at first appears to be to Zola's shoppers or Maupassant's men on the verge of a nervous breakdown. Instead, the numerous windows, glass liqueur bottles, glass perfume bottles, drinking glasses, optometric glasses, display cabinets, and shop windows all exist only to play an active, intentional part in *À rebours*'s reconfiguration of literary modernity.

Contrary to first appearances for today's reader, a reading of *À rebours* alongside the popular culture of the period reveals unexpected parallels between Des Esseintes's aesthetics and everyday popular culture. It suggests that, despite the protagonist's protestations, Des Esseintes is purposely located *within* the paradigms of mainstream Republican society. Glass becomes a tool with which to hyperbolize popular culture and literary debates, and to help create a schism between Des Esseintes's bourgeois-inspired aesthetics and Huysmans's avant-garde writing. Indeed, the significance of glass in this shift towards a new literary style is later evoked in Huysmans's 'Préface écrite vingt ans après le roman' ['Preface Written Twenty Years After the Novel'] in the Cent Bibliophiles edition of 1903. After twenty years, six novels, the *fin de siècle*, and his conversion to Catholicism, the author (or at least, his authorial persona) still deliberately evokes vitreous imagery. He compares Naturalism to a stuffy room, like the bourgeois private sphere, which made him yearn to 'ouvrir les fenêtres, [...] fuir un milieu où j'étouffais' ['to open windows, to escape from an atmosphere in which I was stifling'] (*AR*, xxiii/193). The enclosed-room metaphor is also utilized by Durtal in *Là-Bas* [*Damned*], when he declares that Naturalism produces '[des] romans sans portes et sans fenêtres' ['novels without doors or windows']³ — thus making it impossible to assuage that feeling of *étouffement*. The content of *À rebours* is described as 'des spécialités rangées dans les vitrines' ['specialities displayed in the show-cases'] (*AR*, xxiii/192–93), educing the shopping culture and World Fairs which characterized the consumer world.

Glass and material culture not only root Huysmans's work in Third Republic culture generally, but they also orchestrate a number of oblique gestures towards memories of 1870–71; although these historical events are never thematized directly by Huysmans after *Sac au dos* [*Backpack*] (1880), they are allowed to linger in underlying allusions, just as they do in Zola's *Rougon-Macquart*.⁴ For example, the construction site occupied in clearing the charred remains of the Hôtel de Ville forms the backdrop to André's *crise juponnière* in *En ménage* [*Living Together*] (1881). As André seeks a quiet café for his first assignation with Jeanne, readers may be forgiven for being distracted from the protagonist's mediocre desires as they recall the fire, the ruins, and the harrowing photographs or engravings of the town hall's burned-out skeleton, with its rows of blackened window-frames divested of their once-glittering glass panes (*EM*, 235, 239). Indeed, by placing this crisis of André's increasingly bourgeois lifestyle in such close spatial proximity to an evocative symbol of the Republic's crises, this novel draws a correlation between the flaws of the private and the public spheres.

Moreover, it is often glass imagery, specifically, which brings these disquieting remembrances into Huysmans's writing. Ostentatious window displays in *Le Drageoir aux épices* [*A Dish of Spices*] (1874), where 'des pâtissiers étalaient à leurs vitrines des multitudes de gâteaux' ['bakers displayed multitudes of cakes in their windows'] (*DE*, 71), evoke the windows utterly divested of food during the Prussian siege less than four years previously. In *En rade* [*Becalmed*] (1887), glass amplifies the atmosphere of distress felt by Jacques Marles at the Château de Lourps. Jacques's sense of dislocation and despair is exacerbated by uncanny imagery of windows, mirrors, and glass. His nocturnal fears in the chateau seem to revivify memories of that other recent period of horror, with the disquieting 'vitres brisées, [par lesquels] le vent s'engouffrait, remuant l'ombre amoncelée sous la voûte' ['broken windows, through which the wind billowed, shifting the shadows piled below the vaulted roof']; with the 'fenêtres [...] démantibulées, les volets fracturés, recloués à la hâte, bandés par des planches' ['dilapidated windows, fractured shutters, hastily repaired with a few nails, held together with planks']; and with the shattered glass of its library where 'les armoires avaient perdu leurs vitres dont les éclats craquaient sous ses souliers' ['the wardrobes had lost their glass panels, whose shards cracked under foot'] (*ER*, 15, 54, 71). Notably, Jacques's fantasy of a modest little house in the banlieue at the end of the novel, in complete contrast to the chateau, makes no reference to glass at all (*ER*, 122–24). The location of the chateau is also carefully chosen to evoke the recent conflicts: the Seine-et-Marne region had been overrun by the Prussians in September 1870, and recurrent imagery of a sky of flame and fire cannot help but stir memories of the *année terrible*.[5] Further, Huysmans ensures that it is impossible to dissociate the narrative events from the wider cycle of national crises that had defined French life over the preceding century — we are told that the building's state of disrepair dates from the Great Revolution, and the village is situated just eighteen kilometres from Nogent-sur-Seine, the home of Flaubert's protagonist Frédéric Moreau where he periodically retreats during the unrest of 1848.[6]

Huysmans also plants several insidious references to the *année terrible* in *À rebours* — including in his choice of location for Des Esseintes's retreat. The reader familiar with the events of 1870–71 may notice that all of the windows punctuating the Fontenay house face in one direction; they gaze over the Valley d'Auney in the direction from which the Prussians had attacked during the war (*AR*, 91). The *femme bouledogue* of the syphilis nightmare invades Des Esseintes's dreams, shod in 'des demi-bottes de soldat prussien' ['Prussian military half-boots'] (*AR*, 144/78). Although the region may appeal to Des Esseintes for being 'peu ravagé par les Parisiens' ['free from the depredations of the Parisiens'] (*AR*, 13/9), the reader would be all too aware that the hill fort behind Des Esseintes's house was utterly *ravagé* by the Prussians little more than a decade before.

It is significant, however, that the mono-directional windows scrupulously conceal this ruined fort from view for Des Esseintes — and consequently, for most of the novel, for the reader. The Fontenay house literally turns its back upon the ruins of the *année terrible* and on the constant preoccupation with sociopolitical history. Within its walls, glass objects are toyed with to undermine the reader's tendency to focus on the referential quality of words and so on visualizing material culture. On the one hand, this suggests a fatuous denial of the legacy of social problems persisting in French society; and to some extent this criticism is a true assessment of *À rebours*. On the other hand, whatever the ideological merits of engaged writing, Huysmans cannot enjoy the complete freedom he seeks for aesthetic experimentation if his text is simultaneously plagued by the need to represent distressing memories. It would be impossible to lead the reader to a new, quintessentially modern appreciation of textuality if they are preoccupied by recollections of past suffering and destruction.

Of course, *À rebours* is an extremely dense novel, and glass is by no means the only axis around which Huysmans's innovations turn. Issues of gender and sexuality, and of the relationship between the novel and the art world are among other extremely pertinent approaches to this text; and these have been discussed fruitfully elsewhere.[7] In engaging with the role of glass and material culture in this novel, this chapter seeks to take a narrow but novel approach to one facet of Huysmans's literature which has hitherto been overlooked, and which becomes apparent only when the novel is read in conjunction with the cultural-historical significance of glass in the 1880s.

Des Esseintes and Mainstream Material Culture

Rather than Des Esseintes being *à rebours* of the mainstream in the sense that he turns away from the popular culture of bourgeois society, the cultural-historical context of this novel indicates that *À rebours* forges a Decadent stance vis-à-vis popular culture by *turning Des Esseintes towards it*. This is in notable contrast to Des Esseintes's stance whilst living in Paris in the period prior to his sojourn at Fontenay. While surrounded physically by the bourgeois city, he sought expressly to turn dominant social norms *à rebours*, with sexual perversions and inversion, a white instead of a black suit, his disdain for bourgeois beach resorts, a lack of respect for marriage, and his attempt to foster rather than repress working-class crime. However, once at Fontenay and into the present moment of the novel, his desire to go against the grain of the mainstream is clearly defined as belonging to the past and to Des Esseintes's memory.

Instead, Des Esseintes fully embraces mainstream judgments of aesthetic worth at Fontenay. Huysmans uses his protagonist to exaggerate the kind of values to which any bourgeois might aspire if they wish to be admired for their superiority in taste and wealth. However much the upper bourgeoisie might have disdained the petit bourgeoisie, this did not preclude them from being driven by similar values, such as materialism, conspicuous consumption, a valorisation of wealth and property, and a belief in individualizing oneself by way of possessions. Through Des Esseintes, such values are dramatized; this novel conjectures, with tongue in cheek, about what they might become if fulfilled to the utmost.

To some extent, this is recognized by Rosalind Williams, who has noted Des Esseintes's continued adherence to the driving values of consumer culture, through an inversion of mass-market attitudes rather than their rejection — although her discussion makes only cursory mention of any specific physical objects within his Fontenay home.[8] She suggests that *À rebours* is essentially the portrayal of 'a lonely and agonized attempt to salvage the elitist ideal in an age of mass consumption', but that:

> in the final analysis, Des Esseintes himself is unable to evaluate objects independently of their market value. In a reverse way his mode of consumption is just as dependent on the mass market, and just as devoid of individual integrity as that of the butchers' wives. As soon as an item becomes available to the 'common herd', he rejects it, irrespective of its intrinsic merits.[9]

Alina Clej takes a similar approach, noting that bourgeois culture influences Des Esseintes by giving him a set of standards against which to rebel. She concludes that:

> the carefully crafted retreat the hero has built for himself was not strong enough to resist the pressures of the world outside. In the end, Des Esseintes's 'ivory tower' is itself a mirage obsessively defended by the neurotic recluse precisely because it was already 'contaminated' by the 'vulgar' pleasures of the crowd.[10]

Whilst I agree with both Williams and Clej that common, vulgar pleasures are never out of play in *À rebours*, I question whether Des Esseintes actually makes any genuine effort to escape them, by reversal or otherwise. Huysmans shows no evidence of trying to give Des Esseintes ideas so original that they operate a radical break with popular bourgeois culture.

This is apparent in every inclusion of glass and glass objects at Fontenay. Perhaps in the early Second Empire, before consumer culture gained such a hold upon French society, it would have been easier to make a clear distinction between the aesthete and the mainstream shopper; by the 1880s, however, this has become an impossible endeavour. Janell Watson rightly states that 'the furnishings and bibelots of the 1890s have become what Baudrillard might call empty signifiers, signifying fashion itself'.[11] Watson suggests that, because the collector's item had become a stereotypical element of the bourgeois interior, the dandy might re-appropriate the *bibelot* for art because 'the Dandy is not just a leader in matters of fashion and an arbiter of taste, but also a connoisseur of the arts'.[12] Whilst this may be true of the modish man like Beau Brummel before the bourgeoisification of fashionable life, by the 1880s to lead fashion was to engage with the world of mass production, capitalism, department stores, and a culture which prioritized the bourgeoisie over the aristocratic ideals that had once underwritten 'good taste'. The scope of Des Esseintes's ideas is so close to that of mainstream culture that just five years after the publication of *À rebours*, a reviewer of the 1889 World Fair was able to claim that

> nous avions eu cette fantaisie de décadent de réunir devant nous, sur un plateau, toute la série de ces liqueurs succulents en pensant au personnage du roman de J.-K. Huysmans, *À rebours*, qui s'abandonne si voluptueusement [...] à la curiosité des sensations.
>
> [we had this Decadent fantasy to gather before us, on a platter, the whole collection of succulent liqueurs, thinking of the protagonist of Joris-Karl Huysmans's novel *À rebours* who abandons himself so voluptuously to the curiosity of sensation]

without this fantasy seeming outrageous — despite the fact that this writer is visiting the setting *par excellence* of mainstream consumerism.[13]

The apparently avant-garde aquarium at Fontenay is a clear example of the influence of popular culture on Des Esseintes's aesthetics. In Chapter 2 of the novel, we are given a tour of Des Esseintes's dining room, a room within a room, and between its inner and outer walls is set an aquarium populated with mechanical fish. Utterly abstract, we might think; yet none of this is completely original. Although the aquarium room might strike us today as almost worthy of a Jules Verne science fiction novel, all of its elements are drawn from pre-existing ideas and images which would have been familiar in the 1880s. Aquaria were popular features of both the public and private spheres of Third Republic society. By 1872, a wide variety of aquaria were displayed at the *Exposition d'économie doméstique*, suggesting they had already found a place in even the thriftier bourgeois home.[14] A correspondent for the 1878 World Fair commented that 'en 1867, on ne voyait encore que quelques rares aquariums; ces appareils sont aujourd'hui universellement répandus' ['in 1867, one saw very few aquaria; today, these devices are found everywhere'].[15] So much were aquaria associated with the finer side of Parisian life, that Lisa Quenu — one of those butcher's wives whom Des Esseintes claims to abhor — displays an aquarium in her butcher's shop in *Le Ventre de Paris* to tempt in an aspirational clientele. Additionally, Stendhal had already conceived of the idea of a room within a room for Fabrice's prison cell in his hugely popular novel, *La Chartreuse de Parme* [*The Charterhouse of Parma*] (1839). Even the mechanical fish in Des Esseintes's aquarium are not an entirely new idea: one Paris guidebook from 1878 claims to have known 'un gargotier des environs de Paris qui, pour prouver aux personnes soupçonneuses que ses provisions étaient de la première fraîcheur, avait fait fabriquer un homard mécanique' ['an innkeeper in the outskirts of Paris who, to prove to suspicious customers that his produce was as fresh as could be, had a mechanical lobster constructed'].[16] Although the precise combination of all these elements by Des Esseintes is original, the reader would have no difficulty in visualizing them given the context of contemporary popular culture, and they certainly do not reach as far into the realm of the unconventional as we might initially be led to expect.

Material objects such as this aquarium not only shed light literally into Des Esseintes's home, they also shed light metaphorically upon the nature of his preoccupations. In spite of his wealth, Des Esseintes's concerns often differ surprisingly little from those of Huysmans's splenetic bourgeois M. Folantin in *À vau-l'eau* [*With the Flow*] (1882). Like Des Esseintes, Folantin also fills his home with rows of medicine bottles to treat his perpetual, nameless malaise; he contemplates the problem of appetites both sexual and nutritional; he struggles with the difficulty of solitude; and he gets pleasure from interior decoration, albeit on a different scale (*AV*, 11–12, 22–23, 70). The key difference between the two men's preoccupations is one of proportion, not of inherent nature.

Appreciation of art is a quality generally cited as proof of Des Esseintes's superiority over vulgar philistines like Folantin and the bourgeois townsfolk of Fontenay-aux-Roses. Yet his absorption is not without a hint of pseudo-intellectual posturing. After all, Des Esseintes is not able to paint, write, or create for himself and is thus not elevated above the vulgar crowd by any inherent artistic grandeur; he is just a collector, like the eminently bourgeois Bouvard and Pécuchet or Cousin Pons — all of whom are moved emotionally and sensorily by the objects they collect. Des Esseintes certainly does not fit the definition of Octave Uzanne's 'être qui vit par la pensée' ['being who lives on thoughts']; his flame-orange room utterly contradicts Uzanne's stipulation that the man of taste and superior mind 'capitonne sa cage de couleurs moelleuses et assourdies' ['upholsters his cage with soft, muffled colours'], and his priceless books are antithetical to the thinking man '[qui] n'aime pas les choses qui veulent trop être respectées, tels que livres trop luxueux' ['who doesn't like things that demand too much respect, such as overly luxurious books'].[17]

We might question whether Des Esseintes is so very different from the bourgeoisie that he scorns whilst '[elle] trônait, jovial, par la force de son argent et la contagion de sa sottise' ['confident and jovial, [the bourgeoisie] were lording it over their social inferiors through the power of their money and the contagion of their stupidity'] (*AR*, 334/179). Des Esseintes is confident. He lords it over the people of Fontenay through the power of his money. The decisions he makes are, by any rational standards, rather stupid, and his ridiculously exaggerated materialism would indeed prove contagious since the novel quickly became a cult classic. All that he lacks here is joviality. But then, even joyless spleen had become mainstream by 1884; in Christopher Prendergast's discussion of Laforgue's *Derniers Vers*, he notes that 'Laforgue's ironic point is that "ennui" post-Baudelaire has itself become commodity [...]; it has become Boredom, a mere attitude, cheaply purchased and endlessly recycled'.[18] Huysmans himself wrote satirically: 'allez dans les grands magasins du Temps, on vous y détaillera l'article pessimiste en petites boîtes' ['go into the Department Store of Time, they will sell you Pessimism there in little boxes'].[19]

The blurring between Des Esseintes's appreciation of art and his adherence to popular culture is underlined by his medieval furnishings and his stained-glass window. French society was in thrall to a fashionable medieval revival at the *fin de siècle*, inspired by the Musée de Cluny's collections since the 1840s and made fashionable by Viollet-le-Duc's immensely popular *Dictionnaire raisonné du mobilier français de l'époque carolingienne à la Renaissance* [*Annotated Dictionary of French Furniture from the Carolingian Era to the Renaissance*] (1858–1875). Do-it-yourself stained-glass kits became a pleasurable evening pastime for ladies — nay, an essential one, according to one women's magazine: 'Nous avons dû faire emplette, comme étrennes utiles, de tout ce qui peut faire passer agréablement les soirées. Et d'abord, — les boîtes de choses nécessaires à l'imitation des vitraux gothiques ou à fleurs, avec dessins et explications' ['as useful gifts, we have had to stock up on everything that can make an agreeable evening. And above all — kits for imitation gothic or floral windows, with drawings and instructions'].[20] The windows in the curtain pages of the Bon Marché home-furnishings catalogues incorporated stained glass in a quarter of the images from 1881–1885.[21] Emery and Morowitz discuss the growth of this unusually tenacious fashion, tracing how it blossomed in parallel with the need felt by Republican society to glorify a historical period of French cultural dominance after the *année terrible*.[22] This vogue for the gothic taints any apparently asocial collector; the revival of an art form evoking a period of French glory in Europe incorporates subtle nationalist messages for French society in the wake of recent defeat by the Prussians.[23]

At Fontenay, Des Esseintes has 'vitres, craquelées, bleuâtres, parsemées de culs de bouteille aux bosses piquetées d'or' ['casement windows, [with] bluish, crackled panes, studded with bulging, gold-flecked irregularities of bottle glass'] (*AR*, 25–26/15), recalling this trend for stained-glass — and moreover for modernized, stylized, reproduction stained glass. The choice not to include any authentic medieval stained glass at Fontenay is a critical one; it inscribes Des Esseintes in the mainstream, and leads us to doubt how selective he really is about sourcing, at all times, authentic originals. Furthermore, it questions the very concept of the 'original'. Sacred objects such as stained glass had been produced continuously since the medieval era; they were at all times produced in some quantity in France; and they were generally created by anonymous craftsmen. Consequently, unlike a Moreau painting or Redon charcoal, it is hard to speak in definite terms of unique, original products; how can we know whether the 'authentic' triptych in Des Esseintes's house is actually an apprentice's copy of his twelfth-century master's carving? Or a thirteenth-century reproduction of a twelfth-century artefact?

Where does this stop? Is the cut-off for originality of sacred objects the beginning of the Renaissance, or the Reformation, or the Enlightenment, or the Revolution? Just because these items are made by hand, are they still 'mass-produced' to some extent if they are the product of guilds and workshops — and how can we possibly know how many were made, or how many hands contributed to their production line? Des Esseintes does not seem to trouble himself with such problems, leading us to doubt his aesthetic credentials.

The Conservatory, Exhibition, and Consumption

The conservatory of monstrous plants also implies that Des Esseintes remains within mainstream cultural paradigms. Winter gardens, conservatories, hothouses, and greenhouses were all à la mode in the late Second Empire and Third Republic, as an offshoot of the passion for glass and iron architecture. The vast Palais de l'industrie in 1867 and Palais du Champ de Mars in 1878 both glorified glass and iron architecture; their immense glass roofs filled the halls with light, and they created, in combination with miles of glass display cases, a world of glass fit to rival London's Crystal Palace of 1851. Furthermore, glass structures were sufficiently desirable to be erected by the dozen in the exhibition gardens as well. One guidebook in 1867 enumerated glasshouses 'de toutes les grandeurs et de toutes les formes, serres chaudes, serres tempérées, jardins d'hiver, serres françaises, serres hollandaises, serres rustiques, serres adossées, serres à deux versants, avec ou sans pavillon central' ['of all sizes and all shapes, hot houses, temperate houses, winter gardens, French glasshouses, Dutch glasshouses, rustic glasshouses, conservatory glasshouses, with or without a central pavilion'].[24] It later questioned whether the 'usine électro-magnétique' ['electo-magnetic factory'] was more 'une serre à exposition' or 'une exposition de serre' ['an exhibition glasshouse' or 'an exhibited glasshouse'], implying that no matter what the intention, a glass structure always had significant appeal for the visitor.[25]

The hundreds of brochures for the Fairs were often richly illustrated with images of their many glass buildings: for example, the elaborate coffee-table style souvenir book *Exposition universelle* (1878) included a series of engravings of the exhibition, comprising a bird's eye view over the glass roofs, a view of the heavily-glazed façade of the Pavillon de la Ville de Paris, an image of the glazed dome with its stained-glass panels, an image of the exhibition railway station with its glazed halls, and an image of three magnificent hothouses and conservatories of different shapes and sizes.[26] Faced with these marvellous images, those who had not yet attended the Fair might be seduced into buying their ticket, and those who simply could not attend would still have the chance to be dazzled from a distance by such glittering highlights of the event as these. Yet for Huysmans, such glass and iron structures were already banal by 1867 and he dismisses 'cet essai malencontreux, avec ses affreuses toitures vitrées, [qui] ne saurait nous occuper au point de vue artistique' ['this unfortunate experiment, with its dreadful glazed roofs, which cannot interest us from any artistic point of view'].[27]

Not just the exhibition halls, but the profusion of glass architecture from every corner of the new Paris could be evoked by this conservatory at Fontenay; the reader may call to mind the railways stations, Baltard's Halles, the department stores, and the *grandes serres* at the Jardin des Plantes and Jardin de Luxembourg. Also evoked are literary representations of these glass structures in depictions of the new, bourgeois Paris by Naturalist authors. Examples of this are so numerous that they cannot possibly all be listed here — but in the *Rougon-Macquart* novels which were published prior to *À rebours* alone, we find notable glazed buildings in *La Curée* (1872), *Le Ventre de Paris* (1873), *Son Excellence Eugène Rougon* (1876), *Nana* (1880), and *Au Bonheur des Dames* (1883).[28] Consequently, the conservatory episode of *À rebours* conjures an immense body of intertextual glass imagery from popular culture and Naturalist fiction, locating Des Esseintes firmly within the auspices of the modern, bourgeois-centric culture of Paris. Whatever he stocks within this conservatory, he cannot escape the familiar associations of the setting.

It is noticeable that although we are made perfectly aware of the presence of this glass structure at Fontenay, *À rebours* never elaborates upon this with a detailed description. Indeed, we only find out in Chapter 8 that the Fontenay house even possesses a conservatory, despite the otherwise detailed floor plan of the property in Chapter 5. Once its existence has been revealed, neither the proportions of the conservatory, nor the clarity of the glass, nor the view of the land perceived beyond its panes is depicted — a conspicuous absence in a book which usually invests so heavily in exhaustive and exhausting detail. There are only two occasions on which glass structures are directly mentioned at all in Chapter 8 of *À rebours*. These are not at Des Esseintes's own home but, first, in reference to conservatories and hothouses in modern Paris more widely, where one finds 'les fleurs exotiques, exilées à Paris, au chaud, dans des palais de verre' ['exotic flowers exiled in Paris to the warmth of glass palaces'] (*AR*, 132/72), and secondly in reference to the nursery glasshouses, where 'il avait surprises [ces plantes], confondues avec d'autres, ainsi que dans un hôpital, parmi les salles vitrées des serres' ['he had unexpectedly come upon them, mingled in with others as if in some hospital, within the glassed-in wards of the hothouses'] (*AR*, 136/74). Rather than this entailing a denial or rejection of popular culture, it does in fact replicate the descriptive choices made by accounts of the World Fair in 1878. Whereas the glass aspect of the architecture received considerable attention in the official guides to the 1867 Fair, by 1878 glass barely gets mentioned. For example, in an article on the Palais du Champs de Mars, glass is only finally mentioned after fifteen full pages of description, and then only very briefly.[29] Another guide gives a lengthy enumeration of the dimensions of the walkways, a breakdown of the Fair's finances, and details of the volume of visitors, but never mentions glass.[30] Glass was generally relegated to illustration alone; and in the absence of any illustrative plates in the original editions of *À rebours*, it is necessarily the reader's wider familiarity with glass structures, especially those in Paris, which must be drawn upon to vivify Huysmans's text.

Shopping and the consumerism so inextricably associated with the rise of bourgeois culture in nineteenth-century Paris are also evoked in a number of ways by this conservatory episode. As Des Esseintes shops for plants until he drops, he bears more than a passing resemblance to Zola's shopaholic Mme Marty. Des

Esseintes returns from the nurseries 'éreinté, la bourse vide, émerveillé des folies de végétation qu'il avait vues, ne pensant plus qu'aux espèces qu'il avait acquises' ['exhausted, his purse empty, filled with wonder at the vegetative follies he had seen, his mind fixed exclusively, now, on the species he had acquired'] (*AR*, 134/73). We might well detect an ironic tone here in the authorial voice, but there is no suggestion that Des Esseintes himself assumes this attitude with his tongue in his cheek.

It is clearly not the concept of shopping or the pleasures of acquisition which is overturned here. Nor indeed the general category of objects desirable for consumption — Des Esseintes buys plants and, elsewhere, jewels, Persian carpets, and tea, none of which are fancies alien to the mainstream shopper. Watson observes perceptively that Des Esseintes, 'impossibly rich, implausibly refined, believing passionately in the power of possessions, is the implied subject of the most wonderful of retail catalogues'.[31] Des Esseintes merely chooses less usual examples from within utterly predictable categories. His inscription within mainstream consumer culture is underlined in Chapter 8 by Huysmans's decision to have Des Esseintes purchase, specifically, exotic plants. This necessitates display under glass, usually restricted to the shop, continuing to enshrine these purchases even when they have been taken home. The glass creates a prolonged aura of desirability, that exhibition value which is normally lent to products by their glass display cases at the World Fairs and department stores. With it, the dreaming of commerce and capitalism invade the supposedly aesthetic abode.

Purchases of plants and jewels may perhaps be the expected province of a female rather than a male shopper, thus placing Des Esseintes within the blurred gender position of the dandy; however, despite all the sense of superiority and self-justification voiced by collectors such as Edmond de Goncourt, dandyism is more subversive of masculinity than it is of the concept of consumerism. Janell Watson suggests that the difference between the dandy and the mainstream shopper is that 'the decadent dandy makes fashion into an art, while high society makes art into fashion';[32] yet any attempt to discern where fashion stops and art starts is an impossible task. Ultimately, it emphasizes that the aesthetic consumer is on precisely the same spectrum of consumption and consumer desire as the mainstream bourgeois shopper. Victor Champier paid heed to this in his remark of 1883 that

> la passion de notre temps pour [...] les bibelots a répandu jusque dans les classes bourgeoises le goût de belles choses, a éveillé des curiosités artistiques, a développé des désirs nouveaux pour le superflu élégant et amiable qui est le signe d'un certain raffinement intellectuel.[33]
>
> [our contemporary passion for trinkets has spread the taste for beautiful things even into the middle classes; it has awoken artistic curiosities, and developed new desires for an elegant and amiable superfluity which is the sign of a certain intellectual refinement]

Such elegant superfluity, increasingly accessible to the middle classes, is in evidence in this plant shopping episode. Des Esseintes accepts its cycles of novelty and wastefulness unflinchingly; he soon tires of his costly plants ('la joie de posséder de mirobolantes floraisons était tarie; il était déjà blasé sur leur contexture et sur leurs nuances' ['the joy of possessing astounding blooms had run its course; he had already grown indifferent to their composition and their delicate variations'], *AR*, 151–52/82), and then he fails to care for them properly. The glasshouse itself then becomes superfluous; its emptiness exhibits nothing but the wastefulness of consumerism, and the very sight of it rapidly irritates Des Esseintes — perhaps making a pointed remark about the vast glass Palais which were constructed at great cost for each World Fair, only for their novelty and purpose to wane within a few months (*AR*, 154/83). Indeed, Des Esseintes's wastefulness even extends to his supposedly durable purchases; the Parnassian adoration of gem stones and marble may have sought to counter the transience of consumer culture and modernity,[34] but they too are rendered transient when Des Esseintes abandons the Fontenay house and all its expensive trappings less than a year after moving in.

Furthermore, the location of this chapter within the two glazed spaces of the plant nursery and his own conservatory sets Des Esseintes's plant shopping apart from his other purchases. With these two glass buildings comes an influx of sound which is extremely rare in *À rebours* — precluded as sound is from his daily life by the muteness of his two attendants and the padding around his doors. Unlike in the *orgue à bouche* episode where the sound produced by the beverages is hallucinatory, within the glasshouse the delivery men and Des Esseintes all speak aloud. We might identify here a pastiche on the sonority so enjoyed by Zola's shoppers within the heavily-glazed Au Bonheur des Dames (discussed in Chapter Two). Indeed, when Des Esseintes and the gardeners enumerate each item, it is reminiscent of the staff during Mouret's inventory ('Des Esseintes appelait, vérifiait ses emplettes, une à une' ['Des Esseintes identified and verified his purchases, one by one'], *AR*, 134/73; 'les jardiniers que ces lenteurs ennuyaient se mirent à annoncer, eux-mêmes, à haute voix, les étiquettes piquées dans les pots' ['the gardeners, annoyed at these delays, themselves began to read aloud the labels stuck in the pots'], *AR*, 138/75). Des Esseintes goes on to comment aloud on the various plants, much as Zola's ladies comment on the Oriental carpets ('Sapristi! fit-il enthousiasmé' ['My God! he exclaimed fervently'], *AR*, 136/74; 'Celle-là va loin, murmura des Esseintes' ['That one is truly amazing, murmured Des Esseintes'], *AR*, 139/76). This is in contrast with, for example, the gilded tortoise episode, in which the goldsmith's delivery man bows wordlessly, Des Esseintes chews his nails without speaking as he contemplates possible improvements, the jeweller is stupefied into silence by the request, and finally Des Esseintes's eyes 'se grisaient' ['were intoxicated'] without triggering any impulse to speak (*AR*, 68–69/38).

Des Esseintes's endorsement of consumer culture is also echoed at the textual level by listing and cataloguing which seep into his free indirect discourse. As the new plants enter his conservatory, Des Esseintes enumerates the monstrous plants with a series of unfamiliar words which may seem a moment of pure abstraction to today's reader. However, the proliferating foreign and Latin genera, the grandiose descriptions, and the celebration of the art of modern horticultural cross-breeding mimics the shopping catalogues, exhibition brochures, and guidebooks prevalent in contemporary culture.[35] G. Dorville's information booklet for the 1878 World Fair, for example, included a complete list of all the flowers on display and their provenance, making Des Esseintes's enumeration of plants in *À rebours* seem remarkably normative.³⁶ Huysmans's five pages of plant names, then, produce a concatenation of the tendency to list from non-fiction sources, alongside the tendency for minute description from the Naturalist novel. Such lists are only surprising here owing to the sparse plotline surrounding them; there is more narration than one would anticipate in the pure lists of the catalogue, and far less narration than one would anticipate to justify such lengthy description in a novel. The context differs, therefore, but the content is ordinary.

Watson comments that 'neither Des Esseintes nor Huysmans manages to escape bourgeois society, certainly not by recourse to the catalogue. It is by the catalogue form that the logic of bourgeois culture enters into Huysmans's novel, for, despite his efforts at nostalgic esotericism, he cannot succeed in opposing his lists to those of commerce'.³⁷ I agree with Watson that these lists do not escape the remit of commerce, but I would question whether this was ever the aim. The rendering of this episode in free indirect discourse makes it clear that these are *Des Esseintes's* thoughts and behaviours, and are thus part of his wider appurtenance to mainstream culture. There is no sense of a conflict between his consumer desires and his attempts at expressing them in language; rather, the pleasure of listing is part of the pleasure he experiences as his purchases stream into his conservatory.

However, this glee is predictably short-lived; far from the delightful dreaming which glass palaces are expected to engender, the conservatory triggers a harrowing nightmare. It is important that Des Esseintes be within this glass space when he is tormented by his syphilis dream. As well as the messages this nightmare sends about sexuality and sexual profligacy, the deliberate choice of location implies a direct correlation between shopping culture and the diseased horrors of his nightmare. It suggests that the pleasant fantasies of bourgeois consumer culture are never far away from the brink of disaster. This is emphasized by the inclusion of two distorting glass windows near the climax of Des Esseintes's nightmare. As he tries to escape from the Grande Vérole, 'il était là, derrière une *lucarne ronde*, dans le couloir; plus mort que vif, Des Esseintes se retourna, vit par *l'œil-de-bœuf* des oreilles droites, des dents jaunes, des naseaux soufflant deux jets de vapeur' ['he was there, the other side of a *circular skylight* in the passage: more dead than alive, Des Esseintes turned around, and saw through the *little windows* two pricked-up ears, some yellow teeth, and two nostrils breathing jets of steam'] (*AR*, 146/79 — my emphases). Although Des Esseintes shows no signs of renouncing the pleasures of consumerism after this nightmare, we are certainly not encouraged to follow his example; the text insinuates that the phantasmagoric pleasures offered by these glass spaces of shopping and exhibition are only ever shallow and fleeting.³⁸

Considering this episode in conjunction with Huysmans's Parisian works more widely, we see that he often uses glass to highlight the limitations of mainstream bourgeois culture. One means of achieving this is through a recurrent analogy between glass and the banal minds and lives of women. Whereas in Maupassant's short stories this analogy attacks a fundamental weakness in masculine psychology, in Huysmans's work the emphasis is upon mediocrity rather than irreparable crisis. Significantly, glass décor often characterizes the middle-class marital home; with a wife, both glass and prosaicism enter a man's life. This is particularly marked in *En ménage* (1881). André's wife, the banal Berthe, comes from a bourgeois home with its obligatory standing mirror and glass-fronted barometer. In her youth, she and her girlfriends exchanged gossip and confidences in window seats, and, on marrying André, Berthe sets about establishing a home with glass candlestick holders, large windows, and numerous mirrors (*EM*, 73–74, 86, 22). When André discovers her *in flagrante delicto*, the tense silence is punctuated by the tapping of 'la corde d'une store qui frappait aux vitres' ['the pull for the shutter tapping against the window panes'], and when the couple reunite in the final pages of the novel they move into an utterly bourgeois maisonette, complete with 'une porte avec des vitres de couleur donnant sur le jardin' ['a door inlayed with coloured glass, leading out to the garden'] (*EM*, 16, 382).

Prostitutes — that other group of women essential for the satisfaction of bourgeois male desires — are also given associations with glass but in the public rather than the private sphere. In 'L'Ambulante', the *fille* is to be found in a bar replete with 'le verre en tulipe, le godet, les bouteilles de hauts crus, veloutées de poussière, les grossiers litrons de picolo et de vin bleu' ['tulip glasses, tumblers, bottles of quality vintages, downy with dust, rough litre bottles of sweet plonk and cheap wine'] (*CP*, 63–64). M. Folentin reluctantly becomes embroiled with a prostitute after she enters his restaurant 'et [elle] posa sa voilette et ses gants près de son verre' ['she placed her veil and gloves next to his glass'] (*AV*, 80). André's personal history is punctuated with episodes in bars lined with mirrors, decked with bottles, and laden with glasses. Prior to spending a *nuit blanche* with Blanche — who, on the ambiguous border between prostitute and bourgeoise, also owns a glass display cabinet filled with glassware — André sits with Cyprien, symbolically placed 'sous une glace qui leur mit dans le dos, au-dessus de la tête, l'image réflétée de la dame du comptoir' ['under a mirror which reflected, behind their backs, over their heads, the image of the bar girl'] (*EM*, 180, 175). Similar imagery of glass bottles is echoed at Fontenay by the Benedictine and Chartreuse bottles, which remind Des Esseintes of the sensuous shapes of a woman's body. Indeed, as Armstrong has remarked, glass borrows a corporeal lexicon from the human form, with 'waist', 'lip', 'mouth', 'foot', and 'leg' applying to both glass vessel and the living body.[39] By using glass culture to create an analogy between wives and prostitutes, these texts imply that the sexual and/or domestic comfort provided by women is just another fantasy dreamed up by the bourgeois man — and that the purchase of a wife or a prostitute is equally as likely to end in a syphilitic nightmare as Des Esseintes's conservatory of expensive plants.

Ideal Naturalism

With this perspective upon Des Esseintes's relationship to mainstream culture, we read his sense of superiority in a more sardonic light. Des Esseintes does, after all, cut a rather ridiculous figure with his swooning, his whimsy, and his hysterical mood swings, and there is little about him that Huysmans encourages us to take seriously. And yet the novel does strike the reader as being imbued with seriousness.

Having noted the folly in Des Esseintes's ways and the untenability of his illusions, this seriousness is instead identified with the aesthetics of the novel.

The literary milieu in the 1880s was rife with quarrels about the relative merits of Naturalism and Idealism. In 1887 this would crystalize most famously around the 'Manifeste des cinq' following the publication of Zola's *La Terre* in 1887, but this protest could not have had the influence it did without being part of a long, ongoing debate.[40] However, rather than *À rebours* exploring just one side of this dispute, there is a playful experimentation here; the novel explores what would happen if these antitheses were merged into an Idealized Naturalism. That is to say, not a Naturalism purified of its grime, psychology, and corporeality — that, after all, would no longer be Naturalism — but an ideal form of Naturalism in the sense of Platonic ideal forms, taking the most characteristic elements of Naturalism and producing an epitomic manifestation of their underlying principles.

One key element drawn out by Huysmans is characterization within the text. In Des Esseintes, we find an ideal Naturalist character, with an unchanging and monological value system, with an attachment to the ideas of popular and material cultural, with a fraught psychological state, and with a physical malady and its correspondingly earthy medical treatments. The other key element is the literary style of the text: Naturalism and Realism had always been associated with minute description, which could introduce lyricism into the prose text when their proliferation of descriptive words was arranged with real artistry. Huysmans brings these two ideal Naturalist elements together. The result is a hybrid mixture which refuses generic categorization, and by no means solves the debate; however, it does dramatize the problematic nature of investing in such binaries, and the text progressively drives a rift between the ideal Naturalist character and the idealized Naturalist writing style.

One means of achieving this rift is through a savvy manipulation of material objects to illustrate the tensions between different temporal frameworks within Naturalism, and within contemporary society more widely. In the Naturalist plot, time moves inexorably forwards, but groups of novels often form cycles that imply the eternal return to the same, whilst Naturalist description at its most lyrical reaches towards the intense sense of the present moment characteristic of poetry. Scholarship has often cast its critical eye upon the question of temporality in *À rebours*, particularly in terms of the temporal implications of Des Esseintes's floods of memories. Both Ionna Chatzidimitriou and Elisabeth Donato consider Des Esseintes's attempts to turn time into an object; Chatzidimitriou asserts that Des Esseintes tries to render a threatening past benign by transforming it 'into an artifact, an object of contemplation and delight',[41] and Donato suggests, perhaps rather idealistically, that 'by immersing himself in a past reconstructed in an erudite work of art, Des Esseintes, Huysmans and any Flaubert reader can elevate themselves beyond time'.[42] However, they do not consider his relationship to the many physical objects at Fontenay except those which are most clearly designated as *objets d'art* — although the latter are numerically scarce, in a house filled with bells, furniture, carpets, crockery, fans, fire-grills, drinking glasses, perfume bottles, liqueur bottles, windows, mirrors, and much more. I suggest that this object-laden environment is a crucial contributing factor to the presentation of temporality in *À rebours*.

It has often been stated that, as nineteenth-century Paris modernized, the individual was forced to be more aware of time than ever before.[43] The city was driven by a binary experience of passing time. On the one hand, quotidian life was filled with repetitiveness — characterized by the eternal return of novelty in department stores and World Fairs, the industrial machine, regular office hours, and social rituals. Repetitiveness was also manifested in nostalgia, and the longing for a return of a golden age, be it the medieval world of chivalry,[44] or the early days of the Revolution before factionalism undermined its momentum. During the *année terrible*, the *Moniteur universel* evoked in one breath the return of both ancient Gaul and 1792, proclaiming that 'nos contemporains prouveront qu'ils sont dignes fils des *héros de 92*, et comme eux ils repousseront les *barbares* qui osent fouler du pied la terre de la civilisation' ['our contemporaries will prove themselves worthy sons of the *heroes of 92*, and like them, they will push back the *barbarians* who dare to set foot upon civilized soil'].[45] Circularity is everywhere to be found at Fontenay. Donato has argued that 'bourgeois mediocrity condemns man to the eternal recurrence of the same [...]. The circle becomes the embodiment of the evil forces of modernity'.[46] It is perhaps for this reason that Des Esseintes is surrounded by a considerable number of circles in his material world — the port-hole windows; the empty circular spaces he leaves in his library for future art purchases; the false *œil-de-bœuf* in the library ceiling; the barrels, bottles, and glasses of his *orgue à bouche*; the knotted rope, binoculars, and compasses in his ship room; the gilded *culs de bouteille* of his windows; the baptismal font that he uses for a wash basin; and even the cylindrical device for the insertion of his suppositories.

On the other hand, nineteenth-century modernity created a sensation that time was rushing past in a linear sense — characterized by the steam and speed of trains, and the teleological ideas of cultural and evolutionary 'Progress'. The *État* asserted confidently that 'avec les découvertes de la vapeur, de l'électricité, le développement de l'instruction, les peuples sont assurés de marcher dans la voie de la liberté, de la science, du progrès moral et matériel' ['with the discoveries of steam, electricity, the development of education, people are sure to walk the path of liberty, of science, of moral and material progress'].[47] Linearity characterizes many aspects of Des Esseintes's existence: the progression of his neurosis; the pursuit of new acquisitions, from not having to having; the development of his discussions of literature from the ancient to the contemporary; and the lines of text in his books. Yet the teleology of Progress necessarily negates the retrospective, nostalgic perspective. Either the past was inferior to the present, or we should long for its return, but both cannot logically be true at once.

In *À rebours*, glass is used to illustrate these incompatible temporalities as Des Esseintes willingly manipulates the impression of the passage of day and night. In one room, his windows are glazed, tinged and gilded (*AR*, 25–26/15). Owing to the gilding which covers Des Esseintes's *cul de bouteille* windows, his perception of time is blurred, since '[les vitres] ne laissaient pénétrer qu'une lumière feinte' ['[the windows] allowed only a deceptive light to penetrate'], *AR*, 26/15).

This obtuse version of time is not just caused by one window, but is projected over the world outside by Des Esseintes on every occasion that he gazes through a window. The views through Des Esseintes's windows are described repeatedly without colour, in black and white alone. This colourlessness renders time increasingly ambiguous and gives the impression that this glass is no ordinary glazing, but that the windows are instead akin to a series of lenses. They produce images most often encountered in the zoetrope and zoopraxiscope optical toys, which used rapid sequences of chronophotographic images, such as those taken by Eadweard Muybridge and Etienne Jules Marcy in the 1870s and 1880s. The constant rise in the popularity of photography meant that, increasingly, popular culture invited people to contemplate life through a lens — be it through taking amateur photographs (as Zola famously loved to do), or through the lenses of others via the endless stream of photographic prints for sale. As the product of mainstream culture, Des Esseintes internalizes this obsession with photography; whenever the reader views the outside world through Des Esseintes's eyes, it is sapped of colour as though it were a zoopraxiscope sequence. For example, in a passage more often cited as evidence of Des Esseintes's taste for material rather than temporal artifice, the first occasion on which Des Esseintes gazes from his window reveals an exclusively black-and-white landscape:

> Dans l'*obscurité*, à gauche, à droite, des masses confuses s'étageaient, dominées, au loin, par d'autres batteries et d'autres forts dont les hauts talus semblaient, *au clair de la lune*, gouachés de *l'argent*, sur un ciel *sombre*. Rétrécie par *l'ombre* tombée des collines, la plaine paraissait, à son milieu poudrée de *farine d'amidon* et enduite de *blanc cold-cream*; dans l'air tiède, éventant les herbes *décolorées* et distillant de bas parfums d'épices, les arbres *frottés de craie par la lune*, ébouriffaient de *pâles* feuillages et dédoublaient leurs troncs par les *ombres* barraient de *raies noires* le sol en *plâtre* sur lequel des caillasses scintillaient ainsi que des *éclats d'assiettes* (*AR*, 38 — my emphases).

> [In the *shadows*, to left and right, indistinct shapes rose up one behind the other, while above them, far away, loomed other batteries and other fortifications, whose high supporting-walls seemed in *the moonlight* to have been washed over with *silver* gouache, against a background of *dark* sky. Its size diminished by the *shadow* of the hills, the plain looked as if its centre had been powdered with *dry starch* and daubed with *white cold-cream*; in the balmy air that fanned the *faded* grasses, generating cheap, spicy scents, the trees, *chalk-white in the moonlight*, fluffed out their *pale* foliage, replicating their trunks with *black shadows* that stripped the *limy* soil, on which pebbles sparkled, like *shards of broken china* (21)]

Whilst at first the lack of colour here seems merely symptomatic of the moonlit scene, all of the other instances where Des Esseintes gazes from windows are also depicted with the same black-and-white colour scheme. Several of these moments do ostensibly occur at night. In Chapter 4, the increasing snowfall against a night sky turns the black-and-white configuration of the outside world *à rebours*:

> Ainsi qu'une haute tenture de *contre-hermine*, le ciel se levait devant lui, *noir* et moucheté de *blanc*. Un vent glacial courut, accéléra le vol éperdu de la *neige*, intervertit l'ordre des couleurs. La tenture héraldique du ciel se retourna, devint une véritable *hermine*, *blanche*, mouchetée de *noir*, à son tour, par les points de *nuit* dispersés entre les *flocons* (*AR*, 70 — my emphases).

> [Like some great hanging of *reversed ermine*, the sky rose before him, *black* and

dappled with *white*. An icy wind gusted, intensifying the wild scudding of the *snow*, inverting the proportions of black and white. The heraldic hanging of the sky turned itself over, becoming true *white ermine*, itself dappled with *black* by the tiny patches of night strewn among the *snowflakes* (38–39).]

However, the daytime scene in the rain prior to his aborted voyage to London is equally colourless:

> des fleuves de *suie* roulaient, sans discontinuer, au travers des plaines *grises* du ciel, des blocs de nuées, [...] des torrents de pluie. [...] Les flots d'*encre* s'étaient volatisés et taris, [...] une brume d'eau enveloppa la campagne. [...] *Toutes les couleurs se fanèrent* (AR, 189 — my emphases).

> [across the *grey* plains of the sky, rivers of *soot* were endlessly rolling mass upon mass of clouds. [...] The *ink-black* floods had vaporized and dried up, the jagged edges of the clouds had melted away; [...] a watery mist enveloped the countryside. [...] *All the colours had faded* (103–04)]

The heatwave adds little colour to the scene outside when observed by Des Esseintes from his window; here, white is merely prioritized over black as though in an overexposed photograph — in spite of the emphasis which will later be placed on the 'brouillard verdâtre' ['greenish mist'] once he stops looking through the window and ventures into the garden (AR, 252/136):

> Après les rafales et les brumes, des ciels chauffés à *blanc*, telles que des plaques de tôle, sortirent de l'horizon. [...] Attisé comme par de furieux ringards, le soleil s'ouvrit, en gueule de four, dardant une lumière presque *blanche* qui brûlait la vue; une poussière de flammes s'éleva des routes *calcinées* [...]; la réverbération des murs peints au *lait de chaux*, les foyers allumés sur le zinc des toits et sur les vitres des fenêtres, aveugla (AR, 247 — my emphases).

> [After all the squalls and the fogs, *blazing hot* skies, like sheets of metal, appeared from over the horizon. [...] As though stirred into life by fierce pokers, the sun opened like the mouth of a furnace, shooting down an almost *white* light which burned the eyes; a fiery dust rose up from the *sun-baked* roads [...]; the glare from the *white-washed* walls, the light flaming on the zinc roofs and the window panes was blinding (134).]

Even his maidservant, costumed as a beguine, creates a black-and-white portrait when she passes before his windows, framed with her 'bonnet blanc et large capuchon, baissé, noir' ['white cap and a large black cowl pulled down over it'] (AR, 28/16). It is notable that all these scenes include movement. They do not seem to fix a moment in time like a photograph, but seem to continue progressing in time in a permanent *present* moment — without it being possible to fix any *precise* moment. At the window, Des Esseintes appears trapped between competing timeframes, as circularity and linear progression come into conflict.

Ideal Naturalist Description

A similar conflict is produced at the textual level, as Naturalistic description is idealized to the point that it shifts towards poetry. This manifests itself through the inclusion of deliberately arcane words in the description of the material world at Fontenay. It is unlikely that the majority of readers would be familiar with even half of the Latin authors in Chapter 3 of *À rebours*, the unusual gems in Chapter 4, or the exotic plants in Chapter 8; these signifiers are thrust upon the reader in full knowledge that at least some of these will elude him. Minute, apparently Naturalist description in these passages outreaches the erudition of most readers, and so what seems to be an effort to represent the material world is necessarily an abortive one. Without a known referent, these words strike the reader as empty and mysterious collections of phonemes with no concrete visual image attached — often rendered still stranger by an influx of non-French vocabulary. The reader must then choose between different, incompatible temporal experiences of the novel: first, continuing to read but accepting a failure to understand and to create mental images throughout vast swathes of the novel; second, fragmenting the forward progression of reading by approaching the novel in parallel with an encyclopedia; or third, deferring knowledge to a future moment when the reader will look up these alien words — then inviting a further reading of the novel to benefit from this supplementary research. Accordingly, the reader's reception of the rarefied words and visualization of Des Esseintes's world are separated over time. These scattered reading moments dislocate the familiar temporal experience of the novel, and reach beyond the familiar plot markers of a beginning, middle, and end.[48]

The celebrated *orgue à bouche* episode uses the presence of glass in the text to signpost the chaotic implications of an idealized Naturalism still further, inviting the reader to focus on the writing *as writing* within this episode instead of on writing as representation. At the outset, the 'baril à liqueur' ['liqueur barrel'] evokes a largely conventional image, appropriate to Des Esseintes's adherence to mainstream culture. In the 1880s, *caves à liqueur* were fashionable among the bourgeoisie, and were available from department stores across Paris in a wide variety of designs and for a whole range of budgets. Yet the text raises our suspicion that something here is different with the physical position of the drinking glasses. Unlike the ostentatiously displayed cut-glassware in fashionable *caves à liqueurs*, Des Esseintes's *baril* conceals 'imperceptibles gobelets' ['imperceptible goblets' — translation adapted] (*AR*, 71/39). Importantly, the reader must focus on the poetic use of language rather than on translating words into images if he is to discover such hidden glassware — the *verre* in 'des sensations analogues à celles que la musique *verse* à l'oreille' ['sensations analogous to those which music affords the ear'] (*AR*, 71/39), and in the 'chartreuse *verte*' ['green Chartreuse'] (*AR*, 72/40).

This initial deviation from the familiar *cave à liqueurs* invites a closer examination of the prose. In conjunction with this phonetic game of glass hide-and-seek, the musicality of the passage is established in advance by the implicit juxtaposition of music and glass, in 'des sensations analogues à celles que la musique *verse* à l'oreille'; by the sonority contained within the name given to 'son orgue à bouche' — the /sɔnɔʀ/ within /sɔnɔʀg/; and by Des Esseintes's ability to 'se jouer sur la langue de silencieuses mélodies' ['to play himself silent melodies on his tongue'] — both 'la langue' (his physical tongue) and 'la langue' (the diegetic language) (*AR*, 72/40). There is further phonetic play between the liqueur flavours and their various associated musical instruments: the long /m/ of kummel approximates the bilabial embouchure of the oboe; the /y/ in 'sucrée' ['sugary'] mimics the pursed embouchure of the flute; and the crash and roll of the cymbals are found in the frequency of reverberating /R/ and of a phrase composed almost exclusively of monosyllables akin to Strauss-style cymbal clashes: 'roulent les coups de tonnerre de la cymbale et de la caisse frappés à tour de bras dans la peau de la bouche par les rakis de Chio et les mastics!' ['rolling thunder of the cymbals and the drum as the rakis of Chios and the mastics strike with all their might upon the skin of the mouth!'] (*AR*, 71/39).

The rift between Des Esseintes's material world and the novel's literary aesthetics is heavily underlined here. It initially appears that these poetic threads are woven into the text to aid us to share our protagonist's sensory experience of drink; however, it later becomes apparent that the prose actually *divorces* the reader from identification with Des Esseintes's thoughts and actions. Right at the end of this masterful display of lyrical description, the reader learns that Des Esseintes has not partaken of this experience at all as, 'ce soir-là, des Esseintes n'avait nulle envie d'écouter le goût de la musique' ['that evening, Des Esseintes felt no urge to listen to the taste of music'] (*AR*, 73/40) and instead he only drinks pure whiskey. The episode ends with a cut-glass goblet of whiskey being brought out from its hidden position in the *cave*, transformed from 'imperceptible' to 'perceptible'; but only after a foray into almost incantatory prose poetics. As the potential for lyricism in minute description is amplified here, the text ceases to correlate reliably with the fictional world — and, problematically for a novel, poetics takes precedence over plot.

Glass once more signals the cleft between writing as representation and as text in Chapter 11, when Des Esseintes ostensibly embarks on a journey to London through Paris. Glass is more abundant within this episode than any other. The chapter opens with Des Esseintes drumming on his window (*AR*, 189). He selects his socks from a glass display cabinet in his bedroom (190), he gazes out of the glass windows of a train carriage (191) and of a Parisian cab (194), he stares through the glass shop frontage of the Galignani's Messenger (196–97), he sits in the Bodega surrounded by spectacle wearers (201) and by drinking glasses (which are designated explicitly by the text, unlike the concealed glasses of the *orgue à bouche* — 199–200, 203), and he hears the rain drumming on the glass skylights of the station tavern (206) whilst he drains another series of glasses of alcohol (208–09).

However, in this episode the play on Naturalist traditions is more complex because there is a definite sense of plot here. Des Esseintes travels to Paris, site par excellence of the Naturalist novel, and suddenly adultery, romance, marriage, crime, mystery, corruption, or reform all suddenly became possible trajectories for the plot line of *À rebours*. Des Esseintes immerses himself in modern, Haussmannized Paris; he takes trains and cabs, arrives in new railway stations, travels along new boulevards, visits shops, and eats and drinks in cafés and restaurants. As soon as Des Esseintes announces his intention to travel to Paris, the reader of the 1880s is drawn into a web of intertextual connections; and unlike the intertexts evoked in the conservatory which evoke an array of images, here the direction of the plot itself seems to splinter into a kaleidoscopic variety of plausible forms.

To begin with, glass continues to function as a confirmation of Des Esseintes's mainstream mindset. Even before Des Esseintes leaves his bedroom in Fontenay, the 'bibliothèque vitrée' ['glass-fronted bookcase'] (*AR*, 190/104) in which he keeps his spectrum of socks sheds an aura of exhibition value over this humble footwear, in a clear parody of the displays in bourgeois department stores. There is no sense that Des Esseintes himself is being sardonic; there is an everyday simplicity to his actions that belies any suggestion that he sees his use of the trappings of commodity culture as an act of mockery, any more than Zola's Renée or Denise treat shopping with disdain. Later, when Des Esseintes visits the Galignani's Messenger, he appears to be caught up in the very consumerist passions which he elsewhere scorns, and he stands enraptured before the wide glass display window of the bookshop.

Although glass objects ostensibly represent the material world of consumerism in this chapter, the signifiers for these objects migrate away from their signifieds. They draw our attention instead to the absence of referential reality behind either our ideal Naturalist protagonist, or the idealized descriptive passages. It is apt that glass should be given this role as it too, like text, is generally looked through by the observer, who focuses instead on what it contains, displays, reflects, or magnifies. It is still more apt because of the long literary tradition of using glass and mirrors as metaphors for the close relationship between the text and the world (as discussed in the Introduction). Huysmans plays upon this well-worn analogy to create a text which *refuses* transparency, and foregrounds language itself at the expense of the represented world. Indeed, Huysmans even includes a ludic image to show the reader that text itself is the focus of his endeavours. Des Esseintes is drawn to the Galignani's Messenger by the sight of the shop windows, with its 'verres dépolis couverts d'inscriptions et munis de passe-partout encadrant des découpures de journaux et des bandes azures de télégrammes' ['frosted glass covered with notices, and laden with passepartout-framed newspaper cuttings and blue telegraph forms'], next to 'deux grandes vitrines [qui] regorgeaient d'albums et de livres' ['two huge shop-windows [...] filled to overflowing with picture albums and books'] (*AR*, 196–97/107). Here, glass not only contains text but also becomes text; glass itself is the *passe-partout* between the fantasies of mainstream culture — both in the consumption of commodities and the consumption of narratives — and an appreciation of finely-crafted writing.

The trope of literature as a mirror along the roadway is dismantled as Des Esseintes travels, precisely, along the roadways of Paris. Des Esseintes is not just selective about what he chooses to acknowledge outside the cab window, but he also actively *invents* sights. The interposition of the glass cab window between Des Esseintes and Paris enables him not only to look over but also to overlook the rebuilt roads and buildings where the upheaval of barricades, encampments, and fires had rewritten the city's topography during the *semaine sanglante*. On the route described from Sceaux station to the Rue de Rivoli, he must have passed several sites of burned buildings — at the southern end of the Jardin de Luxembourg, between the Boulevard Saint Germain and the Quai Voltaire in the largest area of fire damage in the whole of Paris, and the charred remains of the Tuileries Palace and western end of the Louvre. His cab drove across the locations of famous Commune barricades — two on the Boulevard d'Enfer (now Raspail), and three on the Rue du Bac.

When he stops the cab at the Galignani's Messenger, he is mere metres away from the Place Vendôme. Indeed, the Bodega on the corner of the Rue Castaglione and the Rue de Rivoli is located exactly where a key Communard barricade defended the southern end of the Place Vendôme from the Versaillais forces. Despite the constant presence of harrowing physical reminders of the Commune and all its attendant horrors, Des Esseintes treats the windows of the cabs as an opaque screen on which to project his fantasies of London, rather than as a window onto the outside world. There is no pretense at a reality effect, and the description does not even pretend to represent a plausible reality.

Glass takes this detachment from expectations further at the Bodega. In this bar, Des Esseintes dives into all-encompassing moments of literary fantasy — and indeed seems unable to do so without a drinking glass in front of him. Of course, each new *verre* brings another unit of alcohol to Des Esseintes's lips, and while his inner monologue may seem at first glance to remain sober in its eloquence, these *verres* seep into the language of the narrative to remind the reader that the inebriated Des Esseintes cannot be trusted to represent the world around him. After at least seven units of alcohol in a couple of hours, he pours one final glass of brandy to 'verser [*verre*-ser] du courage' ['to get up his courage'] (*AR*, 208/113), but instead he is overwhelmed by 'une immense aversion' ['an immense distaste'] (*AR*, 210/114), or 'une immense a-*verre*-sion' at the thought of turning this fantasy trip into a physical one. Believing that literature is a mirror for reality, it would seem, is like believing the proclamations of a drunkard.

Dismantling Des Esseintes

Ultimately, ideal Naturalist description and the ideal Naturalist protagonist are shown to be incompatible. As the lyrical qualities of the descriptive text grow, it becomes impossible to pursue a plotline, or to suspend our disbelief in the protagonist and the material world depicted by the text. Huysmans not only enacts this, but signals overtly to the reader that he is doing so. Des Esseintes's subjectivity seems to dissolve as the novel progresses, in spite of the absence of any external influence from women, workers, foreigners, the (un)dead, or any of the threatening Others which abound in nineteenth-century society and literature.

Despite Des Esseintes's hyperbolized, outlandish nature, the majority of readers will nonetheless have suspended their disbelief and accepted Des Esseintes as a subject in order to engage with the first half of the novel as they might for any Naturalist protagonist in any of Huysmans's previous novels. Yet as *À rebours* progresses, Huysmans makes it progressively difficult for the reader to invest in Des Esseintes as a narrative subject. A subtle clue to this is concealed in Chapter 6 through a pun on Des Esseintes's patronym — that is, on the very noun that officially confers Des Esseintes with subjective existence in language. As his neuroses worsen, Des Esseintes loses the ability to concentrate on his books and, before launching into a rêverie on religion and sacrilege, the narrative briefly states that:

> la solitude avait agi sur son cerveau, de même qu'un narcotique. Après l'avoir tout d'abord énervé et tendu, elle amenait une torpeur hantée de songeries

vagues; elle annihilait *ses desseins*, brisait ses volontés, guidait un défilé de rêves qu'il subissait, passivement, sans même essayer de s'y soustraire (*AR*, 112–13 — my emphasis).

[solitude had affected his brain like an opiate. After first making him feel edgy and strained, it had brought on a lethargy haunted by vague reveries; it annihilated his plans and nullified his desires, marshalling a parade of dreams to which he submitted passively, not even attempting to escape from them (62).]

The four-point assonance between 'ses desseins' (/sedesɛ̃/) that are being annihilated and the name 'Des Esseintes' (/dezesɛ̃t/) points towards the process of 'unsuspension' of disbelief to be effected by the text on its own protagonist.

As his seclusion at Fontenay progresses, glass emphasizes in a number of ways the rift between character and text. This had been prefigured in the 'Notice'; before Des Esseintes ever left Paris, it was his inability to hold a glass without shaking which precipitated his exodus to Fontenay: 'la main remuait, droite encore lorsqu'elle saisissait un objet lourd, capricante et penchée quand elle tenait quelque chose de léger tel qu'un petit verre' ['he could not keep his hand still: if he grasped a heavy object he could hold it straight, but if he held something light such as a small glass, his hand jerked limply about'] (*AR*, 11/8). In parallel, the first sign in Chapter 13 of his decline at Fontenay is that 'son verre lui parut à un lieu de lui' ['his glass seemed a league away'] (*AR*, 249/135), and he goes on to experience pain akin to entrapment in a glass vacuum bell: 'il lui semblait être sous une cloche pneumatique où le vide se faisait à mesure' ['he felt as if he was under a bell-jar in which the vacuum each moment was becoming more powerful'] (*AR*, 251/136). The drinking glass which appeared so far away morphs here, inverted, to imprison and suffocate him two pages later.

Glass is at the heart of the first extended episode in which the protagonist's illusion of subjectivity starts to unravel — the experimentation with perfumes in Chapter 10. This is the first occasion on which there is no pretense that Des Esseintes has any active choice over his departure into reverie and imagination, and this lack of agency is accompanied by an insistent hallucination that a non-existent *flacon* of perfume is lingering somewhere in his room. As the bedroom fills with the smell of frangipane, he searches, distressed, 'si un flacon ne traînait pas, débouché; il n'y avait point de flacon dans la pièce' ['whether a scent bottle might be lying about, unstoppered; there was no scent bottle in the room'] (*AR*, 168–69/92). The multiple repetitions of the signifiers 'flacon' (threefold) and 'frangipane' (fivefold) across the perfume chapter reinforce this. Such repetition effects textually the circular, searching motion that Des Esseintes traces around the room as he seeks the imagined *flacon*, and it mimics the spinning of his head as he is overwhelmed by fragrances. Moreover, the linguistic circling around these signifiers enacts a clear divide between Des Esseintes's world (where the signified glass *flacon* and its essence of *fragipane* do not exist) and its description in the novel (where the signifiers do). This deliberate cleavage brings to the fore that this novel is an object of interpretative reading rather than an act of mimetic writing.

In this episode, glass also brings the mirror and its associations with ego-formation into play. The importance of the mirror for forging identity — and its frequent failure to do so — were thematized so frequently in this period that as soon as a mirror appears in *À rebours*, we suspect that we are going to witness the collapse of Des Esseintes as a subject. Above Des Esseintes's baptismal-font-cum-wash-basin hangs 'une longue glace en fer forgé, emprisonnant ainsi que d'une margelle argentée de lune, l'eau verte et comme morte du miroir' ['a long mirror with a wrought-iron frame which imprisoned the green, lifeless waters of the glass like the stone rim of a well silvered by the moonlight'] (*AR*, 169/92). Yet unlike Maupassant's male protagonists, the dead 'eau verte' of the mirror *never* returns Des Esseintes's image — despite this water metaphor establishing a clear analogy with Narcissus's pool. Even when, on being awakened from an olfactory hallucination of open meadows, 'il se retrouva au milieu de son cabinet de toilette, assis devant sa table' ['he found himself back in his dressing-room, seated at his table'] (*AR*, 180/98), there is no indication that he is reflected in the watery surface of the looking-glass.

This challenge at the mirror to the narrative subject in Chapter 10 is prefigured in the distorting mirrors of Des Esseintes's old dandyish abode in Paris. His mirrors, '[qui] se faisaient écho et se renvoyaient à *perte de vue*' ['which mirrored one another and reflected an infinite series of pink boudoirs'], led to a loss of sight rather than its enhancement (*AR*, 16/10 — my emphasis). Although the reader is told that Des Esseintes's mistresses took pleasure in admiring their reflections in this flatteringly lit room — so we know these mirrors work — Des Esseintes's reflection was, again, absent. Even when he actively gazed into these multiple mirrors, it was the twirling birdcage which he saw, not his own image (*AR*, 17/11). Huysmans gives us an effective mise-en-abyme of the fact that Des Esseintes, like all fictional characters, has no selfhood to reflect in the mirror, in spite of Naturalism's ability to trick the reader into believing otherwise. This provides a ludic explanation for why Des Esseintes seems so distressed on the one occasion that the mirror *does* seem to return a reflection of his face. The reader is told that:

> il se reconnaissait à peine; la figure était couleur de terre, les lèvres boursouflées et sèches, la langue ridée, la peau rugueuse; ses cheveux et sa barbe que le domestique n'avait plus taillés depuis la maladie, ajoutaient encore à l'horreur de la face creuse, des yeux agrandis et liquoreux qui brûlaient d'un éclat fébrile dans cette tête de squelette, hérissée de poils (*AR*, 314).
>
> [he scarcely recognized himself, his face was mud-colour, his lips dry and swollen, his tongue furrowed, his skin rough; his hair and beard, which his manservant had not trimmed since he fell ill, added to the horror of the cadaverous face and the huge, watery eyes which burned with a feverish glitter in that skeletal head covered with bristling hair (168–69).]

The one and only physical description of Des Esseintes's face is reminiscent of an Odilon Redon portrait, a Félicien Rops satanic image, or one of Luykens's engravings of torture victims, rather than a real man's face. The hand mirror reflects facets of the objets d'art with which Des Esseintes initially tried to define himself as a subject, showing the void behind the illusions needed to construct an ideal Naturalist protagonist.

The hand mirror and bathroom mirror draw together various themes and images which have been associated with glass throughout the novel. As Des Esseintes stares into the hand mirror, we recall his transfixed stare into the Galignani's Messenger shop window in Paris. The watery quality of the *cabinet* mirror recalls the aquarium room with its collection of nautical objects, and its complicated layering of fish-tank windows. Des Esseintes's *cabinet* is hung with green Japanese crepe silk wallpaper — indeed, perhaps it is this which was reflected all along in the watery mirror, and we looked straight through Des Esseintes to the paper where, 'simulant le friselis d'une rivière que le vent ride [où], dans ce léger courant, nageait le pétale d'une rose autour duquel tournoyait une nuée de petits poissons dessinés en deux traits d'encre' ['simulat[ing] the rippled surface of a wind-blown river; floating in this light current was a single rose petal, round which swam a swarm of tiny fishes, sketched with a couple of strokes of the pen'] (*AR*, 181/98). While the green, watery silk background reprises the 'eau verte' of the mirror, the colours and images upon the silk clearly evoke Des Esseintes's most cherished books of poetry. They recall the black Chinese ink, rose-tinted paper, and fish-skin binding of his large volume of Baudelaire (*AR*, 214–15/116), and 'la tresse noire [qui] rejoignait la tresse rose [...] comme un soupçon de fard japonais [...] sur l'antique blancheur' ['the black braid met the pink braid [...], added a whisper of powder [...] to the antique whiteness'] of his edition of Mallarmé (*AR*, 300/161). Indeed, the 'eau verte' mirror is itself an intertextual reenactment of Mallarmé's 'Hérodiade', which is later quoted by Des Esseintes. It is hard to miss the parallels between Des Esseintes's remembrances, the refrain of green, and the absence of clear reflection in Mallarmé's verse:

> O miroir! [...]
> Cherchant mes souvenirs qui sont
> Comme des feuilles sous ta glace au trou profond,
> Je m'apparus en toi comme une ombre lointaine (*AR*, 297).
>
> [O mirror! [...] seeking memories (like leaves beneath the icy glass covering your fathomless depths) — have I seen myself appear in you as a distant shadow! (Note 160, 223)]

In this riddle of reflections, it is not a Naturalistic representation of a real person — or even of a plausibly real person — that we can expect to see in the mirror. Baudelaire's works are, after all, filled with references to glass and mirrors, many of which are metaphors for intoxicated, distorted vision and visions,[49] like the 'miroir grossissant, mais un pur miroir' ['magnifying mirror, but a pure mirror'] of hashish.[50] Rather, it is the beauty of lyrical, idealized description itself that is reflected back to us. The image we are offered is the reflected legacy of Huysmans's pre-decadent literary heroes: Baudelaire, Mallarmé, followed by *À rebours* itself.

For the discerning reader, these references to Baudelaire and Mallarmé offer a lesson; they encourage us to look past the splendour of Des Esseintes's wealth and his excesses within popular-cultural paradigms, past the Naturalist emphasis on realistic description of material objects, and to focus instead on the intricacies of writing. There is a warning here to avoid the misguided belief that Des Esseintes's lavishness is evidence of the quality of his aesthetic choices. We are given all possible indicators that this novel is not to be taken as mimesis, that belief should not be suspended, but that it must be read critically *as text*.

* * * * *

Pierre Jourde has suggested that, 'pour être soi-même enfin, il faut cesser d'être "décadent", c'est-à-dire cesser de se chercher à l'extrémité de la prolifération des images culturelles, cesser de vouloir se voir; il faut franchir le miroir. Des Esseintes ne le fait pas' ['in the end, to be one's self, one must stop being "decadent"; that is to say, one must stop looking for oneself at the extremes of culture's proliferating images, stop wanting to see oneself; one must cross through the mirror. Des Esseintes does not do this'].[51] Whilst I agree with Jourde that the integrity of Des Esseintes's subjectivity does deteriorate as the novel progresses, I would contend that it is not through being Decadent that Des Esseintes ceases to be a subject. His increasing lack of agency suggests instead that he ceases to be a tenable narrative subject because he is *not Decadent enough*. The ideal reader will recognize that it is not in Des Esseintes's shopping, pontificating, and dreaming that the novel holds its appeal. Alina Clej has asserted that, 'by the end of the novel, [Huysmans] is forced to admit defeat by opening the cavern in which he imprisoned his hero, and letting him return to Paris, until further notice'.[52] However, far from Des Esseintes's 'defeat' within the text signalling the failure of Huysmans's text itself, instead the very opposite is true. Huysmans experiments with the novelistic form, blending contemporary concerns about Naturalism and Idealism into a playful exploration of what an 'idealized Naturalism' might entail, and whether it could be possible. It becomes clear that, in order for either the Naturalist character or Naturalist description to reach an epitomic form, the other must suffer irrevocably. The reader is never invited to follow in Des Esseintes's footsteps and to seek intoxication in perfume bottles, liqueur bottles, drinking glasses, glasshouses, aquaria, glass-fronted bookcases and display cases, shops, cafés, trains, carriages, windows, or mirrors, or indeed in the Realist mirror along the roadway. The folly and hypocrisy of Des Esseintes's engagement with material culture in this novel justifies Huysmans's prioritization of textuality, and the author develops the lyrical possibilities inherent in Naturalism's verve for minute description; Huysmans produces a text that incorporates correspondences with poetry and investigates the potential for prose poetics. When Des Esseintes is forced to admit defeat within the narrative, it is Huysmans's text that is victorious. Paradoxically, from the unwonted juxtaposition of familiar tropes which go very much *with* the grain, the novel so often hailed as the epitome of Decadence is born.

Notes to Chapter 4

1. Eugène Viollet-le-Duc, *Habitations modernes* (Paris: A. Morel, 1875), p. 1.
2. In 1892, Arthur Symons declared *À rebours* to be 'the quintessence of decadence' (in *The Fortnightly Review* (March 1892)); Matei Calinescu calls it 'the summa of decadence' (*Five Faces of Modernity* (Durham: Duke University Press, 1987), p. 172); and Mary Elizabeth Curtin names it 'the paragon of *fin de siècle* Decadent fiction' ('"Like Bottled Wasps": Beerbohm, Huysmans and the Decadents' Suburban Retreat', *Victorian Literature and Culture*, 39:1 (2011), 183–200).
3. In *Œuvres complètes de J.-K. Huysmans*, ed. by Lucien Descaves (Geneva: Slatkine, 1972), XII, p. 29.
4. For an analysis of allusions to the *année terrible* in the *Rougon-Macquart*, see Colette Wilson, *Paris and the Commune 1871–1878: The Politics of Forgetting* (Manchester: Manchester University Press, 2007), Chapter 4.

5. I have discussed this in more detail in 'Verre versus vert: Vegetal Violence in J.-K Huysmans's *En rade*', *French Studies*, 69:3 (July 2015), 305–17.
6. See Gustave Flaubert, *L'Education sentimentale*, in *Œuvres complètes de Gustave Flaubert* (Paris: Club de l'Honnête homme, 1971), III.
7. For example, Rita Felski discusses the implications of the modern male artist appropriating femininity ('The Counterdiscourse of the Feminine in five texts by Wilde, Huysmans, and Sacher-Masoch', *PMLA*, 106 (1991), 1094–1105); Charles Bernheimer suggests the fetishistic nature of Des Esseintes's collecting and love of artifice as a rejection of the natural to avoid facing the reality of maternal castration ('Huysmans: Writing Against (Female) Nature', *Poetics Today*, 6 (1985), 311–24); and Robert Ziegler marks the distinction between women's suffering — physical, in the bed — and men's suffering — intellectual, on the page — in *À rebours* and Huysmans's work more widely ('The Bed and the Book: J.-K. Huysmans's Crucibles of Suffering', *Nineteenth-Century French Studies*, 38 (2010), 264–75).
8. Williams, pp. 107–53.
9. Ibid., pp. 127, 137.
10. Alina Clej, 'Fabricated Visions: From the Opium-Eater to Des Esseintes', in *Symbolism, Its Origins and Its Consequences*, ed. by Rosina Neginsky (Newcastle-upon-Tyne: Cambridge Scholars Publishing, 2010), pp. 291–308 (p. 303).
11. Watson, p. 152.
12. Ibid., p. 19.
13. Léon Pradel, 'D'Amsterdam à Java', in *Revue de l'Exposition universelle de 1889*, ed. by F. G. Dumas and L. de Fourcaud (Paris: Librairie des Imprimeries Réunies, 1889), pp. 95–99 (p. 98).
14. *La Mode nouvelle et Miroir parisien*, October 1872.
15. Commissariat Général, *Catalogue officiel: Section française. Groupes VII-IX, Classes 69–90* (Paris: Imprimerie nationale, 1878), p. 218.
16. Huart and Draner, *Guide comique*, p. 47.
17. Uzanne, p. 44.
18. Prendergast, *Paris and the Nineteenth Century*, p. 197.
19. Quoted in Huysmans, *En marge*, ed. by Lucien Descaves (Paris: Lesage, 1927), p. 53.
20. 'Chronique parisienne', *Le Miroir parisien*, February 1864, p. 124.
21. Au Bon Marché, *Album de l'Ameublement* (Paris: n. pub., from 1881–85), n. pag.
22. Emery and Morowitz, p. 32.
23. Ibid., p. 32.
24. *L'Exposition universelle de 1867 illustrée*, I, p. 68.
25. Ibid., XV, p. 271.
26. *Exposition universelle* (Paris: n. pub., 1878).
27. J.-K. Huysmans, *Ecrits sur l'art*, p. 234.
28. Furthermore, for readers who did not read *À rebours* immediately upon its first publication in 1884, they could also make connections with the references to hothouses and conservatories in Zola's *L'Œuvre* (1886), *La Bête humaine* (1890), and *L'Argent* (1891).
29. R. Tamisier, p. 97.
30. *Almanach-souvenir de l'Exposition universelle* (Paris: Librairie de Ch. Noblet, 1879).
31. Watson, p. 140.
32. Ibid., p. 77.
33. Victor Champier, reprinted in 'À propos de l'enquête sur les industries d'art: une manufacture modèle', *Revue des arts décoratifs*, 9 (1888–89), 161–76 (p. 355).
34. Brian Rigby, 'Things, Distinction, and Decay in Nineteenth-Century French Literature', in *French Literature, Thought and Culture in the Nineteenth Century: A Material World, Essays in Honour of D. G. Charlton*, ed. by Brian Rigby (Basingstoke: Macmillan, 1993), pp. 86–104 (p. 94).
35. This impulse to list reached an obsessive level in guidebooks to Paris during the exhibitions. One such book, the *Guide pour Paris et ses environs, indispensable aux visiteurs de l'Exposition universelle de 1878. Paris le jour, Paris la nuit* (Paris: M. Paulme, 1878) listed all of Paris's churches, *palais*, hotels, museums, libraries, schools, and lycées; it detailed the principal features of the *rive droite*, the *rive gauche*, the Champ de Mars, and the Trocadéro; it gave all the opening hours and entry points for the Exhibition, theatres and ball, halls and markets, morgues, cemeteries, hospitals, prisons, and

catacombs; it listed the sewers, barracks, and suburbs; it named the senators, ambassadors, and bankers; it gave price lists and locations of post offices, Parisian public transport, and railways; and it enumerated all the road names in the entire city.

36. G. Dorville, pp. 164–65.
37. Ibid., p. 139.
38. In the Introduction to his essay 'Paris, Capital of the Nineteenth Century', Walter Benjamin writes: 'As a consequence of [our] reifying representation of civilization, the new forms of behaviour and the new economically and technologically based creations that we owe to the nineteenth century enter the universe of a phantasmagoria. These creations undergo this "illumination" not only in a theoretical manner, by an ideological transposition, but also in the immediacy of their perceptible presence. They are manifest as phantasmagorias' (*The Arcades Project*, p. 14).
39. Armstrong, p. 226.
40. Articles from the vast debate in the 1880s weighing the relative benefits of Naturalism and Idealism include: Emile Zola, 'Les Romanciers contemporains', in *Les Romanciers naturalistes* (Paris: Charpentier, 1881), pp. 333–87; Ferdinand Brunetière, *Le Roman naturaliste* (Paris, Calmann-Lévy, 1883), and 'L'Idéalisme dans le roman', *Revue des deux mondes*, 1 May 1885; and Auguste Sautour, *Idéal et naturalisme, à propos du roman* L'Amour de Jacques *de Charles Fuster* (Paris: Fischbacher, 1891).
41. Ioanna Chatzidimitriou, 'Against Memory: Remodeling the Past in Huysmans' À rebours', *Nineteenth-Century Studies*, 20 (2006), 113–28 (p. 123).
42. Elisabeth Donato, *Beyond the Paradox of the Nostalgic Modernist: Temporality in the Works of J.-K. Huysmans* (New York: Peter Lang, 2004), p. 192.
43. For example, Christopher Prendergast has suggested that Impressionism with its seemingly hurried, blurred brushstrokes sprang from the experience of fleeting time: the rapid existence of the modern city, Prendergast writes, 'will also implicate the fate of art, both practically through its growing incorporation into the market, and formally in the development of an art more and more committed to the registration of sudden *aperçu*, fluid sensation, mobile point of view and fugitive impression [...]; there can be little doubt as to the validity of Walter Benjamin's argument that the sense of the city as an increasingly uncertain and unpredictable perceptual field is linked to the emergence of an art geared to an ultimately new set of rhythms, an art based on the principles of surprise and "shock", disruption and displacement of any assumption of a coherent "centre" to experience' (*Paris and the Nineteenth Century*, p. 6).
44. Elizabeth Emery and Laura Morowitz have noted that 'innumerable poems, songs, books, plays, school celebrations and artistic commissions sprang up around [Joan of Arc and Roland's] names, while scholars celebrated their selfless contributions to the nation' (*Consuming the Past*, p. 22).
45. *Le Moniteur universel*, 11 August 1870, my emphases.
46. Donato, p. 57.
47. *L'État*, 9 January 1873.
48. Indeed, for the reader who returns to Huysmans's writing in the future to read *En rade*, this idea of linear temporality is undermined further. Unlike other contemporaneous serial novels and novels linked by recurrent characters (epitomized by Zola's Rougon-Macquart family), *À rebours* and *En rade* are not connected by a linear progression of time across the two individual narratives. Of the many intertextual echoes between Huysmans's works, one of the most confusing is the recurrence of the Château de Lourps in these two novels. In the Notice to *À rebours*, the reader learns that the Château de Lourps was Des Esseintes's childhood home. Although no specific political periods or personal ages are ever given in *À rebours*, the reader is led to presume that Des Esseintes's seclusion at Fontenay occurs at some point in the 1880s, and that his childhood therefore took place at some point during the mid- to late Second Empire. However, in *En rade*, the equally splenetic but bourgeois Jacques Marles seeks asylum from financial troubles in the Château de Lourps during the Third Republic, only a handful of years after Des Esseintes would have sold the property. Yet in *En rade*, this building is said to be in long-term disrepair, to be the erstwhile seat of the Saint-Phal family, and now to be the property of a rich boulevard tailor (ER, 6). This poses a string of questions about how the temporalities

of these two narratives interconnect — with repercussions for both novels. If the time scheme proposed by *En rade* is true (and it is certainly more historically accurate) then where does this leave Des Esseintes? Does this completely obliterate the events of *À rebours* in the *En rade* universe? If the reader seeks to reconcile *À rebours* with *En rade*, it becomes necessary to question all the assumptions about time eked from the vague temporal indicators in *À rebours*; this then prompts either a return to *À rebours* to check (thus adding another rereading long after the novel was first finished, and once more destabilizing the conventional beginning-middle-end pattern of narrative reception), or a mental rewriting of the time frame of *À rebours* (thus diverging from Huysmans's timeframe for the narrative, and so further dissolving Des Esseintes's attachment to temporality). Or, more complex still, the reader may wonder whether it is possible for the same, real-life Château de Lourps to harbour two, concurrent fictional universes — and if this is the case, the reader may only fully understand their relative temporalities by holding both novels in their mind simultaneously.

49. Mirrors appear either literally or metaphorically in 'Bénédiction', 'Les Phares', 'L'Homme et la mer', 'La Beauté', 'Tu mettrais l'univers', 'L'Invitation au voyage', 'La Musique', 'L'Héautontimorouménos', 'L'Irrémédiable', 'Le Cygne', 'La Mort des amants', 'L'Invitation au voyage' (prose version), 'La Belle Dorothée', 'Les Yeux des pauvres', 'Le Miroir', and 'Portraits de maîtresses'. Bottles are mentioned in 'Le Flacon', 'Spleen' (76), 'L'Ame du vin', 'Le Vin du solitaire', 'Une martyre', 'La Chambre double', 'Le Chien et le flacon', 'La Femme sauvage', 'Les Tentations', and 'Portraits de maîtresses'. Windows are mentioned literally or metaphorically in 'Tu mettrais l'univers', 'L'Irréparable', 'Le Gouffre', 'Paysage', 'Le Cygne', 'Je n'ai pas oublié', 'Rêve parisien', 'La Chambre double', 'Le Mauvais vitrier', 'La Femme sauvage', 'Les Projets', 'Les Yeux des pauvres', 'Le Joueur généreux', 'La Corde', 'Les Fenêtres', and 'La Soupe et les nuages'.
50. Charles Baudelaire, 'Les Paradis artificiels', in *Œuvres complètes*, I, pp. 75–227 (p. 89).
51. Pierre Jourde, *Huysmans: " À rebours": L'Identité impossible* (Paris: Champion, 1991), p. 57.
52. Clej, p. 298.

AFTERWORD

In 1889, Boulanger's revolutionary aspirations waned and a new generation came of age — politically and socially — who had never known anything but the Third Republic. The 21-year-olds of 1889 had no personal recollection of the *année terrible*. Essential repairs had been conducted to private homes within months of May 1871, and by 1880 most of the public buildings were repaired with their windows once more intact and large mirrors hanging again in their galleries. Memories were waning of the daily horror of shells, bullets, or fires shattering windows and mirrors, and of the analogy between windows and spies, look-out posts, or gun-emplacements. The handful of ruins still lingering in the cityscape — notably, the Tuileries Palace, Hôtel de Ville, and remnants of the Rue de Lille — did not in themselves transmit to the next generation the distressing visual and aural experience of shaking and breaking glass witnessed during the Prussian bombardment and *semaine sanglante*. Whilst the new generation certainly received from their parents second-hand messages of nationalistic fervour, bitterness against Germany, and suspicion of the lower classes, these would have been transmitted without the memories attached specifically to glass culture.

As this new generation reached adulthood, material culture began to endow glass with fresh meanings — unconcerned by, or perhaps oblivious to, its embroilment in such recent crises. The early years of Symbolism and Art Nouveau demonstrated a return of widespread artistic interest in glass. In the 1880s, there was revived fascination with the medieval art of stained glass, which enjoyed considerable popularity and formed an integral part of the 'La Pierre, Le Bois, La Terre, et Le Verre' exhibition in 1884. Stained glass offered a means of reconfiguring perception — not just perception of the *année terrible*, but of a whole century of revolution: of political, social, technological, and aesthetic upheavals, and of repeated blows to national pride. Stained glass works inscribed glass with positive narratives. As Shoshana Felman observes in her article on Flaubert's 'La Légende de saint Julien l'Hospitalier', 'le vitrail entretient [...] un rapport ambigu avec la lumière: sa fonction n'est pas simplement — en laissant infiltrer les rayons de lumière — *d'exhiber une représentation*, mais aussi — en faisant écran à ceux-ci — *de déformer une perception*. Le vitrail — ou ce qui doit être lu — en même temps donne à voir et aveugle' ['the stained-glass window fosters an ambiguous relationship with light: its function is not simply, by letting light through, *to put forward a representation*. It is also, by framing that representation, *to deform perception*. The stained-glass window, or that which must be read, both shows and blinds at the same time'].[1] The stained-glass window at once blinded the reader/viewer to the turmoil of recent history, and provided an alternative, more agreeable narrative.

So powerful was the draw of stained glass that it was translated into oil-on-canvas form by Symbolist painters such as Emile Bernard, Paul Sérusier, and Pierre Bonnard in their *cloisonniste* works. Glass was now elevated from the plaything of bourgeois, Haussmannized Paris and its World Fairs to being valued in high art. As the Third Republic progressed, glass became increasingly polysemantic, appreciated and endowed with meaning by artists, by architects, and by popular culture alike. Art Nouveau epitomizes this verve for the regeneration of glass. Alastair Duncan describes Art Nouveau, not so much as a movement, but as an anti-movement that helped to discard old modes of representation rather than inaugurate new ones.[2] A much-needed discarding it would seem, to judge by the popularity of Art Nouveau at all levels of society: works in the new style began appearing in familiar, day-to-day locations as well as art exhibitions and expensive private mansions. Shop windows were often the first stages for Art Nouveau displays; Bing's Maison de l'Art Nouveau, for example, opened in December 1895 and presented the passer-by of any social class with an exhibition of ten windows designed by members of the Nabis.[3] Art Nouveau permeated the décor of fashionable restaurants such as Maxim's, but also enlivened the daily commute of the middle classes with its elaborate canopies for Metro stations.

To some extent of course, this repeats the influx of glass into Haussmann's new bourgeois cityscape in the 1840s and 1850s. However, there are a few fundamental differences in the sphere of Art Nouveau. First, glass was now a material affordable for the masses, and if Tiffany lamps and Baccarat crystal were beyond the financial reach of the working classes, reproductions giving a similar experience of form, shape, light, and colour were widely available. Secondly, Art Nouveau glass tends to eschew both transparency and reflectiveness, favouring opaque or translucent surfaces, and thus refusing the sight lines and power relations fostered by Second Empire windows and mirrors. Thirdly, Art Nouveau is characterized by organic lines and natural imagery rather than framing and reflecting the urban experience. Of course, the Art Nouveau movement was by no means unique to France — indeed, it saw considerable success in Belgium, Germany, America, and Great Britain — but it took root more firmly and in more creative fields in France than elsewhere.[4] Its simplification of form, flattening of space, and elaboration of undulating, vegetal lines offered escapism and a bucolic nostalgia that all city dwellers could share, whatever their motives — rather than harbouring associations with the recent urban past. Instead of the memories of national defeat, class division, and the problems of modernity which this study sketched out in Chapter One, glass in the Art Nouveau provided pleasantly affirmative, even euphoric images of nature, of pure youthful virginity, and of regeneration for both the older generations and the new.

This is particularly notable in the works of the glassmaker and furnisher Emile Gallé. With a utopian vision reminiscent of Zola's *Quatre Evangiles* (1898–1902), Gallé explicitly related natural imagery with social reconciliation and peace in his 1900 article for the *Revue des Arts Décoratifs*. He wrote that a décor inspired by nature 'sera un décor éloquent, fraternel. Le décor du meuble contemporain ne sera pas de parti pris mélancolique. Il sera sincère. Il sera donc volontiers joyeux' ['will be an eloquent, fraternal décor. Décor with contemporary furnishings will not take a melancholic stance. It will be sincere. It will thus be willingly joyful'].[5] By the turn of the century, nature became the primary focus of Gallé's glass works, with *objets d'art* incorporating images of thistles, being shaped like mushrooms, and displaying reliefs of seahorses, among many others. For Gallé, glass was a way to represent and return to nature, peace, and purity, rather than vegetating in an atmosphere of urban conflict and corruption.

The parallel study of *Au Bonheur des Dames*, Maupassant's short stories, and *À rebours* in this book has revealed a common concern with the interplay between material and literary culture. Literature, Zola hopes, may go some way to influencing meaning in the world of things; Maupassant embraces the world of things to influence the reading of literature; and Huysmans narrates Des Esseintes's engagement with material culture with the aim of ultimately leaving it behind, in favour of an exploration of literary aesthetics. This concern persists in Gallé's works; but instead of inscribing glass into literature, he inscribed literature into glass. He repeatedly quoted poetry (especially by Baudelaire) in the notices for his *objets* at exhibitions,[6] and — moreover — he inscribed poetry into the physical surface of his *verreries parlantes*. For example, his 'Têtards' vase (c. 1889–1900) includes an extract from Gautier's 'Le Château du souvenir' ['The Castle of Memories']; his 'Pasteur' coupe (1892) displays several lines from Hugo's 'Les Malheureux' ['The Unfortunates']; and his elaborate 'Raisins' decanter (1900) is engraved with a section from Baudelaire's 'Le Poison'. Like Zola, Maupassant, and Huysmans, Gallé recognized the fruitfulness of the relationship between material culture and writing; he knew that objects as well as words contain '*la signification*, que toujours l'esprit humain voudrait requérir' ['*significance*, which the human mind always wants to seek out'].[7]

This study has looked in detail at three very different examples of how authors in the 1870s and 1880s chose, in the wake of the *année terrible*, to play upon the symbolism of glass culture in writing. These examples by no means give an exhaustive view of the ways in which literature manipulated this vitreous symbolism. However, as authors of repute and of large readerships, Zola, Maupassant, and Huysmans were ideally placed to stylize the obsessive return to imagery of windows, mirrors, and broken glass, so characteristic of newspaper and diary accounts from the Franco-Prussian War and Commune. As we have seen, Zola used glass to recast mass, violent uprising into a purely commercial context: the suffering of Parisians in the siege and the Commune is projected upon the commerce of the past in this novel, and glass in the new department store of the future has a conciliatory role. Glass architecture veils conflict with the unthreatening associations of exhibition, rendering the upheaval less abhorrent to the reader, before offering both a degree of freedom to the ruled classes, and a relief from the threat of revolution for the rulers.

Maupassant, in contrast, has no desire to cleanse glass of its distressing associations. On the contrary, memories of trauma and threats to established patriarchal order are vital to Maupassant's writing, and are deliberately brought to the fore in his short stories. Glass objects are fundamental to tales of erotic perversion, psychosis, murder, and suicide, none of which have a happy ending; unlike Zola, Maupassant is clearly not in the business of comforting his reader with a brighter vision of the future. The reader is subjected to a plethora of short but unsettling tales, which often appear benign but which are woven with distressing symbolic undercurrents by glass — particularly the mirror, as a traditional linchpin for the ego and identity-formation. Maupassant's texts themselves are also often shaped to mimic glass, and as such they invoke something of those feelings of disquiet which assail his fictional characters. However, in a manner almost exactly antithetical to Zola, Maupassant does offer a source of pleasure through his writing — an opportunity for catharsis as a reward for grappling with the anxieties and aggression inflicted by the text.

In Huysmans, glass plays quite a different role, and as we have seen, it is no longer a question of placing memories of the *année terrible* at the fore. Glass shows the reader that Des Esseintes, who thinks himself above the common crowd, cannot think beyond mainstream material culture even in his most eccentric moments. Glass inscribes Des Esseintes within a world of material objects; however, its symbolic associations with 1870–71 are deliberately distanced from the narrative to avoid social history becoming the central concern of the novel. Instead, Huysmans conducts a literary experiment, at a time when aesthetic debates constantly centred on the relative benefits of Naturalism and Idealism. *À rebours* does not aim to argue in favour of one genre or the other, but plays with the idea of an Idealized Naturalism: the protagonist is the ideal Naturalist *détraqué*, existing to drive the plot forwards with his folly in a race, milieu, and moment of folly; and the language of the text drives lyrical and extensive description towards the realms of prose poetry. Material objects provide the contrast needed to distance the ideal Naturalist character from ideal Naturalist description, and the traumatic past associations of glass are not so much changed as rendered insignificant.

The blend of material culture and literature, of non-literary and literary texts at the foundations of this study has sought to take objects beyond Marxist and materialist criticism and their focus upon consumption in order to explore a broader approach to the juncture between material objects and linguistic signifiers. The learned relationships between linguistic signifiers and material signifieds are enriched at each moment of French cultural history by further, fleeting associations between the material *as signifier* and the events it evokes *as signified* — offering authors the chance to explore how objects may manipulate the meaning of words and, conversely, how words may reconfigure the meaning of material objects in the 'real world'.

Objects, in this study, have not been set upon a pedestal as the ultimate traces of a culture. I have not questioned, as Baudrillard did, 'de quelle façon ce système de la "parole" *oblitère-t-il* celui de la langue?' ['by what means this "speech" system [of objects] *overrides* the system of language?'].[8] Nor is language hailed for its ability to master a troublesome material world. Rather, this book bridges the rich intersection between object and text, and the complex layers of meaning that this intersection may bring into literature. The apparently innocent details of the everyday provide a fruitful means of writing about and thinking about the wider world. With such a reading, literature is no mere liminal, fictional phenomenon, but is a functional part of our understanding of human life.

Notes to the Afterword

1. Shoshana Felman, 'La Signature de Flaubert: *La Légende de saint Julien l'Hospitalier*', *La Revue des sciences humaines*, 181 (1981), 39–57 (p. 56).
2. See Alastair Duncan, *Art Nouveau* (London: Thames and Hudson, 1994), p. 36.
3. Including Toulouse-Lautrec, Pierre Bonnard, Paul Ranson, Félix Vallotton, Edouard Vuillard, and Henri Ibels.
4. Alastair Duncan discusses the varying impact of Art Nouveau across different nations in *Art Nouveau*, pp. 106–12.
5. Emile Gallé, 'Le Mobilier contemporain orné d'après la Nature', *La Revue des arts Décoratifs*, 20 (1900), p. 336.
6. See Emile Gallé, *Ecrits pour l'art: floriculture, art décoratif, notices d'exposition 1884–1889*, ed. by Henriette Gallé-Grimm (Marseille: Lafitte Reprints, 1980).
7. Gallé, 'Le Mobilier contemporain', p. 368.
8. Baudrillard, p. 17, my emphasis.

BIBLIOGRAPHY

Primary Sources

M. L'ABBÉ PETIT, *Petit Miroir du dix-neuvième siècle* (La Rochelle: n. pub., 1862)
Almanach-souvenir de l'Exposition universelle (Paris: Librairie de Ch. Noblet, 1879)
Au Bon Marché, *Album de l'Ameublement* (Paris: n. pub., 1881–85)
Au Bon Marché, *Maison Aristide Boucicaut, Articles pour Etrennes* (Paris: n. pub., 1882–85)
Au Bon Marché, *Vêtements pour Hommes et Jeunes Garçons* (Winter 1884–Summer 1885).
BALZAC, HONORÉ DE, *La Comédie humaine*, ed. by Pierre-Georges Castex, 12 vols (Paris: Gallimard, 1976)
BAUDELAIRE, CHARLES, *Œuvres complètes*, ed. by Claude Pichois, 2 vols (Paris: Gallimard, 1975–76)
BELL, GEORGES, *Paris incendié: Histoire de la Commune de 1871* (Paris: n. pub., 1872)
BLEIGNERIE, H. DE, *Paris incendié 1871. Album historique contenant: I. Historique, par H. de Bleignerie; II. Notice sur les monuments, les rues incendiées, par E. Dangin; III. Vingt photographies artistiques des plus remarquables ruines de Paris* (Paris: A. Jarry, 1871)
BONNETAIN, PAUL, 'Les Enfants', in *Les Types de Paris*, ed. by Jean-François Raffaëlli (Paris: Editions du Figaro, 1889), pp. 55–64
Catalogue-almanach du Musée Grévin (Paris: n. pub., n.d. [1883?])
CHAMPIER, VICTOR, 'À propos de l'enquête sur les industries d'art: une manufacture modèle', *Revue des arts décoratifs*, 9 (1888–89), 161–76
CHAUMELIN, MARIUS, *Chefs-d'œuvre et curiosités de l'industrie à l'Exposition universelle de 1878* (Paris: Larousse, 1878)
CLÉMANDOT, LOUIS, *Visites des ingénieurs anciens élèves de l'Ecole centrale des arts et manufactures à l'exposition universelle de 1878* (Paris: n. pub., 1878)
COMMISSARIAT GÉNÉRAL, *Catalogue officiel: Groupe 2–6, Section française, classes 6 à 68* (Paris: Imprimerie Nationale, 1878)
——*Catalogue officiel: Section française. Groupes VII-IX, Classes 69–90* (Paris: Imprimerie nationale, 1878)
DABOT, HENRI, *Griffonages quotidiens d'un bourgeois du quartier latin, du mai 1869 au 2 décembre 1871* (Péronne: E. Quentin, 1895)
DALÈS, ALEXIS, *La Clé d'or des époux, ou les Vœux du poète, suivie du Miroir de la femme parfaite, poésies* (Paris: n. pub., 1861)
DEJOUX, ETIENNE, *Souvenirs du siège de Paris* (Paris: Moulin, 1871)
DORVILLE, G., *Les Renseignements sur l'exposition universelle de 1878: Guide des exposants* (Paris: n. pub., 1877)
DUMAS, F. G., 'Fontaines lumineuses', *Revue de l'exposition universelle de 1889*, 1 (1889), 341–46
L'Exposition universelle de 1867 illustrée, ed. M. Fr. Ducuing, 60 vols (Paris: n. pub., 1867)
Exposition universelle (Paris: n. pub., 1878)
FLAUBERT, GUSTAVE, *Œuvres complètes de Gustave Flaubert*, 16 vols (Paris: Club de l'Honnête homme, 1971)
——*Carnets de Travail*, ed. by P. M. de Biasi (Paris: Baillard, 1988)

——— *Correspondance*, ed. by J. Bruneau and Y. Leclerc, 5 vols (Paris: Gallimard, 1973–2007)
FOURNEL, VICTOR, *Paris nouveau et Paris futur* (Paris: Jacques Lecoffre, 1865)
FRANKLIN, ALFRED, *Les Ruines de Paris en 4875* (Paris: Librairie de l'Echo de la Sorbonne, 1875)
GAUTIER, THÉOPHILE, *Poésies complètes de Théophile Gautier*, ed. by René Jasinski, 3 vols (Paris: A. G. Nizet, 1970)
——— *Mademoiselle de Maupin*, in *Œuvres complètes: Romans, contes et nouvelles*, ed. by Anne Geisler-Szmulewicz, 5 vols (Paris: Honoré Champion, 2004)
GENTILINI, R., *La Société anonyme des manufactures de glaces et produits chimiques de Saint-Gobain, Chauny et Cirey à l'exposition universelle de 1889* (Paris: Publications du journal *Le Génie Civil*, 1889)
GONCOURT, EDMOND DE, *Paris under Siege, 1870–71: From the Goncourt Journal*, trans. by George J. Becker (Ithaca and London: Cornell University Press, 1969)
——— *La Fille Elisa* (Paris: La Boîte à Documents, 1990)
——— *Chérie*, ed. by Jean-Louis Cabanès and Philippe Hamon (Jaignes: La Chasse au Snark, 2002)
——— *Journal: Mémoires de la Vie Littéraire, 1866–1886*, 2 vols (Paris: Laffont, 2014)
GONCOURT, EDMOND DE, and FERNAND LOCHARD, *Maison d'Edmond de Goncourt à Auteuil: Photographies et gravures représentant l'intérieur des appartements avec légendes manuscrites par Edmond de Goncourt* (n. pub., 1883)
GOUDEAU, EMILE, 'Ascension à la Tour Eiffel', *Revue de l'Exposition universelle de 1889*, 2 (1889), 280–88
Guide des étrangers à l'exposition universelle et Itinéraire dans Paris (Paris: n. pub., 1878)
Guide pour Paris et ses environs, indispensable aux visiteurs de l'Exposition universelle de 1878. Paris le jour, Paris la nuit (Paris: M. Paulme, 1878)
HANS, LUDOVIC, and J.-J. BLANC, *Guide à travers les ruines. Paris et ses environs, avec un plan détaillé* (Paris: A. Lemerre, 1871)
HENRIVAUX, JULES, *Le Verre et le cristal*, ed. by M. Frémy (Paris: Dunod, 1883)
HUART, ADRIEN, ET DRANER, *Guide comique dans Paris pendant l'exposition* (Paris: n. pub., 1878)
——— *L'Exposition comique* (Paris: n. pub., 1878)
HUYSMANS, JORIS-KARL, *Écrits sur l'art, 1867–1905*, ed. by Patrice Locmant (Paris: Bartillat, 2006)
JOANNE, PAUL, *Paris-Diamant* (Paris: Hachette, 1878)
KNIGHT, CHARLES, *Cyclopedia of London* (n. pub., 1851)
MALOT, HECTOR, *Miss Harriet: Souvenirs d'un blessé* (Paris: Flammarion, 1895)
MATTEI, ANTOINE, *Projet d'un jardin d'hiver public à faire dans la cour des Tuileries* (Paris: De Dubuisson, 1876)
MAUGARS, A., *Miroir de l'enfance* (Paris: n. pub., 1851)
MAUPASSANT, GUY DE, *Sur l'eau, Blanc et bleu, Livre de Bord* (Paris: Louis Conard, 1921)
——— *Correspondance inédite*, ed. by Artine Artinian (Paris: Editions Dominique Wapler, 1951)
——— *Chroniques*, ed. by Hubert Juin, 3 vols (Paris: Union Générale d'Editions, 1980)
——— *Romans*, ed. by Louis Forestier (Paris: Gallimard, 1987)
MORÉAS, JEAN, *Œuvres* (Geneva: Slatkine, 1977)
Observations présentées à l'Assemblée nationale par les Fabriques de Glaces françaises (Paris: n. pub., 1874)
POURCIN, *Visite à l'exposition universelle: itinéraire* (Paris: Au Petit Financier, 1878)
PRADEL, LÉON, 'D'Amsterdam à Java', in *Revue de l'Exposition universelle de 1889*, ed. by F. G. Dumas and L. de Fourcaud (Paris: Librairie des Imprimeries Réunies, 1889), pp. 95–99

RACHILDE, *Monsieur de la Nouveauté* (Paris: E. Dentu, 1880)
RAMPAL, BENJAMIN, *Souvenirs du siège de Paris* (Marseille: n. pub., 1871),
SAINT-VICTOR, PAUL DE, *Barbares et Bandits: La Prusse et la Commune* (Paris: Michel Lévy, 1871)
SAND, GEORGE, *Journal d'un voyageur pendant la guerre* (Paris: Michel Lévy frères, 1871)
SAULLE, LEGRAND DU, *Le Délire des persécutions* (Paris: Plon, 1871)
—— *Les Hystériques: état physique et mental, actes insolites, déliciteux et criminels* (Paris: J.-B. Baillière et fils, 1883)
SÉBRUN, MME MARIE, *Journal d'une mère pendant le siège de Paris* (Paris: Didier, 1872)
Société centrale des architectes: Série des prix applicables aux travaux de bâtiments exécutés pour le compte des particuliers dans la ville de Paris 1883 (Paris: Imprimerie et librairie centrales des chemins de fer, 1883)
Souvenirs d'un garde nationale pendant le siège de Paris et sous la Commune par un volontaire suisse. La Capitulation (Neuchatel: J. Sandoz, 1871)
STECKEL, MAURICE, *Notice sur l'emploi des glaces et des verres* (Paris: Melet, 1890)
STENDHAL, *Le Rouge et le Noir*, ed. by Béatrice Didier (Paris: Gallimard, 1972)
TAMISIER, R., *Les Annales de l'exposition universelle de 1878* (Paris: n. pub., 1878)
TRAPADOUX, MARC, 'Le Métier du chiffon', in *Paris qui s'en va, Paris qui vient: publication littéraire et artistique*, ed. by Léopold Flameng (Paris: Alfred Cadart, 1859–60)
UZANNE, OCTAVE, *Le Miroir du monde: notes et sensations de la vie* (Paris: Quartin, 1888)
VALLÈS, JULES, *Le Tableau de Paris* (Paris: Messidor, 1989)
VEUILLOT, LOUIS, 'Pensées de nuit d'un bombardé', *L'Univers* (18 January 1871)
VIOLLET-LE-DUC, EUGÈNE, *Habitations modernes* (Paris: A. Morel, 1875)
WYZEWA, T. DE, 'Le Palais de l'alimentation', *Revue de l'exposition universelle de 1889*, 2 (1889), 137–44
ZOLA, EMILE, *Le Roman expérimental*, ed. by François-Marie Mourad (Paris: Flammarion, 2006)
—— *Correspondance*, ed. by Alain Pagès (Paris: Flammarion, 2012)

Secondary Sources

ABRAMS, M. H., *The Mirror and the Lamp: Romantic Theory and the Critical Tradition* (New York: W. W. Norton, 1953)
ARAGON, LOUIS, *Le Paysan de Paris* (Paris: Gallimard, 1926)
ARMSTRONG, ISOBEL, *Victorian Glassworlds: Glass Culture and the Imagination 1830–80* (Oxford: Oxford University Press, 2008)
BARROWS SUSANNA, 'After the Commune: Alcoholism, Temperance, and Literature in the Early Third Republic', in *Consciousness and Class Experience in Nineteenth-Century Europe*, ed. by John M. Merriman (New York: Holmes and Meier, 1979), pp. 205–18
—— *Distorting Mirrors: Visions of the Crowd in Late Nineteenth-Century France* (New Haven and London: Yale University Press, 1981)
BARTHES, ROLAND, *Œuvres complètes*, ed. by Eric Marty, 3 vols (Paris: Seuil, 1993–95)
BAUDRILLARD, JEAN, *Le Système des objets* (Paris: Gallimard, 1968)
BELL, DAVID, *Models of Power: Politics and Economics in Zola's* Rougon-Macquart (Lincoln, NE: University of Nebraska Press, 1988)
BENJAMIN, WALTER, *The Arcades Project*, trans. by Howard Eiland and Kevin McLaughlin (Cambridge, MA: Belknap Press, 1999)
BERGSON, HENRI, *Matière et mémoire*, in *Œuvres*, ed. by André Robinet (Paris: Presses Universitaires de France, 1963)
BERNHEIMER, CHARLES, 'Huysmans: Writing Against (Female) Nature', *Poetics Today*, 6 (1985), 311–24

BIELECKI, EMMA, *The Collector in Nineteenth-century French Literature: Representation, Identity, Knowledge* (New York and Bern: Peter Lang, 2012)
BOWLBY, RACHEL, *Just Looking: Consumer Culture in Dreiser, Gissing and Zola* (London and New York: Methuen, 1985)
—— *Shopping with Freud* (London and New York: Routledge, 1993)
—— *Carried Away: the Invention of Modern Shopping* (London: Faber and Faber, 2000)
BREVIK-ZENDER, HEIDI, *Fashioning Spaces: Mode and Modernity in Late Nineteenth-Century Paris* (Toronto: University of Toronto Press, 2015)
BRONFEN, ELISABETH, *Over Her Dead Body: Death, Femininity and the Aesthetic* (Manchester: Manchester University Press, 1992)
BUCK-MORSS, SUSAN, *The Dialectics of Seeing: Walter Benjamin and the Arcade Project* (Cambridge, MA: MIT Press, 1989)
CALINESCU, MATEI, *Five Faces of Modernity* (Durham: Duke University Press, 1987)
CALLÈ, LUISA and PATRIZIA DI BELLO, *Illustrations, Optics and Objects in Nineteenth-Century Literature and Visual Cultures* (Basingstoke: Palgrave Macmillan, 2010)
CHATZIDIMITRIOU, IOANNA, 'Against Memory: Remodeling the Past in Huysmans' *À rebours*', *Nineteenth-Century Studies*, 20 (2006), 113–28
CHESSID, ILONA, *Thresholds of Desire: Authority and Transgression in the* Rougon-Macquart (New York: Peter Lang, 1993)
CLEJ, ALINA, 'Fabricated Visions: From the Opium-Eater to Des Esseintes', in *Symbolism, Its Origins and Its Consequences*, ed. by Rosina Neginsky (Newcastle-upon-Tyne: Cambridge Scholars Publishing, 2010), pp. 291–308
CNOCKAERT, VÉRONIQUE, 'Intimité publique. L'exemple d'*Au Bonheur des Dames*', *Les Cahiers naturalistes*, 83 (2009), 205–12
CURTIN, MARY ELIZABETH, '"Like Bottled Wasps": Beerbohm, Huysmans and the Decadents' Suburban Retreat', *Victorian Literature and Culture*, 39:1 (2011), 183–200
DICKSTEIN, MORRIS, *A Mirror in the Roadway: Literature and the Real World* (Princeton, NJ: Princeton University Press, 2005)
DONATO, ELISABETH, *Beyond the Paradox of the Nostalgic Modernist: Temporality in the Works of J.-K. Huysmans* (New York: Peter Lang, 2004)
DUFRENNE, ROLAND, JEAN MAËS and BERNARD MAËS, *La Cristallerie de Clichy; une prestigieuse manufacture du XIXe siècle* (Clichy-la-Garenne: La Rose de Clichy, 2005)
DUNCAN, ALASTAIR, *Art Nouveau* (London: Thames and Hudson, 1994)
EMERY, ELIZABETH and LAURA MOROWITZ, *Consuming the Past: The Medieval Revival in fin-de-siècle France* (Aldershot: Ashgate, 2003)
FELMAN, SHOSHANA, 'La Signature de Flaubert: *La Légende de saint Julien l'Hospitalier*', *La Revue des sciences humaines*, 181 (1981), 39–57
FELSKI, RITA, 'The Counterdiscourse of the Feminine in five texts by Wilde, Huysmans, and Sacher-Masoch', *PMLA*, 106 (1991), 1094–1105
FOURNIER, ERIC, *Paris en ruines: Du Paris haussmannien au Paris communard* (Paris: Imago, 2008)
FREUD, SIGMUND, *Beyond the Pleasure Principle*, in *Standard Edition of the Complete Pscychological Works of Sigmund Freud*, trans. and ed. by James Strachey, 24 vols (London: Hogarth Press, 1955)
GALLÉ, EMILE, 'Le Mobilier contemporain orné d'après la Nature', *La Revue des arts Décoratifs*, 20 (1900)
—— *Ecrits pour l'art: floriculture, art décoratif, notices d'exposition 1884–1889*, ed. by Henriette Gallé-Grimm (Marseille: Lafitte Reprints, 1980)
GENETTE, GÉRARD, *Figures II* (Paris: Seuil, 1969)
GILLOCH, GRAEME, *Myth and Metropolis: Walter Benjamin and the City* (Cambridge: Polity Press, 1996)

GREEN, ANNE, *Changing France: Literature and Material Culture in the Second Empire* (Cambridge: Cambridge University Press, 2012)
GROSZ, ELIZABETH, *Jacques Lacan: A Feminist Introduction* (London and New York: Routledge, 1990)
HADLOCK, PHILIP, 'Telling Madness and Masculinity in Maupassant's "Le Horla"', *L'Esprit Créateur*, 43:3 (2003), 47–56
HARRIS, TREVOR, *Maupassant in the Hall of Mirrors: Ironies of Repetition in the Work of Guy de Maupassant* (Basingstoke: Macmillan, 1990)
HARROW, SUSAN, *Zola, The Body Modern: Pressures and Prospects of Representation* (London: Legenda, 2010)
HENNESSY, SUSIE, 'Consumption and Desire in *Au Bonheur des Dames*', *The French Review*, 81:4 (2008), 696–706
HOSKINS, JANET, *Biographical Objects: How Things Tell the Stories of People's Lives* (London and New York: Routledge, 1998)
HUET, MARIE-HÉLÈNE, 'Unsettled Memories: the Revolution Buries its Dead', in *Unfinished Revolutions: Legacies of Upheaval in Modern French Culture*, ed. by Robert T. Denommé and Roland H. Simon (University Park, PA: Pennsylvania State University Press, 1998), pp. 121–37
JAOUEN, FRANÇOISE, 'Le Bonheur des Dames ou la Machine du Célibataire', *Qui Parle*, 2:1 (1988), 98–112
JOURDE, PIERRE, *Huysmans: "À rebours": L'Identité impossible* (Paris: Champion, 1991)
KRISTEVA, JULIA, *Pouvoirs de l'horreur: Essai sur l'abjection* (Paris: Seuil, 1980)
LACAN, JACQUES, *Ecrits: A Selection*, trans. by Alan Sheridan (London: Tavistock, 1977)
—— *The Seminar. Book I*, ed. by Jacques-Alain Miller, trans. by John Forrester (New York: Norton, 1988)
—— *The Seminar. Book II*, ed. by Jacques-Alain Miller, trans. by John Forrester (New York: Norton, 1988)
LAMB, JONATHAN, *The Things Things Say* (Princeton, NJ: Princeton University Press, 2011)
LINDNER, CHRISTOPH, *Fictions of Commodity Culture: From the Victorian to the Postmodern* (Aldershot: Ashgate, 2003)
MAGRAW, ROGER, 'Producing, Retailing, Consuming, Spending', in *French Literature, Thought and Culture in the Nineteenth Century: A Material World, Essays in Honour of D. G. Charlton*, ed. by Brian Rigby (Basingstoke: Macmillan, 1993), pp. 59–85
MARX, KARL, *Capital. A Critical Analysis of Capitalist Production*, trans. by S. Moore and Edward Aveling, ed. by Frederick Engels (London: Lawrence and Wishart, 1974)
MCGUINNESS, PATRICK, 'Belgian Literature and the Symbolism of the Double', in *From Art Nouveau to Surrealism: Belgian Modernity in the Making*, ed. by Nathalie Aubert, Pierre-Philippe Fraiture, and Patrick McGuinness (London: Legenda, 2007), pp. 8–22
MICALE, MARK S., *Hysterical Men: The Hidden History of Male Nervous Illness* (Cambridge, MA: Harvard University Press, 2008)
MILLER, DANIEL, *The Comfort of Things* (Cambridge: Polity Press, 2008)
MILLER, MICHAEL, *The Bon Marché: Bourgeois Culture and the Department Store, 1869–1920* (Princeton, NJ: Princeton University Press, 1981)
MOGER, ANGELA, 'Narrative Structure in Maupassant: Frames of Desire', *PMLA*, 100:3 (1985), 315–27
MOREAU, JOHN, 'Maupassant's Empty Frame: A New Look at "Boule de Suif"', *French Forum*, 34:2 (2009), 1–16
MULVEY, LAURA, *Visual and Other Pleasures* (Basingstoke: Palgrave Macmillan, 1989 [2009 second ed.])
NELSON, BRIAN, 'Speculation and Dissipation: A Reading of Zola's *La Curée*', *Essays in French Literature*, 14 (1977), 1–33

―― 'Zola and the Counter Revolution', *Australian Journal of French Studies*, 30:2 (1993), 233–40
OLIVER MILLS, KATHRYN, *Formal Revolution in the Work of Baudelaire and Flaubert* (Newark, MD: University of Delaware Press, 2012)
OPITZ, MICHAEL (ed.), *Walter Benjamin: Ein Lesebuch* (Frankfurt am Mein: Surkamp, 1999)
OUTKA, ELIZABETH, *Consuming Traditions: Modernity, Modernism, and the Commodified Authentic* (Oxford: Oxford University Press, 2009)
PENROD, LYNN, 'Shopaholic Space: From Zola's *Au Bonheur des Dames* to The Gap', in *New Approaches to Zola: Selected Papers from the 2002 Cambridge Centenary Colloquium*, ed. by Hannah Thompson (London: The Emile Zola Society, 2003), pp. 21–30
PRENDERGAST, CHRISTOPHER, *Paris and the Nineteenth Century* (Oxford and Cambridge, MA: Blackwell, 1999)
RAMAZANI, VANEED K., 'Gender, War, and the Department Store: Zola's *Au Bonheur des Dames*', *Substance*, 113 (2007), 126–46
SALATO, ELEANOR, 'Shopping for an "I": Zola's *The Ladies' Paradise* and the Spectacle of Identity', in *L'Ecriture du féminin chez Zola et dans la fiction naturaliste*, ed. by Anna Gural-Migdal (New York and Bern: Peter Lang, 2003), pp. 449–70
SANDVOSS, CORNEL, *Fans: The Mirror of Consumption* (Cambridge: Polity Press, 2005)
SCHOR, NAOMI, *Zola's Crowds* (Baltimore, MD and London: Johns Hopkins Press, 1969)
SCOTT, HANNAH, 'Symphonic Shopping: From Masculine Visuality to Feminine Aurality in Zola's *Au Bonheur des Dames*', *Dix-Neuf*, 18:3 (November 2014), 259–71
―― 'Verre versus vert: Vegetal Violence in J.-K Huysmans's *En rade*', *French Studies*, 69:3 (July 2015), 305–17
SCOTT, WILLIAM, *Terror and Repression in Revolutionary Marseilles* (London: Macmillan, 1973)
SONTAG, SUSAN, *On Photography* (London and New York: Penguin, 1977)
STARR, PETER, *Commemorating Trauma: The Paris Commune and its Cultural Aftermath* (New York: Fordham University Press, 2006)
STOUT, JANIS, *Willa Carther and Material Culture: Real World Writing, Writing the Real World* (Tuscaloosa: University of Alabama Press, 2005)
TERDIMAN, RICHARD, *Present Past: Modernity and the Memory Crisis* (Ithaca, NY and London: Cornell University Press, 1993)
THOMPSON, HANNAH, 'A Battle in the Feminine? The Gendered Body and the Franco-Prussian War', in *Visions/Revisions: Essays on Nineteenth-Century French Culture*, ed. by Nigel Harkness (Bern: Peter Lang, 2003), pp. 157–73
VINKEN, BARBARA, 'Temples of Delight: Consuming Consumption in Emile Zola's *Au Bonheur des Dames*', in *Spectacles of Realism: Body, Gender, Genre*, ed. by Margaret Cohen and Christopher Prendergast (Minneapolis, MN: University of Minnesota Press, 1995), pp. 247–67
WALKER, PHILIP, 'The Mirror, the Window and the Eye in Zola's Fiction', *Yale French Studies*, 42 (1969), 52–67
WARD, JANET, *Weimar Surfaces: Urban Visual Culture in 1920s Germany* (Berkeley, CA: University of California Press, 2001)
WATSON, JANELL, *Literature and Material Culture from Balzac to Proust* (Cambridge: Cambridge University Press, 1999)
WILLIAMS, ROSALIND, *Dream Worlds: Mass Consumption in Late Nineteenth-Century France* (Berkeley, CA: University of California Press, 1982)
WILSON, COLETTE E., *Paris and the Commune 1871–1878: The Politics of Forgetting* (Manchester: Manchester University Press, 2007)
ZIEGLER, ROBERT, 'The Bed and the Book: J.-K. Huysmans's Crucibles of Suffering', *Nineteenth-Century French Studies*, 38 (2010), 264–75

ŽIŽEK, SLAVOJ, 'The Fetish of the Party', in *Lacan, Politics, Aesthetics*, ed. by Willy Apollon and Richard Feldstein (Albany, NY: State University of New York Press, 1996), pp. 3–29
—— *The Žižek Reader*, ed. by Elizabeth Wright and Edmond Wright (Oxford: Blackwell, 1999)

INDEX

Abrams, M. H., 3
aesthetic of anxiety 81, 95
alcohol 38–39
Armstrong, Isobel 7, 22, 23, 26, 27, 59, 99, 119
Art nouveau 136–37

Balzac, Honoré de 2
Barrows, Susanna 4
Barthes, Roland 5, 95
Baudelaire, Charles:
   mirrors in 134 n. 49
   peintre de la vie moderne 3, 94
   windows in 134 n. 49
   'Les Yeux des pauvres' 16
Baudrillard, Jean 2, 51, 75, 138
Bell, David 60, 61
Benjamin, Walter 1, 4, 26, 33, 133 n. 38
Bergson, Henri 40
Bielecki, Emma 2–3
Bleignerie, H. de, *Paris incendié 1871*: 36
Bon Marché 22, 25, 48, 54, 62, 113
Bonnetain, Paul 88
Bowlby, Rachel 50, 58, 73
Brevik-Zender, Heidi 69–70
Bronfen, Elisabeth 62

Caillebotte, Gustave 16, 20–22
Champier, Victor 116
Chatzidimitriou, Ionna 120
Chessid, Ilona 49
chiffonnier, 25–26, 39
Clej, Alina 110, 131
cloisonnisme 136

Dabot, Henri 28, 29, 38
defenestration 22, 43 n. 45
Degas, Edgar 16
Dejoux, Etienne, *Souvenirs du siège* 29
department stores in 1870–1871: 48, 53–54
Dickstein, Morris 4
Donato, Elisabeth 120, 121
Duncan, Alastair 136

Emery, Elizabeth 4, 113
exhibition effect 70, 75

Felman, Shoshana 135
fetishism 85–87, 103 n. 21

Flaubert, Gustave 2
   Bouvard et Pécuchet 17, 112, 103 n. 16
   L'Éducation sentimentale 23, 89
Forain, Jean Louis 16
Forestier, Louis 96
Fournel, Victor, *Paris nouveau et Paris futur* 47
Fournier, Eric 27
Franklin, Alfred, *Les Ruines de Paris en 4875*: 39

Gallé, Emile 136–37
Gautier, Théophile 2, 3, 54
Gervex, Henri 21
Gilloch, Graeme 56
glass:
   in aftermath of 1870–71: 40–42
   in architecture 13, 15–17, 115
   in bibelots and trinkets 22
   in Commune 5, 8, 33–39
   in Franco-Prussian War 5, 8, 20, 26–33
   industry 1, 14, 26, 32, 34
   for lower classes 24–26
   mirror industry 13
   in painting 16, 20–22
   in private sphere 20–26
   for technology 14
   window making 15
   at World Fairs 15, 17, 18, 19, 114, 115
Goncourt, Edmond de:
   Auteuil photographs 23
   Chérie 88
   La Fille Elisa 16, 24
   Journal 29, 35
Green, Anne 2–3, 7, 18, 70
guidebooks to the ruins 20, 40

Hadlock, Philip 99
Hans and Blanc, *Guides à travers les ruines* 20
Harris, Trevor 4
Harrow, Susan 70
Henrivaux, Jules, *Le Verre et le cristal* 25, 83
Hoskins, Janet 6
Huart and Draner, *Guide comique dans Paris* 16
Huysmans, Joris-Karl:
   À rebours 9
      aquarium 111
      allusions to 1870–71: 108
      on Baudelaire 130
      Commune locations in Paris 126–27

conservatory 114–18
des Esseintes's subjectivity 127–31
gender bending 132 n. 7
glass and women 118–19
Idealism vs. Naturalism 119–31, 133 n. 40
London voyage 125–27
mainstream culture 110–19
on Mallarmé 130
mirrors 128–30
orgue à bouche 124–25
photography 122
poetics 123–27
shopping culture 115–18
stained glass 113
temporality 120–24
windows 121–23
À vau-l'eau 112, 119
Croquis parisiens 16, 24, 25, 119
Le Drageoir aux épices 22, 108
Écrits sur l'art 16, 114
En ménage 108, 119
En rade 108, 133 n.48
Là-Bas 108
Marthe, histoire d'une fille 24
on Naturalism 3, 108
Pierrot sceptique 39

Impressionism 133 n. 43
see Caillebotte, Degas, Manet, Morisot

Jourde, Pierre 131

Knight, Charles 26
Kristeva, Julia 100–102

Lacan, Jacques 59–60
Laforgue, Jules 113
Lamb, Jonathan 5, 6, 7
  things and objects 5
Legrand du Saulle, Henri 21, 22, 43 n. 41&42

madness, clinical 80, 81, 105 n. 44
Magraw, Roger 4, 24
Malot, Henri, *Miss Harriet* 28
Manet, Edouard 16
Marx, Karl 26
material culture 1–3, 6–7, 9 n. 9
Maupassant, Guy de:
  absent reflections 87, 90
  'L'Ami Patience' 95
  breakdowns at the mirror 81–85, 93
  breaking glass in 92–93
  'Le Chevelure' 86–87
  'La Confession' 81
  Contes et nouvelles 8
  'L'Enfant' 82, 95
  'En voyage' 95–96

'L'Ermite' 98
'Fini' 82–85
frame narratives in 95–96, 104 n. 35
glass and femininity in 87–92
'Histoire d'une fille de ferme' 82
'Le Horla' 82, 99
'Imprudence' 88–90
'Lettre d'un fou' 90–91, 97
'Le Lit' 29, 91
'Madame Hermet' 82
'Menuet' 95
'Moiron' 81
'Monsieur Parent' 92–93
'La Morte' 87–88
'La Petite Roque' 99–101
'Le Port' 93
'Promenade' 82
'Rencontre' 86
repetition in 97
'La Serre' 91–92
'Le Signe' 21, 90
'Suicides' 82
Sur l'eau 6, 22, 94
'Un cas de divorce' 85–86
'Un Lâche' 93–94, 98
writing and glass in 95–101
'Yvette' 82
McGuinness, Patrick 6
medieval revival 113, 135
Micale, Mark S. 80
Miller, Daniel 6
mirrors 22–23
  in the brothel 24–25
  as a metaphor for representation 3–4
Moger, Angela 95
Moréas, Jean 6
Moreau, John 95
Morisot, Berthe 20
Morowitz, Laura see Emery, Elizabeth
Mulvey, Laura 50
Musée Grévin 87

Nelson, Brian 49

Oliver Mills, Kathryn 27
optical toys 44 n. 52

Penrod, Lynn 49
photography 14, 83–84
  during the Franco-Prussian War 31
  of ruins 36
Prendergast, Christopher 49, 55, 113
  on Impressionism 133 n. 43

Rachilde 64–65
Rampal, Benjamin, *Souvenirs du siège de Paris* 30
Rigby, Brian 2

ruins, representing the 27, 28, 36, 37, 40, 41–42

Saint-Victor, Paul de, *Barbares et Bandits* 38
Sand, George 31
Schor, Naomi 48
Sébrun, Marie 30–31
Sontag, Susan 83
speculum genre 79
Starr, Peter 69
Steckel, Maurice 13, 15, 35
Stendhal, 3, 95, 112
Symbolism, 7, 136

Terdiman, Richard 20
textualizing 1870–71: 41
Thompson, Hannah 81, 91

Uzanne, Octave 23, 112

Vallès, Jules, *Tableaux de Paris* 21, 22, 39, 43 n. 40
Versailles 5–6, 32
Veuillot, Louis 5
Vinken, Barbara 60
Viollet-le-Duc, Eugène 113

Walker, Philip 49
Watson, Janell 2, 111, 116, 118
Williams, Rosalind 71, 110
Wilson, Colette 42

Zola, Emile:
  L'Assommoir, 24, 25, 66–67
  Au Bonheur des Dames 8
    gender conflict 77 n. 43
    glazing 47
    light 54–56
    mirrors 58–65
    petit commerce 52–54
    seduction of women 49–53, 76 n. 16
    shop windows 49–55
    social conflict 64–70
    and sound 71–73
    and the visual 47–58, 75 n. 2
  La Curée 25, 88, 89
  La Débâcle 33
  'Lettres parisiennes' 41
  theory of screens 3–4
  Le Ventre de Paris 65–67, 70, 72, 112

www.ingramcontent.com/pod-product-compliance
Lightning Source LLC
Chambersburg PA
CBHW082248220526
45469CB00009B/2917